• • • •

Weldon Kees, April 1954. Photograph courtesy of Michael Grieg

Weldon

K·E·E·S·

and the Midcentury Generation · Letters, 1935–1955

≡

Edited, and with Commentary, by Robert E. Knoll

≡

University of Nebraska Press · Lincoln and London

≡

Copyright 1986 by the
University of Nebraska Press
All rights reserved
Manufactured in the United
States of America

The paper in this book meets
the minimum require-
ments of American National
Standard for Infor-
mation Sciences-Permanence
of Paper for
Printed Library Materials,
ANSI Z39.48-1984

Library of Congress Cataloging
in Publication Data

Kees, Weldon, 1914-1955?

Weldon Kees and the midcentury
generation

Bibliography: p.
Includes index.
1. Kees, Weldon, 1914-1955? –
Correspondence.
2. Authors, American – 20th
century – Correspondence.
3. Artists – United States –
Correspondence.   1. Knoll,
Robert E.   11. Title.
PS3521.E285Z48   1986
811'.52 [B]   86-1288
ISBN 0-8032-2709-4
alkaline paper

To The Heritage Room

Bennett Martin Public Library

Lincoln, Nebraska

CONTENTS

More than three decades after his mysterious disappearance, Weldon Kees has become a figure of great artistic and literary interest. His poems have been included in major anthologies of midcentury American verse, and in 1960 Donald Justice edited *The Collected Poems* for a limited edition published by the Stone Wall Press, Iowa City. This edition was reprinted with six additional poems as a Bison Book by the University of Nebraska Press in 1962. For a revised edition in 1975, Donald Justice rewrote his introduction. Several of the Kees poems are reprinted so frequently that they are nearly classics of their time.

Kees's prose has not received as much attention as the poetry, but it is not entirely forgotten. His essay on popular culture, "Muskrat Ramble: Popular and Unpopular Music," and his book with Jurgen Ruesch, M.D., *Nonverbal Communication* (1956, still in print), are sometimes noted, though his sketches and short stories are uncollected. James Reidel and Timothy Nolan assembled eight of these pieces in *Columbia: A Magazine of Poetry and Prose,* no. 8 (1983), with a cover reproducing a black and white painting by Kees. In 1983 Abattoir published a limited edition of Kees's fiction entitled *The Ceremony and Other Stories,* containing a picture by Kees. The following year this volume, edited and with an introduction by Dana Gioia and amplified by five additional pieces, was reprinted by Graywolf Press. Dana Gioia has also prepared *Two Prose Sketches* (1984) for Aralia Press; these are not in any of the other volumes, and, though slight, help fill out the body of Kees's work. Weldon Kees, who was a connoisseur of printing, would be gratified to see in what handsome dress his poems and stories make their contemporary reappearance.

Critical studies of Kees have appeared in a variety of places. My own essay, "Weldon Kees: Solipsist as Poet," came out in *Prairie Schooner* in spring 1961; and Howard Nemerov published his essay, "The Poetry of Weldon Kees," in *Poetry and Essays* (1963). *Sequoia: Stanford Literary Magazine,* edited by Ted Gioia, devoted its spring 1979 issue to Kees. That year a retrospective showing of Kees's paintings, collages, and drawings was held at the Sheldon Memorial Art Gallery at the University of Nebraska–Lincoln. In 1985, Jim Elledge prepared a collection of essays for Scarecrow Press in a volume including a comprehensive bibliography by Robert Niemi. Also in 1985, William T. Ross published a book-length study of Kees, and Raymond Nelson completed a sensitive brief biography. A selection of Kees's New York letters was published in the spring 1985 issue of the *Hudson Review* and his play, "The Waiting Room," was published in the spring 1986 issue of *Prairie Schooner.* Robert Helm has tried on a number of occasions to get a hearing for Kees's music. Altogether, there seems to be some rising interest in the work of Weldon Kees.

• • •

Before Sarah Green Kees died in April 1964, she gave a collection of her son's papers to the Lincoln City Libraries to be used "for scholarly purposes." They are kept in the Heritage Room of the Bennett Martin Public Library. The letters, manuscripts, clippings, offprints, advertising fliers, and memorabilia had been assembled by her and by Weldon's father, John Kees, who died in October 1961. They had put 210 letters in an accordion file; some were letters to Weldon but others were copies of letters that he had written to his friends and business associates. Clearly proud of what he wrote, Weldon may have had some idea that these might eventually be published. In addition, Mrs. Kees gave the library three scrapbooks. One, prepared by Weldon himself, includes reviews, news stories, and the like, dated and annotated in Weldon's own hand, from 1941 to 1950. A second, also by Weldon, covers the years from 1950 to 1955. A third volume, carrying the notation "Scrapbook prepared by John Kees Summer 1957," contains family pictures, Weldon's juvenilia, and miscellaneous printed materials. John Kees must have assembled it from family collections and from what he found in Weldon's San Francisco house in 1955.

In addition to letters, papers, and scrapbooks, the bequest also contains six professionally bound volumes of poems, articles, and stories by Weldon Kees. One volume is a typescript of stories, but the rest consist of offprints, typed indexes and pages, bibliographical notes, and a few pictures—all carefully if unprofessionally arranged, footnoted, and dated, usually with accuracy, by John and Sarah Kees. Typescript copies of Kees's unpublished novel, *Fall Quarter;* of radio scripts; and of sketches for skits are boxed and labeled separately. Everything that Weldon published, plus typescripts of fugitive pieces, is thus conveniently assembled. The Kees bequest does not contain books, but a complete collection of books by and about Kees has been gathered at Bennett Martin's Heritage Room.

Kees's major correspondent was Norris Getty, to whom he wrote from 1935 until 1955; and though Weldon retained only a few of Norris's letters, Norris kept nearly all of Weldon's. After Getty retired from Groton School, he gave his collection to the Lincoln City Libraries in October 1972, presumably because he knew that the Kees family had already deposited papers there. He had 172 letters, mostly from Weldon, but a few were copies of his letters to Weldon. Before Getty died, at home in Nebraska in January 1983, he endorsed the publication of this correspondence.

When Cathryn Stenten became curator of the Heritage Room in 1978, she counted nearly four hundred letters to and from Weldon Kees in the collections, and she noted the considerable mass of supporting materials. Encouraged by Carol J. Connor, the director of the Lincoln City Libraries, Mrs. Stenten called their existence to the attention of the Center for Great Plains Studies at the University of Nebraska–Lincoln; and the Center invited Virginia Faulkner, then editor-in-chief of the University of Nebraska Press, to assess them. Recommending publication, Miss Faulkner noted, "This collection will stand as one of the most revealing self-portraits of a gifted individual likely to come our way." She considered the collection "unique because of its breadth—it takes in the state of the literary, musical, art, and film worlds during a period when everything was in flux—the end of the Thirties, World War II, and most of the postwar decade—and Kees knew just about everybody" (report to Center for Great Plains Studies, July 18–24, 1980). Upon her recommendation, the Center for Great Plains Studies asked me to edit the letters. I began in the summer of 1981 with a grant from the Research Council of the University of Nebraska–Lincoln, for which I am grateful. The librarians and staff of the Lincoln City Libraries have given me support at every turn. The Kees papers have been fully indexed by Cathryn Stenten; her successors, Pamela Gossin and Joann Casullo; and their assistants, John Stephen Smith and James Gullick. I wish to acknowledge my debt to all of them and to Pamela Gossin in particular. I also want to thank Carol J. Connor, her assistants Joyce Coppinger, Dan Piersol, Vivian Johnson, and the rest of the staff, particularly those in the Information/Reference department.

Though the Getty letters and the Kees papers are voluminous, I found that they did not cover the full range of Weldon's career. At this point Nancy Johnson made available letters from Kees to her husband, Professor Maurice Johnson. The correspondence between them conveniently supplemented that between Getty and Kees and contained more than sixty items written from July 1935 to January 1954. Mrs. Johnson has kindly given me permission to quote from her husband's correspondence, and I thank her and her family. She has also let me use some of her family pictures.

Weldon Kees's friends of later years were as generous as those of the earliest years. Anton Myrer, by 1981 a celebrated novelist, provided me with copies of his correspondence with Kees extending from 1948 to 1955. In addition, he and Judith Rothschild wrote me fully of their memories of Ann and Weldon Kees. All of Kees's friends, except one, encouraged me in this project, confident that Kees would have approved it. None had been in touch with Ann Kees for many years; they report that she did not respond to their offers of friendship. According to the California Office of Vital Statistics, Ann S. Kees was found dead August 15, 1975, in her Berkeley apartment. She had been dead for perhaps a week and was buried, unknown to her family in Wyoming, ten days later at Mt. View Cemetery. A monument was

placed on her grave by her friends, Janet and Charles Richards, in
1983.

In this volume I include only a fraction of the total surviving letters,
for I want to present a clear self-portrait of a gifted individual who
participated in some of the major artistic movements of the midcentury generation. I have not aimed for a complete "life and letters" but
have selected to provide the essential facts and spirit of Kees's life. I
have had to omit many pieces that Kees's friends wrote to him as well
as pieces that he wrote to them: I did not want to be redundant, and I
wanted the story to march directly from its beginning to what seemed
its fated conclusion. The collection, with my editorial additions, is to
read rather like an epistolary novel.

To this end Kees's stylistic idiosyncrasies are retained where possible.
Contractions, ellipses, decorative stars, dropped apostrophes, and curious punctuation have been kept to give personal flavor to the total.
Inside addresses of letters have been omitted except where they serve
to clarify or set a new scene. Salutations usually have been retained,
but closings only when a postscript follows them. Titles in the letters
have been italicized or put in quotes according to standard practice.
Paragraphing has also been regularized. The military style of dating
that Kees habitually used has been retained in the letters. Occasionally
the date appears in the upper left corner of the letter (in parentheses if
inserted by me), and occasionally it appears in parentheses after a
brief excerpt. Generally, for the sake of continuity, the date appears in
the text leading into the letter.

I have occasionally quoted poems as they appear in the letters, for
they define Kees's insistently double life. In his letters Kees was often
gay, sardonic, social, and gossipy; in the poems he revealed the dark
caverns through which he traveled in both daylight and nighttime
hours. Since the *Collected Poems* is easily available, the poems do not
need extensive quotation here, but I hope enough are included to
indicate the counterpoint of his life.

In order to make this volume readable, I have kept annotation to a
minimum but have included the footnotes that Kees himself appended
to his letters. These are marked with his initials: [W.K.]. Notes sig-

naled by asterisks occur at the bottom of the page and identify people, events, and other references in the text. Notes carrying numbers, at the end of the book, provide source information. Ordinary ellipses are Kees's; my ellipses appear within brackets: [. . .]. Since Kees speaks of so many persons, I have provided a guide to his friends and associates at the back of this book. It is as complete as I can make it. Taken together, these identifications form a kind of gallery of writers, painters, and musicians, prominent and not so prominent, between 1935 and 1955. The entries are generally intended to provide information on their activities between those dates.

Most of the material in this edition comes from unpublished papers assembled in the Heritage Room at the Bennett Martin Public Library in Lincoln, Nebraska, and from unpublished letters and papers held in various other libraries around the country. Where I have expressly drawn on published material, I have indicated sources in the notes at the back of the book. If I have not otherwise indicated, the reader may assume the materials cited are in the Heritage Room.

Many people remember and talk of Weldon Kees, even after his long disappearance. Ethel Baziotes, Fritz Bultman, Byron Bryant, Herbert Cahoon, Malcolm Cowley, Evelyn Knoll Dorr, Nesuhi Ertegun, Wilbur Gaffney, Ervin Getty, Burket Graf, Michael Grieg, Robert D. Harper, Robert and Kathryn Helm, Pauline Kael, Ruth McDuffee Knight, James Laughlin IV, Kathryn Renfro Lundy, Dwight Macdonald, Harvey McCaleb, the Honorable Hale McCown, Esther Montgomery, Wright Morris, Anton Myrer, Howard Nemerov, Laure Pollack, Harvey Powelson M.D., Harold Renaud, Janet and Charles Richards, Judith Rothschild, Jurgen Ruesch M.D., Margaret Smith, Robert H. Swan, Maisie Swan Wilkinson, and Rudolph Umland have all written or talked to me about Weldon Kees. I am grateful to all those people.

I am indebted to scholars and friends for getting me information, for checking libraries, and for giving advice. I want particularly to name Dudley Bailey, Barbara Day, the late Virginia Faulkner, Norman Geske, Dale Gibbs, Lee Lemon, Howard Norland, Wallace Peterson, James Rawley, the late Bernice Slote, and Dorothy Zimmerman. I am also beholden to Richard L. Brengle, Richard Flamer, Donald Justice,

David Lipset, John McKernan, William T. Ross, and Kenneth Seib. I have a heavy debt to Robert Niemi, Raymond Nelson, James Reidel, and, most of all, to Dana Gioia. Marian Salzman Carman and LeAnn Messing typed my manuscript thoughtfully. My wife, Virginia, has helped me with every page. I thank them all.

This edition of the letters of Weldon Kees from 1935 to 1955 is in some respects a continuation of my earlier volume, *McAlmon and the Lost Generation* (1962, reprinted 1976). In that book I traced the history of "advanced" writers in America and Paris from about 1915 to about 1935, as recorded in the work of a man who seemed to know everybody. In this book I have continued that history, tracing the "advanced" artists in America from 1935 to 1955 as presented in the letters of a man who seemed to know most of the influential figures of his generation. The two volumes, taken together, are a history of American literary experience, as seen from the edge of the picture. Altogether, I have had a wonderful time. As for Weldon Kees himself: I count myself now, after these years, one of his circle of friends; and my hand reaches out to him.

Acknowledgement is gratefully made to the following persons, publishers, and institutions for permission to use materials:

Sterling Library, Yale University, for letters of Weldon Kees to James Laughlin IV dated December 1938; January 1940; June 12, 1940; and November 30, 1943.

The Dwight Macdonald Papers, Yale University Library, for a letter from Kees to Dwight Macdonald dated June 22, 1949.

The Malcolm Cowley Papers, The Newberry Library, for portions of letters from Kees to Malcolm Cowley dated September 15, 1943, and November 3, 1952; and for Cowley's testimonial and note to Kees and Kees's reply on November 30, 1954. One paragraph from *The Literary Situation* by Malcolm Cowley. Copyright 1954, renewed © 1982 by Malcolm Cowley. Reprinted by permission of Viking Penguin Inc.

The Huntington Library, San Marino, California, for two items in the MSS of Conrad Aiken: AIK 691, Weldon Kees to Conrad Aiken, May 22, 1951, and AIK 695, Ann Kees to Conrad Aiken, May 25, 1957.

Daniel Aaron, Harvard University, for portions of letters by Kees to Newton Arvin dated November 28, 1942, and February 21, 1943.

Rare Book and Manuscript Library, Columbia University, for selected sentences of letters from James T. Farrell to Weldon Kees, March 26, 1942, and April 13, 1942.

Gordon C. Harvey, editor, *Sequoia: Stanford Literary Magazine,* for material from essay "Weldon Kees" by Norris Getty, *Sequoia,* vol. 23, no. 2 (Spring 1979): 21–22.

Charles Richards for passages from Janet Richards, *Common Soldiers: A Self-Portrait and Other Portraits* (Archer Press, 1979, 1984), pp. 145, 147, 148, 149, 288, 295, 299–300, 301–2; for personal letters and conversations about Kees from 1982 to 1985; and for photographs loaned from the Richards collection.

The Everson Museum of Arts, Syracuse, New York, for one paragraph from Dorothy Gees Seckler, "History of the Provincetown Art Colony," in *Provincetown Painters, 1890s–1970s,* edited by Ronald A. Kuchta (Everson Museum of Arts, 1977), p. 65.

Michael M. Grieg for passages from *Intro Bulletin: A Literary Newspaper of All the Arts,* vol. 1, no. 8 (May 1956), p. 4, dealing with the disappearance of Weldon Kees in July 1955; and for selected photographs of Kees and friends.

Norris Getty for private letters to and from Weldon Kees.

Fritz Bultman for paragraph from unpublished essay, "Enemy of Obfuscation," deposited in Sheldon Memorial Art Gallery, Lincoln, Nebraska; and for selected photographs.

Nesuhi Ertegun for passages from private letter to Robert E. Knoll, September 23, 1981, about Weldon Kees.

Robert D. Harper for passages, including quoted letters, from essay "Weldon Kees' Denver Years," deposited in Heritage Room, Bennett Martin Public Library, Lincoln, Nebraska, 1980.

Rudolph Umland for selections from unpublished essays "Looking Back at the Wimberly Years" and "More Beerdrinking with Wimberly," both deposited in Heritage Room, Bennett Martin Library, Lincoln; and selected photographs from the Umland collections.

Robert and Kay Helm for correspondence between Kay and Robert Helm and Weldon Kees; for private letters to Robert E. Knoll; and for photographs from their collections.

Nancy Johnson for selections from the correspondence of Maurice Johnson and Weldon Kees, 1935–55; and for selected photographs of Kees, Nancy and Maurice Johnson.

Anton Myer for passages from letters by Weldon Kees to Anton and Judith Myer, 1949–55; for a few sentences from letters from Anton Myer to Weldon Kees, 1949–50; and for selected passages from private letters by Anton Myer to Robert E. Knoll about Weldon Kees, July 13, 1981, and later.

Laure Pollack for brief passages from the correspondence between Weldon Kees and Lou Pollack. From LP to WK: November 19, 1950; December 30, 1950; May 18, 1951. From WK to LP: November 26, 1950; December 2, 1951; December 29, 1951. Deposited by John and Sarah Kees in Bennett Martin Public Library, Lincoln.

Judith Rothschild for a few sentences from private correspondence between Judith Rothschild and Robert E. Knoll about Weldon Kees, January 2, 1983.

R. E. K.

Before he vanished in 1955, Weldon Kees thought of himself as "the
most versatile artist now working in America," and his famous friends
agreed that he was. In the late thirties and early forties, James Laughlin IV, editor of New Directions, and Edward J. O'Brien, editor of the
Best Short Stories annuals, published his fiction; Malcolm Cowley
praised his poetry, and *Poetry* printed it. In the midforties Philip Rahv,
Edmund Wilson, and Dwight Macdonald admired his critical acumen,
and the *Partisan Review* included his essays in its pages. *The New
Yorker* published his verse. Both the *New York Times* and *The New
Republic* found place for his reviews. Later in the decade his paintings
and collages were exhibited in important New York galleries, including the Whitney. His association with Hans Hofmann, Willem de
Kooning, and Robert Motherwell linked him to the New York School
of Abstract Expressionism. When he succeeded Clement Greenberg as
art columnist on *The Nation* in 1949, his judgments earned general
respect. After 1950 Nesuhi Ertegun, later an impressario in popular
music, Turk Murphy, and persons in the San Francisco jazz revival
gave his music their attention. He now experimented with both still
and moving photography, in collaboration with Jurgen Ruesch, the
psychiatrist, and Gregory Bateson, the anthropologist-psychologist.
With Ruesch he worked on a book, *Nonverbal Communication*. Also
in the midfifties he became involved in stage shows, what later were
called "total happenings," performing on the jazz piano, and writing
for actors and singers. Poet, painter, critic, photographer, musician—
he seemed to have his hand in everything.

For fifteen years Weldon Kees participated actively in the literary and artistic life of the nation. Originally from Nebraska, he made his way in a competitive, national scene. Standing a bit apart from the parade and committed to no coteries, he reported with charm and irony all that he saw in letters to his friends around the country. He was gifted, his work was meritorious, and he had wit. Satiric in temper, he yet inspired affection in those he met, many of whom never forgot him. He was a man of some accomplishment, with the promise of more to come.

When Weldon Kees disappeared in July 1955, he was near the general acceptance that he sought and had been approaching for twenty years. He was taking his place in the national establishment. At age forty-one he was, one might say, ten minutes from triumph. And then his car was found on the north approach to the Golden Gate Bridge, where it had been abandoned in the deep fog of midsummer. He has not been seen nor heard from since. His book with Ruesch was published in 1956, some of his lyrics and music got a brief hearing, his pictures continued to be exhibited, and his poems and essays were reprinted. But Kees was gone. The beginning of a major career was cut off in midpassage. With success imminent, why did he withdraw?

One hesitates to say. Perhaps he was defeated, paradoxically, by his own achievement. From his earliest years, Kees was impatient with the comfortably traditional. As poet, critic, and artist, he went his own way, separating himself from popular standards. He lived with his antennae up, anticipating what other artists and ultimately the general public would respond to, or even need. He lived in the cultural vanguard. But he was not a bohemian. His ideas of dress and social conduct were suggested by the Ivy League and Scott Fitzgerald. And he was no revolutionary, for he admired the craft of the Pound-Eliot-Joyce generation even as he anticipated the sensibilities of his own generation, many of whose leaders he came to know. Weldon Kees had the singular ability to know where the action was to be, and to participate in it: he foresaw the shape of art to come. Solitude was the price of his achievement, and it may have been greater than he could pay, emotionally fragile as he was. Still, he chose his life, and he stuck to it.

• • •

Born on February 24, 1914, in Beatrice, Nebraska, Weldon Kees grew up in the normalcy of Warren G. Harding: silent movies, open cars, and large yards trimmed with hand-propelled lawn mowers. But from his earliest years Kees had a critical temper in a world of automatic acceptance. Coming of age in the Great Depression, he felt equally removed from the genteel traditions of his mother's garden club and the political agitation of the radicals. He may have looked like a "pinko" to Gage County, Nebraska, but to the urban crowd of *The New Masses,* which he read, he was Old Guard. He thought the radicals of the thirties no more the total, or even the defining, experience of the thirties than the Ladies' Clubs, and he stood aloof from both.

Throughout his life Weldon Kees sought to examine all possibilities. After graduating from the University of Nebraska in 1935 with a bachelor of arts degree, he went at twenty-one to the Hollywood never-never land of Robert Taylor, whom he had known in Nebraska as Arlington Brugh. Shortly he returned to Nebraska to join the Federal Writers' Project. The FWP gathered people who flirted with socialist solutions to social inequities, but Kees had no share in this. In the thirties, when numbers of the nation's literati joined the Party or sought economic solutions to moral problems, Weldon Kees had already gone on to a kind of New Criticism: he thought that a work of art was a formal construct of human experience which deserved to be examined on its own terms. Before he was twenty-one he had seen through the political simplifications that charmed some of the brightest young people of the Great Depression.

Through the Federal Writers' Project, writers gave one another mutual support. In Lincoln, Nebraska, Kees lived for a time in a literary circle that included Loren Eiseley, Mari Sandoz, and others. There Kees found stimulation and a pretty wife named Ann Swan. Though from the start he was eager to play on the national scene, he may have had an advantage in maturing in the hinterland. Perhaps the geographic isolation encouraged his independence of judgment: big names never intimidated him for all his eagerness to know them, nor did he admire books simply because famous critics praised them.

In Lincoln, Weldon Kees found a hospitable publisher in the *Prairie*

Schooner, one of those noncommercial, small-circulation "little maga-zines" existing far from ancient, authoritative cultural centers. The little magazines fostered poetry and prose not yet acceptable to *Harper's* and *The Saturday Evening Post.* The *Prairie Schooner,* whose motto was "talent scout of the midlands," was open to writers from everywhere so long as they wrote to the editor's high standards. Eu-dora Welty first published there, and so did Loren Eiseley. By the time Kees appeared in its pages, the *Schooner* was known as an excellent showplace for new talent, and literary agents watched its pages.

The *Schooner* did more for him than exhibit his prose. Through re-viewing their books for the quarterly, Kees made the acquaintance of critics, poets, and publishers; and they in turn introduced him to other literary persons. He felt himself, and was, in the literary avant-garde. When he moved to Denver in 1937 to become a librarian, he continued his association with the *Schooner,* and in 1938 he began publishing verse in *Poetry,* the most prestigious periodical of its kind since Ezra Pound, T. S. Eliot, and Robert Frost first appeared in its pages. By the time he was twenty-five, Kees had a place, if a minor one, in the writers' trade.

From Nebraska and Colorado, Kees made his way into the national life with astonishing speed. Edward J. O'Brien, who always published stories from the little magazines in his important annual volumes of *Best Short Stories,* began citing Kees's work while Kees was still an undergraduate; and in 1940 he dedicated his last annual volume of *Best Short Stories* to Weldon Kees. By then, too, *New Directions* was publishing him. In 1943, when Kees went from his library job in Denver to Manhattan, he was received by the *Partisan Review* crowd—the *Partisan Review* had an even more formidable reputation then than now—and he spent evenings with Edmund Wilson, Horace Gregory, and Allen Tate. His writing appeared in *Time, The New Republic,* and the *New York Times* as well as in *Poetry, Partisan Review,* and *Furioso.* Although he knew Malcolm Cowley and Dwight Macdonald and Philip Rahv, all literary Leftists, Kees remained aloof from Marxist and Freudian doctrines. He was concerned with the human predicament, not political and psychological orthodoxy.

In New York, Kees observed various groups without joining any of them. He learned what Manhattan was like for ambitious young writers. Having begun to make his mark as a poet and critic—he stopped writing fiction about this time—he took up painting and exhibited with such influential artists as Hans Hofmann and Willem de Kooning. Peridot Gallery gave him four one-man shows. His pictures went unsold. Kees knew many of the Abstract Expressionists, but just as he had observed the genteel world of his mother's Nebraska, the social protest of the Depression, and the Freudian and Marxist controversies of the *Partisan Review,* he observed the New York School of Art but stood apart from it. When Kees succeeded Clement Greenberg as art critic on the *Nation,* he was not yet thirty-five.

Kees understood how powerful the New York scene was in advancing a career, but he knew too that New York remained but a part of a very large nation; coming from Nebraska, he had some awareness of continental reaches. Weary of urban dirt and decay, he and his wife in 1950 left New York for California, where in the Bay Area a new artistic life was stirring. He arrived ahead of Lawrence Ferlinghetti's City Lights Bookstore and the excitement that was to surround the Beat Movement. He sensed a growing ferment: he seemed destined always to be the first at the party.

Continuing to publish his poems and to exhibit his pictures, he now addressed himself to classical jazz, just then reviving in California. For years he had been a serious critic of the popular arts. He had written an appreciation of Fats Waller for *Time* in 1943, long before Waller was fashionable, and in May 1948 he wrote a piece on popular music for *Partisan Review.* Now he took to composing tunes and lyrics, anticipating the midcentury explosion of popular music. At the same time, he experimented with both still and moving photography. And in 1954 his third book of poems, *Poems 1947–1954,* was brought out in San Francisco, published by Adrian Wilson and underwritten by funds from his parents.

But he did not stay the course. Subject from early youth to extreme swings in mood that both he and his friends recognized as cyclical, in 1955 he disappeared. Perhaps like Ambrose Bierce, whom he talked of, he had gone to Mexico to "start again"—he had proposed to one of his friends that they go off like this, and he had talked of Mexico to his mother. But who can say? After 1955 the Weldon Kees of Nebraska, New York, and San Francisco drops from sight, leaving poems, stories, paintings, and a sizable packet of remarkable letters. The letters tell it all. They are collected here because they present an interesting man, sensitive, shrewd, witty, and intelligent. Their critical astuteness deserves our respect. So does the man. These letters help to fill in the history of their time as it is experienced by somebody a bit out in front. If Kees's enigmatic withdrawal throws a gray pall over all his life, it also drives a collection of his letters into unity.

It may be, as Weldon Kees suggested sometimes, that his letters were the chief accomplishment of his creative life. Certainly who touches them touches a man. In his poems, his paintings, his cinema, and in his fiction he gave expression to a subjective nightmare; but in his letters, he gossips about people and his world, and he is often full of intellectual excitement. His poems may be subjective, sometimes near-ly solipsistic, but his letters reach out to their reader.

Kees's chief correspondents saved his letters, aware that they had something special in their hands. The art of letter writing is not dead, as Kees showed in letters that seem as compulsive, as driven, as his stories and poems. Over the years Norris Getty, a college friend, accumulated a large file of Kees's letters. Getty, of Waco, Nebraska (population 350), became a classics master at the Groton School, where the Roosevelts educated their sons. He was Weldon's chief edi-tor, critic, and correspondent all his life. Maurice Johnson was an-other of Weldon Kees's major correspondents. An undergraduate colleague who took his Ph.D. at Columbia, he became a distinguished scholar of eighteenth-century literature at the University of Pennsylva-nia. He and Weldon were alike in their detached, satiric tempers; in his letters to Johnson, Kees offers sketches of events that call up those fading years.

In his last years Kees wrote to Anton Myrer, who was his third major correspondent. In time Myrer was to become a best-selling novelist; but in the 1950s he was just learning his craft, with Weldon Kees as one of his teachers. To him Kees sometimes hinted at recurrent fears, and even asked for sympathy. Only to Tony and Judith Rothschild Myrer does he sign himself "with love." One could wish that he had extended his "love" to Maurice Johnson and Norris Getty, not just his "sincerity," but in their inexpressive Nebraska way, perhaps they did not know how to invite testimonies of affection. In the end Kees needed love more than many men; but, for the most part, these letters remain witty documents, not cries from the heart; in poetry he unlocks his profoundest fears. Weldon Kees practiced letter writing for its own sake, and in the letters we go down the intellectual highways of two decades.

Identifications of persons mentioned in the letters and commentary appear in "Kees's Friends and Associates," pages 203–39 of this book.

From his earliest years Weldon Kees was fascinated with words and writing. In 1921, at the age of seven, he began to "publish" a family newspaper with masthead, headlines, and continued stories; by the time he was ten, he was typing out the newspaper on a machine provided by his father. His first printed piece was a column about movies, written when he was fourteen, which his father got published in the local newspaper. In it he gave an account of the talkies that he and his father had gone to on a recent trip to Minneapolis.

His imagination, like the imagination of many of his generation, was touched by films; and for him, even at twelve or fourteen, the movies were not simple entertainment: they were objects to which he could give his critical attention. For a sensitive boy like Weldon, Beatrice, Nebraska, seemed remote from the glamorous centers of movies and fiction. The Hollywood glitter of the picture shows at the Rialto or the Rivoli theater was in contrast to the solidity of the Richardsonian granite of the courthouse and the beaux art decorations on the Carnegie Library in the park. Thanks to voyages of his imagination, Weldon knew that the foundations of life about him were less monolithic than many assumed them to be. From the start, he lived in divided and distinguished worlds. Twenty years later, in a frequently anthologized poem, Kees recalled his childhood. The movies and his apprehensions of instability were joined in his memory. (Milton Sills—Silly Milt, as Weldon and his friends called him—and Doris Kenyon were among his favorite movie stars):

1926

The porchlight coming on again,
Early November, the dead leaves
Raked in piles, the wicker swing
Creaking. Across the lots
A phonograph is playing *Ja-Da*.

An orange moon. I see the lives
Of neighbors, mapped and marred
Like all the wars ahead, and R.
Insane, B. with his throat cut,
Fifteen years from now, in Omaha.

I did not know them then.
My airedale scratches at the door.
And I am back from seeing Milton Sills
And Doris Kenyon. Twelve years old.
The porchlight coming on again.

[*Harper's Magazine*, August 1949;
reprinted *Collected Poems*, p. 104]

Beatrice, a prosperous county seat of ten thousand, was full of standard American contrasts: dirt farmers in overalls and bankers in dark suits, a dozen splendid houses and rows of comfortable frame cottages, a few businessmen like Weldon's father who traveled to Chicago and many townspeople who thought Lincoln forty miles to the north rather exciting. Townspeople pronounced the name of their city with a heavy accent on the second syllable: Be*at*rice. The John Kees house, a handsome bungalow with leaded windows and wide porch, stood next to one of the mansions, the Kilpatrick estate, which was to become a retirement home for the PEO sisterhood in the thirties. In Weldon's childhood, it was a private dwelling just over the side fence.

John Kees, who was president of the family hardware manufacturing company founded by his father, a locksmith, was interested in books as well as in business. At the state university he had edited the campus newspaper, and in Beatrice he served as secretary of the library board. He read Hardy, Cervantes, and James Joyce and subscribed to *Punch*. He was a Democrat in a sturdily Republican County. Weldon addressed his father as John from the time he went off to college, and John always referred to his wife as Sarah in letters to his son. The Kees family, of German stock, referred to Sarah as Sadie, which she did not like. She was a member of the National Society of Magna Carta, the Sons and Daughters of Pilgrims, the Americans of Royal Descent, and she became a regent of the Daughters of the American Revolution. She christened her son Harry Weldon, but the family always called him Weldon, which was part of the name of Sarah's mother. Local people thought she coddled, overprotected, even indulged him.

Accustomed to being the center of attention at home, Weldon seemed to expect to be the center everywhere he went. In high school he was a little out of the mainstream because he was more interested in artistic matters than in sports. Even as a kid he was more eager to find an audience for his puppet shows, presented in his mother's living room, than in sledding in the street or kicking a football on the playground. Active in music and drama, editor of the senior yearbook, he did not endear himself to his teachers, perhaps because he was supercilious. Local people observed that, though obviously very bright, he got mediocre grades. Always meticulously groomed, he was a rather elegant boy and young man. He graduated from high school in 1931.

Weldon spent his first two undergraduate years at Doane College in Crete, a small town twenty miles west of Beatrice. He wrote plays and acted in college shows; but he found insufficient intellectual and artistic community there. He began to smoke heavily, too heavily, his parents thought. In his junior year he transferred to the University of Missouri at Columbia, which was famous for its school of journalism, but he found that the community there was no more to his exacting requirement than Doane had been. After he left Columbia one of his teachers wrote him that most would-be poets "hung their lyres up on some willow tree as they left our gates or sent them back with their caps and gowns," their passion for words only a temporary, adolescent itch, but that Weldon was different. He wrote constantly, without tutorial prodding, for he meant to write as a professional, to hold himself to standards his contemporaries hardly knew existed. Though he had grown up in a Booth Tarkington society, he did not intend to live in it.

In the spring of 1934 Kees sent a story to Lowry C. Wimberly, founder and editor of the *Prairie Schooner,* a literary quarterly published at the University of Nebraska. He got a quick and encouraging response, with suggestions for revision. Amenable to criticism throughout his life, Kees lengthened his story according to the editor's suggestion and thought it much improved. Wimberly published "Saturday Rain" in the fall 1934 issue of *Prairie Schooner.* In the story a young man returns to his hometown to discover his sweetheart with another man, her emotional life clearly different from what he had assumed it to be. Edward J. O'Brien awarded it three stars in his "Index of Distinctive Stories of 1934" in *Best American Short Stories 1935.* Thus Kees had an auspicious launching as a writer. He was twenty years old.

Encouraged, Kees packed up for Lincoln, ostensibly to get his baccalaureate degree but also to look for literary colleagues. In Lincoln he made important and lasting friendships. Orin Stepanek, a colorful professor of comparative literature, within days took him home to meet his brilliant young wife. Their beautiful house filled with Navajo rugs and Czech pictures was central in whatever artistic circles existed in Lincoln. In one of Stepanek's classes, Kees met Maurice Johnson, a senior who like Kees planned a literary career. A protégé of Louise Pound, the celebrated philologist, Johnson was to become a leading scholar of Jonathan Swift. He and Kees hit it off, for both had splendid aspirations. Kees's correspondence with him began in the summer of 1935, and continued for the rest of his life. In that year he also met Ann Swan, a complex girl from Douglas, Wyoming, whom he was to marry in 1937. She had come down to Lincoln from Wyoming and had pledged a fashionable sorority, but had no real part in undergraduate life.

The central figure in Lincoln for Kees as for many other aspiring writers was L. C. Wimberly. Although Wimberly published his own stories irregularly in *American Mercury* and *Harper's,* by 1934 he had begun to resign himself to being a teacher of writers more than a writer himself. Robert Lasch, an admiring student who later won a Pulitzer Prize in journalism, referred to him in print as "Gloomy Gus" because of his obsession with the dark side of human experience, including suicide. In Wimberly, Kees had a mentor whose judgments he could respect and whose disposition he found congenial. Behind

his satirical gaiety, Weldon was at least as concerned with the dark
side of human experience as Wimberly. Rudolph Umland, one of
"Wimberly's boys," has written an account of Wimberly, Kees, and the
writer's life in *Prairie Schooner* country:

> Loren Eiseley said he could remember that there was a certain magical
> quality in the air of Lincoln. Mari Sandoz said a Bohemianism sud-
> denly took root and flourished. Lincoln in those years had been a kind
> of Greenwich Village to its literary aspirants often seen sitting around
> tables in cafes discussing lofty subjects like Communism, Fascism,
> Democracy and such people as Proust, Henry Mencken, D. H. Law-
> rence, Dos Passos and Sherwood Anderson. They discussed too the
> flashy clothes that Barney Oldfield wore, the satirical stories of
> Weldon Kees, and poetry which appeared in the *Schooner*. They dis-
> cussed, in fact, every article, story and bit of verse that appeared
> between the yellow covers of that little magazine. The literary life in
> the city centered around the *Schooner* and its editor.

Umland provided an account of Wimberly:

> Wimberly would be remembered as a teacher certainly as long as any
> of his students remained alive. He made himself an unforgettable
> teacher because he had had the creative urge of a writer strong within
> him. Although the urge had been beaten down and allowed to wither
> by other things, it had given him an awareness of what good writing
> was and what was required to accomplish it. He had been able to
> express, in his quiet way, the things about literature that make it the
> most unique experience in life and had exposed the sham, pomposity
> and superficiality that is in some of it too. He had shaken his students
> out of their complacency and opened the doors of a liberal education
> to them by introducing more things than literature in his lectures. As
> editor of *Prairie Schooner*, his influence had spread far beyond the
> cornfields and prairies of the Midwest. "Nebraska—? Oh yes," enthu-
> siasts in Mississippi, California, Wisconsin, New York exclaimed,
> "that's where L. C. Wimberly edits the *Prairie Schooner!*"

Perhaps Umland exaggerates, but the *Schooner* was important for new
writers. He recalls that Wimberly occasionally introduced the subject
of suicide into conversations:

He spoke gently of it as though it held a dread fascination. He said that in ancient times in England suicide victims were buried, along with unbaptised infants and executed criminals, in graves on the north side of churches. He was deeply learned in the lore of burial customs. When I told him that I had had a brother and a cousin who had committed suicide, one by slashing his wrists, the other by hanging, he wanted to know the reasons and just how they had set about it. A young person had to have a lot of determination to go through with it, he said. Generally there was no logical reason for suicide. Wimberly said he had never thought about killing himself because he had been brought up believing God wouldn't like it. Moreover the thought of the pain and agony that frequently precedes death gave him the shivers. He confessed he had always wanted to write a short story about some frustrated writer killing himself after having a manuscript returned by an editor. He admitted he worried every time he sent back a batch of manuscripts to *Schooner* contributors because he didn't know which one or how many might cause a suicide.

After Weldon's suicide [Umland here is making a common assumption], Wimberly sometimes expressed a feeling of guilt because he hadn't asked Weldon, during his visit in 1950 when he appeared to be at loose ends, to stay in Lincoln and become an English instructor at the university. A stint of teaching might have changed the patterns in Weldon's life so he would never have heard the singing of the strange bird by day as well as by night. But then he might not have become the poet he did either.[1]

Wimberly understood Weldon Kees. He saw that his talent, essentially lyrical and satiric, was incapable of sustained flight, as Kees himself came eventually to recognize; but friends to whom Kees wrote long letters and showed manuscripts did not seem to understand this. In his first letters to his friend Maurice Johnson, Kees presents himself as an ambitious young novelist, eager to participate in the great world of letters with works of lengthy fiction. In the summer of 1935 Johnson was at home in Norfolk, Nebraska, with his parents, preparing to return to Lincoln to take his master's degree. Weldon wrote him an account of summer school in the heat of a Depression July:

The summer wears on slowly: the highschool superintendents in crinkly seersucker suits meet in campus washrooms and while micturating discuss higher education of the Madrid (Nebr.) publicschools, the salaries there, and the unparalleled value of a Master's thesis on "How Far Should a District School Be From the Road?": Wimberly has a doublebreasted robinseggblue suit with clarkgable pockets and a shirred back: he becomes a bit boring in his particular brand of mysticism which he ladles out in the sweltering Seventeenthcentury Prose class: here in the Beta Theta Pi house a poker game runs day and night: so does the radio: and the drunks in the dormitory: and the debate *re* how many of his original men Duke Ellington had with him when he played Capit(a)l Beach: the sun burning: the blank faces: the schoolteachers from Weeping Water and Hayes Center approaching the menopause slowly but surely in their darkblue eyelet dresses with pink slips underneath: the gin (legal) cooling: the assignments long: the nights maddening: the bed lumpy: the summer wearing on

From which you should deduce that I have recently read MacLeish's DosPassos-dedicated *Panic,* and it is not the sort of thing to give the troops, especially after *Frescoes [for Mr. Rockefeller's City,* 1933] and *Hamlet of A. MacL.* [1928]. I cannot agree with Arch that the speech of the man on the street is trochaic: not that it matters a damn. Perhaps it would play well. The speeches of the bankers and streetpeople are the speeches of MacL. in his : : : : spotted manner and no other . . . I expected much more of Emily Hahn's postmanalwaysringstwicetypography novelette, *Affair;* but it didnt, as Fred Christensen [assistant editor of *Prairie Schooner*] might observe, have quite enough . . . I liked much better the three plays of Clifford Odets: especially *Waiting for Lefty.* The format is in the fine Random House tradition.

Stepanek excused me from World Lit classes: instead I have to read critical works—when I have time. I'm working on a bibliography of Joyce, and if you know of any articles or books that I might not know about, I'd appreciate learning of them. As far as I know there has been no complete bibliography of J.J.—and it may be I can get my M.A. on this. . . . Although I still think that "The Influence of *Ulysses* on Certain Novels of Conrad Aiken, John Dos Passos, and William Faulkner" can't be improved upon for a fine topic. . . . If I can manage it, I'm going to the University of Chicago rather than California. Reasons: numerous. . . . You'd better come along. As Steppy ob-

served: "Nebraska has given you all She has to offer, Maurice." After
all, there's Robert Morss Lovett offering a course in the English
Novel. * * *"

After graduating from the University of Nebraska, Weldon wrote on a
novel, *Slow Parade,* in a cabin in Colorado. On August 14, 1935 he
wrote to Maurice Johnson:

> After my lunch of cornedbeef sandwiches (the Forum Restaurant:
> wonder if that pimplyfaced Joyce-imitator is still there?) and goats-
> milk I walked down to the little store across the Big Thompson river
> for the mail. I was planning on coming back here to our cabin (iron-
> ically named Dinna Fret) and working on the book for the rest of the
> afternoon. But I have been out of touch for a week with most forms of
> talk I love (womangabble: womancackle: allthetime) that your letter
> and the one from Ann disturbed me so much that I won't be able to
> get back to it for an hour or so at least.
>
> Where I'll be for school: I wish to God I knew. It seems fairly certain
> that Ann will be in California. That fascist country doesn't attract me;
> neither does the thought of graduate work anywhere. I'm working like
> hell on this novel, trying to get it finished before the summer is ended.
> And it terrifies me a little because there always seems to be so damn
> much more I want to put in it and I know now that there are some
> things in it already that I don't want: things that must come out; but
> perhaps it will amount to something and some people will like it and
> at any rate it isn't anything to be ashamed of: yet. [. . .] And so I work
> from five to eight hours a day on a screenedin porch with the river
> flowing by making rainsound twenty feet away, with the pines behind
> me, with the typewriter squatting on a stand I made out of a peach-
> crate. . . .

He described the book:

> I am working with a technique that is similar to Dos Passos', but in
> one sense his method inverted: where he (and Charles Dickens) take
> isolated characters and bring them slowly closer and closer to each
> other, I'm trying to take the members of one family and show them
> growing farther and farther away from each other. I hope that you'll
> be able to read it in MS. before the final draft: it seems to me there is
> a greater need for criticism before books are published than after.
> (Vide: Thomas Wolfe.)

1. Weldon Kees and his mother,
about 1919. Photograph courtesy
of the Heritage Room, Bennett
Martin Public Library

H Weldon Kees

Ann Swan

2. Weldon Kees at the University of
Nebraska in September 1934. Pho-
tograph courtesy of University of
Nebraska Archives

3. Ann Swan at the University of
Nebraska in September 1934. Pho-
tograph courtesy of University of
Nebraska Archives

4. Maurice Johnson, about 1936.
Photograph courtesy of Nancy
Johnson

5. Federal Writers' Project, Lincoln, Nebraska, 1936. Weldon Kees in the center, Norris Getty immediately to his left, Rudolph Umland third man to his left, Dale Smith sixth person to his left, J. Harris Gable seated. Photograph courtesy of Rudolph Umland

6. Weldon Kees, Norris Getty, and Dale Smith at the State Capitol, Lincoln, Nebraska, April 1937. Photograph courtesy of Margaret Smith

In a postscript, Kees continues a youthful discussion:

> Anent your art-for-art's sake Proust quotation: it doesn't mean very
> much when you take into consideration that any writer who takes his
> work seriously at all writes "propaganda" of one sort or another.
> What I'm trying to say is that any work of merit or value has a "point
> of view" behind it. Isn't it evident that *Gulliver's Travels, Anna Ka-
> renina, Madame Bovary, Magic Mountain,* etc., etc., all aim at reform,
> solution, or whatever you want to call it? Isn't Joyce trying to put
> something over other than merely setting down beautiful wordpat-
> terns, despite wordobsession? Isn't Faulkner trying to "sell" us on the
> futility of futility? Isn't Wolfe trying to put across his "lostness"? T. S.
> Eliot is the poet who sings the song of Oswald Spengler, that's rather
> evident. . . . All right, you say, what is art-for-art's-sake? It seems to
> me that anyone can be a futilitarian right now: it's the easiest, sim-
> plest thing in the world—because it is *negative.* All this sounds pretty
> platitudinous, and I'm not sure that you'll agree. But surely we should
> have more admiration for those writers with some guts, those who are
> trying to find a rational solution and are willing to fight a little, than
> for those pale and hopeless young men who have little more to say
> than Booth Tarkington and Kathleen Norris . . . And what do you
> think?

Late in September 1935, Weldon rather reluctantly enrolled in the
graduate school of the University of Chicago; but he quickly discovered that the meticulous world of professional scholarship was not
for him. He was much more interested in writing his own novels than
in studying other people's. That month Weldon wrote to Maurice
Johnson from the Mira-Mar Hotel in Chicago:

> Dear Maury—
>
> You were right. Be content with your lot at Nebraska. When I can find
> sufficient time I'll write you at length about the University of Chicago.
> If I can last a quarter, I'll be greatly surprised. I've never been quite so
> disappointed in a place in my life. Please regard Nebraska favorably.
> You would loathe this as much or more so than I do, I'm sure.
>
> I think you'll agree that the enclosed story ["Letter from Maine"] is in
> much better shape than the first draft that you saw. Try to get it in the

Schooner for me. I think Wimberly will like it. And the sooner I get a decision on it, the happier I'll be.

All the nice things you had to say about *Slow Parade* give me heart, and I hope you won't be disappointed in the rest of it. I'm working hard on the closing sections; think I'll be able to finish it this month, with luck. [. . .]

Kees remained in Chicago only briefly and, after a stop in Nebraska, went on to Los Angeles, hoping to get a job as a writer. Robert Taylor was making it big in pictures. Born in Gage County, where his physician-father had been a friend of the Kees family, Arlington Brugh (now known as Robert Taylor) and Weldon Kees had known each other from childhood and both had been involved in theatrical activities at Doane. Virginia Faulkner, of Lincoln, was also making it big. After a spectacular success in writing for popular magazines like *The Saturday Evening Post,* she had been called to Hollywood to work on scenarios for Gable and Garbo. Weldon Kees reported seeing her careening about Hollywood in an open car. She and Robert Taylor proved to him that success in the big time was possible. In letters to Maurice Johnson during the winter of 1935–36, Kees reported on what he saw in Hollywood, as though he were a part of it all:

Dear Maurice:

I meant to write to you before this, but I always experience horrible agony (oh lost! lost!) when I'm thrust into a new environment. It is tremendously difficult for a couple of weeks while I'm trying to make the adjustment. Coming from the relative calmness of Nebraska to the largest of all American cities is little short of terrifying. The damned hurry, the noise, the goddamned lights enjoining you to mobilize your car chew Ex-lax and keep regular dine and dance without overcharge see Dick Powell subject yourself to colonic irrigation, the gasfumes, the freaks, the hurry hurry hurry, the seers, the Christian Scientists, the pitchmen, the unending rainy season, the hurry. . . .

I stayed two days in Hollywood with the Beatrice contingent and was more than happy to escape. Merely call to mind all the wild stories you've ever heard about that mad and terrifying region, augment them with recollections of all the satires written about it, and that is the actual and genuine Hollywood. Ben Hecht's remark, to the effect that out here they're all "either drunk or crazy" is fairly accurate. . . . But on the other hand, and this strictly confidential—a great many writers, actors, and executives are violent Communist sympathetizers, but have to keep it very quiet. There is one prominent director for instance, who pours half or more of his salary into the C.P. . . . Things are very hot here: for instance: Joel Faith (pseud.) who wrote that article in *New Theatre* on Louella Parsons and Marion Davies, is currently hiding out somewhere outside of the state. Hearst has given orders to his vigilantes to shoot to kill. . . . This is becoming pretty gossipy, and I hope you don't mind. [. . .]

He gives an account of the fate of *Slow Parade:*

Covici turned down the book. Three of the men there wanted to publish it, Straus and some other person didnt. From Harold's letter—I'd like to have your reaction to it: ". . . We have finally been forced to come to an adverse decision, however, on the score that in the last analysis you do not dig deeply enough into the psychology of the four children. You tend to describe them as types in broad terms which would fit hundreds of similar characters and you do not work down to the special flavorsome qualities of the individual. . . ." Special flavorsome qualities, indeed! What do you think of that? My own feeling is that while they may be what Mr. Strauss calls "types," people today seem in a broad sense, to fall into such classifications. To be anything but a type you have to be Thomas Wolfe or something like that. Surely Emma Bovary is a type; so are Studs Lonigan (there are thousands of him), Babbitt, the people of Dos Passos, Herrmann, Caldwell. Or am I wrong? I'd very much like to know your views. . . . At least there has been no uniformity of opinion on *Slow Parade* from those who have read it. Covici at least had the good grace to say nothing about it being "unrelievedly grim". It's at Vanguard now. I still have much hope for the book. . . . Now working away at notes on the new one, *A Good American;* and on a novelette, *The Dead Are Friendly.*

• • •

Weldon Kees did not find a place for himself in the movie business; and so in the summer of 1936 he returned to Nebraska. Because his father was generous, he was never destitute. By Depression standards, the Keeses were well off, and Weldon was an only son. He lived in a rooming house and ate at a boarding house, but his dress and manner separated him from the others.

When Weldon Kees reappeared in Lincoln, Wimberly proposed that he join the Federal Writers' Project, then preparing a guidebook to the state of Nebraska. Kees agreed, though taking the job meant that he had to go on relief, over the protests of his parents, especially his mother. The FWP was very nearly a Wimberly fiefdom, for Wimberly nominated candidates to its director, a former student, and kept a close eye on its activities. Kees's associates in Lincoln were now the young and not-so-young aspiring writers of the town.

Life at the Federal Writers' Project was not without its sophomoric gaieties. Kees and other young writers occupied their minds with plans to embarrass and annoy their supervisors. His particular friends were Dale Smith, an unpublished novelist, and Norris Getty, whom some people thought he rather overwhelmed. Because of their spiteful tongues, the three young men became known as the "unholy trio" around the FWP offices. The three were particularly contemptuous of J. Harris Gable, the director of the project; Gable was, in fact, rather punctilious, the kind of person irreverent young men like to deflate. One of his great ambitions, for example, was to be listed in *Who's Who in America*. Years later Norris Getty recalled those days and Weldon's temperament:

> My acquaintance with Weldon Kees began across a desk—or two desks, actually, shoved back to back in the loft of a warehouse in Lincoln, Nebraska. Before that, in the middle 1930's, we had been students at the University of Nebraska, probably attending some of the same lectures. But in college I was usually the talkative student who sat on a front seat, waving an arm and eager to take the floor. Kees, who was never a show-off, would be sitting quietly in a back seat, probably beside the girl he was later to marry. At any rate, we were now [1936–37] fellow-editors in the Nebraska section of the WPA Writers' Project, an enterprise designed to turn out a guidebook for the state. As copy came in from a WPA writer in, say, the settlement of Broken Bow, it would go first to our typing section. Then the

original copy and the typescript would come to the double desk, where either Kees or I would read aloud the manuscript while the other held a red pencil, menacingly, above the typed version. If it was Kees's day to hold the pencil, a good deal of pencil lead was worn away; hardly a sentence would get by without some slashing emendation that made for greater clarity or smoothness. In fact, I probably learned more from Kees about the writing of expository prose than I learned from any of my English teachers. [. . .]

Back in the Writers' Project period, there was a day when the director asked Kees and me to visit a graveyard somewhere in Lincoln; apparently the original reporter had overlooked this tourist attraction. The day of our jaunt was pleasant and sunny, and we found the cemetery easily enough. But as soon as we stepped into the place, Kees headed for the shade of the nearest evergreen tree and sat down. He was ready, he explained, to vouch for anything and everything that I might write about the cemetery. For himself, however, all the conventional trappings of death—the coffins, the graves, the services and all the rest—were simply detestable. "More and more," he said, "I think Hart Crane had the right idea." Years later, when I was crossing the Golden Gate Bridge for the first time, I recalled those words. And I remember them still, as I shall continue to remember many things about a remarkable person and a fine artist.[2]

Hart Crane, whose poem "The Bridge" (1930) is a landmark in American literature, disappeared from a ship bound for New York from Mexico, a presumed suicide.

The quality of Kees's life during the FWP year can be gathered from the letters that he wrote to Maurice Johnson the following summer. He was living near the campus, reading and writing and talking and planning. On July 14, 1937, he wrote:

Wimberly talks dolefully about suspending publication of the *Schooner* for a year and then starting up again. He asked me, on the one occasion that I've seen him in weeks, if that was ever done. I said I didn't think so, though now and then some of the stuffier of the academic journals sometimes did that. He shook his head sadly (scattering cigarashes on his summer suit), emitted one short anglosaxon word, and changed the subject to the preponderance of grasshoppers

> on the prairie in this sad season. (smalltown teacherscollege people
> with sweaty armpits are typing their masters' theses in the Osthoff
> house and the dog Tike is yapping and the electricfan hums regularly
> while outside automobile horns are sounding in the sunshine)

Ann Swan, who had been in California, was about to return to the
Midwest, which pleased him. The satiric insouciance in Weldon's letters contrasts with the somber tone of the first poem which he published that fall. Its use of the movies and its note of threatening futility
anticipates much of his later work. Kees reprinted this poem as a
preface to his first volume of verse, *The Last Man*, published in 1943
and dedicated to Norris Getty and Maurice Johnson.

> Subtitle
>
> We present for you this evening
> a movie of death: observe
> these scenes chipped celluloid
> reveals unsponsored and tax-free.
> We request these things only:
> all gum must be placed beneath the seats
> or swallowed quickly, all popcorn sacks
> must be left in the foyer. The doors
> will remain closed throughout
> the performance. Kindly consult
> your programs: observe that
> there are no exits. This is
> a necessary precaution.
> Look for no dialogue, or for the
> sound of any human voice: we have seen fit
> to synchronize this play with
> squealings of pigs, slow sound of guns,
> the sharp dead click of empty chocolatebar machines.
> We say again: there are
> no exits here, no guards to bribe,
> no washroom windows.
> No FINIS to the film unless
> the ending is your own.
> Turn off the lights, remind

the operator of his union card:
sit forward, let the screen reveal
your heritage, the logic of your destiny.

[*Signatures*, 3 (1937–38)]

In August 1937, Weldon Kees decided to go to the University of Denver to study to be a librarian. Increasingly discontent with academia as he saw it and as Johnson and others reported it to him, he yet wanted a life with books, and he knew he could not make a living as a free-lance writer. John and Sarah Kees were glad to pay his tuition; and the prospect of marrying Ann Swan was further inducement to leave the Federal Writers' Project, a professional deadend, and to get into a career.

The life that Weldon Kees found in Colorado was outside a social community, though one of his classmates remembered later that he created a stir among the women in his classes in library science, handsome as he was. For the most part he was without friends like Norris Getty and Maurice Johnson to whom he could talk of new writing, but he continued to be alert to experimental work wherever it appeared, and he read the little magazines from everywhere. He kept abreast, as they say. He explained his views and exhibited his literary tastes in a review of *New Directions 1937:*

> Writing of an experimental nature makes up its own rules as it goes along, but the finished work usually runs the risk of being judged by rules that are not at all new. What finally determines the quality of any piece of writing rests upon what light it sheds on the phases of doing and being; in short, the old stuff: characterization, mood, movement, etc. Although Mr. T. S. Eliot expects the "serious" reader to go over difficult works six or seven times, taking "at least as much trouble as a barrister reading an important decision on a complicated case," the best experimental work usually reveals most of its worth in a first reading. To insist upon such serious attention and study is to relegate literature to a leisure class minority activity that ends in pointless philological investigations or worse. It is a commonplace of our time that on one hand our mass reading sinks lower and lower (both in style and matter), while the "new writing" veers more and more towards private concerns and unintelligibility.[1]

34

In conversation as well as in print Kees tried to reconcile the popular culture of movies, journalism, and jazz with the high culture of Proust, Eliot, and Mann; and though an aspiring artist himself, he deplored the affectations of those whom Professor Stepanek identified as "the arty guys." In his first letter from Denver to Norris Getty, Kees gave a full account of his day and week. His pleasant job in the public library paid him enough to allow him and Ann Swan to get married immediately, if Ann got a job too:

> 25 September 1937
>
> Dear Norris,
>
> I was glad to get your good letter: up to the time it came, the only communication I'd had from Lincoln was a disturbing screed from Mamie Meredith, who teaches English at the University of Nebraska. It seems she wanted me to pick out a bunch of little magazines to send to some fellow she'd had in class last year and who had chucked It All to get married and live in Deadwood, S.D., or some such place. Evidently she thought Denver newsstands were laden with experimental publications: there she was very wrong: if you can find *New Masses* youre mighty lucky. Or *are* you? . . . Anyway, in my spare moments, I've been staring at her letter rather wistfully, and wondering if the Public Library in Deadwood takes the *Yale Review.* I can see the librarian there now, a wee little lady wearing black cotton sleeveprotectors, muttering to herself in her office and wondering *when* in Heaven's name that nice Louis Bromfield is going to do another book one-half so lovely as *The Man Who Had Everything,* or whatever it was. . . . Well, I wrote Mamie and gave her some addresses of little magazines, and I hope they dont all fold before she writes them. . . . Life is pretty baffling at times.
>
> I've been having my little adventures and surprises. Frankly, Getty, when I left Wymore [the Nebraska town from which he took the train to Denver], the 7th of this month on that unpleasant slowmoving train, I wondered whether I had done the right thing or not. I was damned glad to get away from the FWP, let's not forget that; but the whole plan sounded so uncertain and there was a fine chance of it all working out about as well as the Versailles Treaty. . . . I now feel somewhat differently. A couple of days after I got here, I learned from

one of the men who works at the Denver Public Library that there were a couple of vacancies in the circulation department there, and why didnt I apply? I went in and saw Mr Wyer and talked to him for some time and hit him for a job. He had evidently heard of me from someone or other (besides J. Harris Gable, I mean) and spoke more or less encouragingly; told me to come back the next day and he'd give me a definite answer. Next day I went back; Wyer said (after we had talked for some time of such things as the *Southern Review,* hayfever, rose colds, the Federal Writers' Project, the Soul of J. H. Gable, library schools and Their Place in a Changing Democracy, etc,)—anyway— he said, "How would you like to work here fulltime?" I gasped that that would be fine indeed. All right, he said, you can start tomorrow: it's the beginning of a pay period. . . .

So now I am working 41 hrs a wk at about the same money I got from Harry Hopkins and his little group, taking half of the li- braryschool course, and wondering how I find time to write involved letters like this one. . . . I am going to take the library course in two years: taking Book Arts this year, and Cataloging and Administration next. This relieves me of considerable anxiety as to money, and will make it possible for me—at the end of the period—to have had two years of work and experience in a firstrate public library in a good-sized town. This should be of some value, in addition to the BS degree in Librarianship, when I go after a job. And if Ann doesnt find work right off, we will still be eating, if only the fresh vegetables, reasonably priced, which Colorado offers to its residents.

Much of the work at the library is good stuff, and I like it. Of course there is the usual number of bitches—on a staff of 105, 90% of them women, what can you expect?—but there are other things that make up for that. One is switched about from one place to another so often that, so far at least, I havent been bored. A typical day, in case youre interested. . . . 8–9:40: library school class. 9:40 coffee and cigarette. 10:00: report at library, work at loan desk. 11:30: return desk. 12: slipping room. 12:30; loan desk again. 1:00: lunch. 2:30: registration desk (not so good). 4:00: openshelf room, handling reference work and the rental collection of new books: a little like working for Beryl Black, but on a slightly higher level, I hope. 5:00: special work (re- serves, indexing, extra reference work, exchanges, etc.). . . . And this schedule is so varied that I've never yet worked the same hours at the same places in my eleven days there. . . . There are all sorts of amusing things: the little Russianjew who is writing a lengthy letter to some friends and comes in every day to have me help him with his English. Frankly, I think the man's an exhibitionist of sorts. You should see the letter. It goes on and on, and would delight the Spirit of Ring Lardner . . . Nuns who come in, after G. K. Chesterton or H. H. Munro or some other Pope-sanctioned hack . . . Shy virgins wanting to reserve *Married Love* by Marie Stopes . . . The deaf-and-dumb lady who handed me a piece of paper with this legend: "goon with the wing." [. . .]

I appreciated a lot your lengthy notes on the Lincoln front: let's have more of that sort of thing . . . Am going to write Maurice and urge him to start a magazine. Ernest Brace wrote me that this one that's up in Woodstock is to be rigorously DHLawrencesque: Brace was asked to help edit it, but wasnt very sympathetic. It seems the editor went down to Taos and met Mabel Dodge Luhan and Aldous Huxley and Frieda and really thought he had something. Poor Brace has been laid up in bed, first with la grippe and then with diarrhea: he wrote me that he's written eight novels in the last 14 years and has been able to publish only one of them (*Commencement,* Harpers, 1925).

This address will be permanent, so far as I know.

Give my regards to people there, tell Dale to write (novelettes and a letter to me), and put a sharp tack in the chair of Assistant Director Umland.

Yrs,
Weldon

What's the new man like?—the one who took my unenviable place on the F (for Futile) WP.

The letter that he wrote on the day before he married Ann Swan is almost unnaturally cool, concerned as it is with literary, not human, affairs. He and Ann had met at the University of Nebraska, Weldon transferring from the University of Missouri at Columbia and Ann from two years at Pomona College in California. Exactly one year younger than Weldon, she had grown up in Douglas, Wyoming. Ann and Weldon were constant companions during their year in Lincoln, and though they had no formal "engagement" as the custom then was, they had planned for some time to be married. The marriage was delayed because Weldon had no money and his job paid too little to support both himself and a wife.

[2 October 1937]

Dear Maurice:

Tomorrow is my wedding day and it is meet that I write you before the married life, school, work, writing, etc. prevent me from writing you with any degree of intelligence. (Not that you may expect much from this screed: I have just returned from a somewhat arty cocktail party given for the benefit of the Spanish Loyalists at the apartment of Michael Stuart. You may remember seeing Stuart's stuff in *transition* and elsewhere: he had a story in that issue of *transition* we ordered, the one with the comb on the cover and the thousandleggedworm piece of Franz Kafka's. Stuart was Joyce's confidante and aide in Paris for a good many years: prominently displayed in his apartment is an autographed picture of J.J.)

I shouldnt like to see the body of this letter enclosed in parentheses.

Ann is coming here on the train tomorrow and we are to be married by the local Unitarian minister. I do not anticipate that she will have too bad a time of it finding work, but for the time being we can make it on the salary I am now getting from the City of Denver. No doubt you have by this time learned from Getty or Dale or someone that I am working for the Denver Public Library. The job has, so far, helped my natural neuroticism—which was spurred on by Gable and his little group—a great deal; and although it will take me two years to get my degree in librarianship, I'm not saddened at the prospect. One runs into enough amusing things in a day to balance the odious features of library work . . . As I wrote Getty, I'm particularly delighted with the little man who comes into the reading room, removes his aircushion from his briefcase, blows it up, and sits in pneumatic comfort.

To come to the main point of this letter, I wonder if you are still enthused over the idea of a little magazine of your own. Leonard Thompson, my printer friend, is back in Beatrice, and told me that he could put out a magazine the size of *Hinterland* for $35 an issue. And 500 copies at that. This is certainly a figure you could handle, and God knows a place is needed where people like Louis Mamet, Eudora Welty, Erling Larsen, D. A. Davidson, etc., can publish their stuff that other magazines wont print. A good editor could get out a damned good publication, and I am very anxious for you to consider it seriously. An appeal for fund, if handled properly, would certainly bring in enough to get out a couple of issues; and it would give you such a great deal of satisfaction to run something like that. I really wish you would do it. If you're interested, I'll put Leonard in touch with you.

Nortons sent me Horace Gregory's *New Letters in America,* which contains good things by Auden and Eugene Joffe, and I'm going to review it, along with *American Stuff* and *365 Days,* for the *Schooner* . . . The Goncourt Journals are full of fascinating material: I especially like this: "Flaubert said to us today (March 17, 1861): 'The story or plot of a novel is of no interest to me. When I write a novel I have in mind rendering a colour, a shade . . . In *Madame Bovary* all I was after was to render a special tone, that colour of the mouldiness of a wood louse's existence [. . .]."

In later letters, wit and literary matters fill pages that might have contained expressions of honeymoon euphoria. On November 28, he wrote to Maurice Johnson, beginning with a rather jejune imitation of T. S. Eliot:

> Dear Maurice,
> It is
> SUNDAY MORNING
> and here is a poem
> for you:
>
> The purple sky curdles, chewed by the Sunday sun,
> a pleasant sight for Gloria Onderdonk
> (last of the Onderdonks: a long line)
> washing out undergarments
> in the kitchen sink.

Sunday brings
her favorites (colored) in the funnies,
respite from the day-in-day-out dimestore,
and Father Duffy on the radio.

It is
Sunday: there are newsboys calling:
cars sputter at the curb.
And the soul of Gloria Onderdonk
mingles gratefully
with the tepid soapsuds.

....

SCRAPE YOUR TONGUE AS YOUR DOCTOR ADVISES! With a
Gem Tongue-scraper. *Ooodles of Noodles. says Fred MacMurray* the
bogey branded "Business" is a myth, but fortunately there are individual businesses and businessmen—tens of thousands of them. They
are the workers, doers, pay their bills, bear a major part of the nation's tax load, provide jobs and all the things that raise standards of
living and make life on the American plan *inviting, stimulating* and
worth while. TROUBLED WITH GETTING UP NIGHTS? i always
use it, Ginger Rogers says

* * *

Things go along with some degree of stability here. Ann was lucky
enough to fall into a temporary job here in a lawyer's office shortly
after she arrived. That lasted for three weeks, while some girl was
having her appendix removed. Then that was over. That was over
three weeks ago. As you have no doubt heard, we are having a slump.
People are jittery here: one of my informants, who listens regularly to
the great heartbeat of the coupon-clipping classes, reports a state of
mind among that group that borders on the mass hysteria of pre-
election times. The thing to do, it seems, is to kill off all the govern-
ment employees: that will fix things up fine. And then Roosevelt has
syphilis, you know—that's what's wrong with the country. Roosevelt
has syphilis and that's why business is shot to hell and that's why the
market is in the doldrums and that's what is causing business uncertainty and may even account for the noted escapist quality of Ele-

anor's recently published *This Is My Story.* Anyway, a million people
have been fired in the last two months; but that isnt what is disturbing
these latter-day Adam Smiths: no: the money isnt coming in so fast,
and there's a great flurry and lots of anger and the old talk about
Mussolini and his doctrines and the good they might do here is getting under way again. . . . And now Ann has a lousy job with an
insurance company. 250 girls were fired by Montgomery Wards here
last week. At the library yesterday morning a man who had been out
of work for sometime, and who had been hired by the city to clean
the ice off of the library steps, slipped, fell, struck his head on the
concrete, died. They brought him in the library and after a while a
sleek man from the coroner's office came but they havent decided yet
whether his wife and 3 kids will get any compensation from the city.
Not a regular city employee you know.

After all that it seems absurd to say that I like my job better than any
of the others I've ever held; but it's true. I thought for a while I might
have made a mistake in choosing this in preference to teaching, but
now I think not. After these two years are over, if there are any jobs
then, we'd like to go to San Francisco for a while. But that's a long
way off.

I wonder if I've written you about Bob Hutchison. He's the best
person I've yet met here; have lunch with him almost every day, and
he's over here at the apartment a lot. Comes from a wealthy family
here but is considered a black sheep by them; has been on the Art,
Writers,' and Theatre projects, both here and in San Francisco. Knows
lots of people: Saroyan, Pound, Robert McAlmon, etc. Good friend of
Kenneth Rexroth. Some talk that Rexroth, Bob and I may start a
magazine. We have a prospective backer here who has hinted that he
might kick in a good-sized amount if the market goes up again. I
might say that Denver is full of vaguely arty people who live off of
accrued interest and the market [. . .] .

Within a few months Weldon was suffering from what he came to call
"the old despair." Mari Sandoz, whose *Old Jules* had been a notable
recent success, was living in Denver at this time; and she had recom-
mended him and his novel, *Slow Parade,* to several publishers. After
lengthy deliberation Doubleday Doran rejected the novel, and Kees

was understandably disappointed, even bitter. He wrote to Norris
Getty on January 23, 1938:

> Sunday. Berlioz (uneven) on the radio, with Mr. Enesco or whatever
> conducting. The highschool boy across the hall whistles with quasi-
> cheer (close the transom, we cant hear the goddam Berlioz); the psy-
> chopathic dog downstairs whimpers, barks, is mildly scolded; the gas
> splutters; dark sky: snow coming, they say. Ann reads a translation of
> one of Cocteau's plays by Dudley Fitts. A note to myself is stuck in the
> mirror: "Remember get book at lib." Too many cigarettes. The old
> despair. The soot peacefully floating in the cold Colorado afternoon.
>
> Much to say: don't know how to begin. I'll not dwell on my work at
> the library, or on library school; away from both, thoughts of them
> depress me. But while working at the library, I halfway enjoy most of
> my duties: it is at least a better way of making a living than other
> things I've done. There is considerable pettiness; evidently libraries all
> over are fraught with it. (You know, of course, from your contacts
> there.)
>
> WRITING//// I'm not doing what I want to do; is anyone? In
> my stories, I'm being much influenced (I think) by William Carlos
> Williams, whose *White Mule* impressed me greatly. A story I wrote a
> few weeks back coughed up memories and ideas that set me to think-
> ing of this new novel—the one I wrote Dale about. I cant tell you
> baldly of its content and nature; if I could, I would't even think of
> writing the book: but here's a rough idea. The "artist": theme. The
> treatment: entirely objective. I would stick entirely to "known" mate-
> rial; what I mean is, things that have happened to me, things heard,
> seen, etc. Principal character: an approximation of myself. (You *cant*
> write about yourself, really; try it; it's impossible.) Principal character
> (whom we will call X because that's an interesting letter and of value
> in mathematics) is never seen from *within*. That is: the artist theme is
> carried out in its externals; no Joycean, Wolfesque, handling. Treat-
> ment would be kaleidoscopic. [. . .] . . . This explanation is hor-
> rifically composed, but perhaps you can get some meaning from what
> I'm attempting to say. . . . . . But so much of the time I feel a desper-
> ate apathy towards writing: the apparently insurmountable difficulties
> entailed in writing as one wants, the discouraging business of trying to

get your stuff in print, the realization that nobody much gives a damn whether you write or take dope or read the *American Magazine*. And I'm not talking of myself alone: I'm thinking also of Dale and Erling Larsen (from whom I received a very gloomy letter about his difficulties the other day) and Bradford (who has declared a year moratorium on writing: he's too disgusted to write a line) and the hundreds and hundreds of others. I wish to Christ I had the money to publish a magazine! Maybe no one would read it, but there must be some people who want more than the crap dished out by the *New Masses* "Literary" Supplement, *Story,* and *Esquire.* . . . . . . Then, too, my experiences with *Slow Parade* have been pretty sad. Late in September, Don Elder, the editor at Doubleday Doran wrote me: "Your book has had several readings, and everyone has been almost unqualifiedly enthusiastic about it. I've never seen a first novel get such a hand as yours has. I think it is extraordinarily fine, and I think we're going to publish it. However, there is one obstacle, a matter of house policy, which prevents me from making you an offer immediately. So I am writing you off the record to explain the peculiar situation. DD is a very conservative house, and it has a long established policy of strict censorship. I dont agree with the policy at all, and if I had the authority, I wouldn't hesitate to publish *Slow Parade* as it stands. I think it has every kind of integrity and its candor is one of its many virtues. But since it's a house policy that I cant do anything about, I have to take it into consideration. Frankly, we are all very keen about having you on our list. It is with some hesitation that I make this proposition to you, since I respect the honesty of the book and the admirable way you have handled it: but if you would consent to making some changes to enable the book to pass the censorship requirements without weakening it, I think that we can work out a very satisfactory contract for this book and for future ones . . . (Then there is some more about other matters: not very interesting. WK). . . . The part which requires change is Cynthia's sexual aberration. There is also a good deal of the dialogue which doesn't meet the purity standards. I think it's almost a crime to tamper with the dialog—it's so well done and rings so true—but that is the only way we could publish it. I would require some deletion. The only major change would be that involving Cynthia. . . . . [. . .]

. . . There was much more to this letter; I quote it at such length merely to give you some indication of the state of mind it put me in. I wrote him, and said that I'd consent to minor changes if it would get the book in print. Then Elder wrote, saying it was all set; he'd mail the contracts in a few days, etc. . . . Then, early in October: "It's very hard to tell you that DD's final word on *Slow Parade* is no. It has been decided, practically over my dead body, that the book couldn't be adapted to conform to the policy of the firm. I can only congratulate you on joining a very distinguished group of modern American writers whose books have had similar luck at our hands. Our Purity Dept. backed down on his promise to consider a revised version, and there is nothing I can do about it. When he speaks ex cathedra on a matter of faith or morals, he is infallible. I'm terribly sorry to have held out hope to you. . . ." And much more. A week later, Elder demanded a three month's leave from work. He's in Mexico; I've heard from him there several times. . . . The book has since been very politely turned down by Viking (publishers of Munro Leaf's "gorgeous bit of fun" *Ferdinand*) and Reynal & Hitchcock (publishers of Mrs. Pearl S. Buck.)

Think I'll go to the toilet.

* * *

Back again, immeasurably refreshed. [. . .]

Vanguard sent me Farrell's *Collected Short Stories* which I'm going to review for the Schooner. James Laughlin sent me *New Directions 1937* which is full of excellent things: have you ever heard of an American writer named Henry Miller who lives in Paris and is a sort of combination of Joyce and Wolfe? His work is damned exciting, and so is Cocteau's play translated by [Dudley] Fitts, and the work of Delmore Schwartz. . . . Did you subscribe for *Partisan Review?* They're publishing much good stuff (you cant get in there of course, unless you live in NY and know the editors); if you haven't seen it, let me know; I'll mail you an extra copy I have of their first issue. . . . I was going to have a story in Horace Gregory's *New Letters II*, but it's not going to come out again, I'm sorry to say. [. . .]

In the late thirties all persons who were concerned with new writing watched James Laughlin IV. While still an undergraduate at Harvard,

Laughlin—through his teacher, the poet and translator Dudley Fitts—
became aware of the publishing difficulties faced by noncommercial
writers; and so in 1936 he issued a volume of poetry and prose he
called *New Directions*. He supported this venture with money ob-
tained from his family of Pittsburgh steel magnates. Very shortly he
was producing not only an annual volume but books and pamphlets,
and New Directions was established as the most important publishing
house in the United States for current serious writing. *Time*
(November 21, 1938) called it the "centre for experimental writing in
the U.S." Kees was delighted when Laughlin accepted some of his
work: "Wish I could convey to you how pleased I was over the acceptance of the story ['I Should Worry'] for *New Directions 1939*," he
wrote to Laughlin in December 1938. "Who all do you have lined up
for next year?"

Kees could begin to feel himself launched on a literary career. *Slow
Parade* did not find a publisher, but other pieces got placed. Between
1934 and 1939, he brought out more than thirty sketches and short
stories in various little magazines, and a dozen and a half poems and
reviews in *Poetry* and elsewhere. His name was on the masthead of
both the *Prairie Schooner* and the *Rocky Mountain Review*. When in
the summer of 1939 he and Ann made their first trip to the West
Coast, he could look up writers in some confidence that he would be
accepted as one of them. Back in Denver after the trip, he wrote to
Maurice Johnson:

> 17 July 1939
>
> Dear Maurice,
>
> You are amazed at the compactness of San Francisco: that it is but a
> few minutes' walk from Telegraph Hill to the Italian district and from
> there to Chinatown, and that Fisherman's Wharf is no distance at all
> from Nob Hill. You grunt and puff climbing the hills, but you do not
> really mind because the weather is fine and cool; you are constantly
> being startled that even the most tawdry restaurants serve better food
> than it is possible to get in expensive places in other towns; you have a
> feeling that you are in a European city, and that the town gives the
> impression of having everything New York has (except the Theatre)
> without the monstrousness, the noise, and the hysteria of New

York. . . . As for Portland, Yakima, Tacoma, Seattle, and Boise—Seattle is the only one with even a modicum of attractions. Portland is a frightfully smug, nose-in-the-air place; I think it unlikely that there has been any sexual intercourse there in some years.

Kenneth Rexroth is not only a good poet, but a fine abstract painter and composer of modern music. He also has the reputation of knowing the California mountains about as well as anyone; spends months in them by himself; and for a time supported himself as a guide and as a cook for the U.S. Forest Service. He is a German who looks like the best type of Irishman; volatile, anarchistic, and very witty. Marvelous mimic. He cannot merely tell you of someone; he has to imitate him, and he does this excellently. I particularly liked his imitations of Lionel Abel, Harry Roskelenko—"Better equipped to write bad poetry than anyone of his time," Ford Madox Ford—"I spent a whole afternoon sitting across the table from him and couldn't understand hardly a goddamn word," a duck, a snake he once encountered in the woods, a Communiste laying down the law with clichés from the *Daily Worker.*

* * *

We returned a week ago, and since I don't have to go back to work until day after tomorrow, I have been doing very little. I finished typing the final draft of my [new] novel [*Fall Quarter*] before we left and it is now with the agents in New York, being looked over, I hope, by Harcourt Brace. The feeling induced by getting that out of the way after many months is one of emptiness combined with a desire to get on to something else that I can take a long time to. I have been writing quite a little poetry; and among others, John Crowe Ransom accepted one for the *Kenyon Review.* Do you see the magazine? [. . .]

Getty lives next door. He was transferred to Denver from Alburquerque (?) and works for the *Los Angeles-Albu[querque] Express* as a dispatcher-bookkeeper at ungodly hours; sometimes he works from 8 to 10. He is rather in the dumps and wonders where he is going; talks some of going to library school but says he can't save money, occasionally speaks with some nostalgia of the teaching profession. [. . .]

With Getty as critic and Ann as guardian of his time, Weldon had a productive year. In January 1940, he wrote to Laughlin of "my old harangue. *Why don't you start a magazine?* The time is ripe, if not already rotten." In May 1940, he suggested a book to Laughlin that has since become a modern classic: Harry Levin's study of James Joyce. Laughlin does not remember that Kees's suggestion prompted the book. Levin was an old friend of Laughlin's from Harvard days and needed no nomination from Kees. Still, the suggestion shows how close Kees was to literary currents and how shrewd his critical judgment often was.

In February 1940, Laughlin accepted Kees's ambitious story, "The Evening of the Fourth of July," for *New Directions 1940*. This was a kind of allegory that contained what Kees called "fantastic and caricatural effects," played out against a fearful background of Independence Day celebrations. Kees was responding to what he took to be the exaggerated patriotism growing from the European war. In this work one can see that he admired Nathanael West. "With hell breaking loose it's terrible hard to think or work, but I manage to do it and I'm going to continue," Kees wrote to Laughlin on June 12, 1940. "The calamity-howling is terrific here; I suppose it's far worse in the East." In the spring Edward J. O'Brien asked permission to reprint Kees's disenchanted study of academic life, "The Life of the Mind," in *Best American Short Stories 1941;* and that spring Mavis McIntosh in New York City became his literary agent. Encouraged by Norris Getty, he gave increasing attention to writing poetry.

Kees wanted to be involved in the widest literary scene, and he knew that Manhattan was where reputations were made. He had met prominent writers of his region and the West Coast; but this was not enough. In the summer of 1940 he wrote to a number of New Yorkers, and when he and Ann arrived in Manhattan that fall for a visit he met everybody he wanted to know. He was ecstatic. On September 12, Ann Kees wrote to Getty from the Hotel Albert in Greenwich Village:

> Dear Norris—
>
> Weldon is spending all his days at the English Institute [an annual conference of English professors and writers held at Columbia University] (and took the fountain pen with him, damn it). So I have appointed myself official letter writer for the family.

The mail has been coming forward and we are truly grateful for all the trouble it must cause you. What is your new address to be? I might want to send you a picture of the Statue of Liberty.

This is the pace that kills. Everyone we've met fidgets. The P. R. [*Partisan Review*] boys fidget with cigarette holders and D. Mac. [Dwight Macdonald] plays with his beard. D. [Don] Elder has the DTs or something like. J. L. IV [James Laughlin] looks into space and rubs his head against the side of the booth like a friendly dog, that Laughlin is pronounced as in Lock Lomond. He drives a long red-upholstered coupe. He is a very long man. He neither drinks, smokes nor chews. Just a little beer, no coffee. Probably training for the ski championship. In Jack Delaney's, where we ate last week, the gent's room has a sign 'colts—geldings—studs': J. L. seems to be definitely stud. Between courses he made telephone calls—and had to leave in a hurry. I believe that is what is called Hot Pants. I pictured at the other end of the wire something tall and blonde and wonderfully dumb.

N. Holmes Pearson fidgets with his eyes. He says the Eng. Inst. is an Elks Convention and he is being an Elk.

We had an abortive 10 minutes with Parker Tyler. He was preparing his costume for the surrealist ball. His pretty face is beginning to sag and his shape suggests 8 months gone with child. But more of that later.

There's really too much to tell in a letter. I wouldn't live in N.Y. if I had the gross income from Rockefeller Center. There's an undercurrent of gossip that has small towns beaten every which way.

A letter from Weldon followed:

14 September 1940

Dear Norris,

Mr. and Mrs. Dwight Macdonald entertained a select group of their friends last night at their Greenwich Village apartment, the honored out-of-town guests being Mr. Richard Eberhart, Mr. Morton Dauwen Zabel, and Mr. Weldon Kees. Those present were Mr. and Mrs. Lionel Trilling, Mr. and Mrs. Walker Evans, Mr. Philip Rahv, Mr. and Mrs. William Phillips, Miss Margaret Marshall (in her smartest *Nation* rationalization), Mr. Clement Greenberg, Mr. and Mrs. Culbertson Myers, Mr. M. J. Lasky, Mr. Herbert Solow, and Mr. Jas. T. Farrell. Mr. Farrell entertained the group with a lively account of his newly-acquired carbuncle. Mrs. Weldon Kees did not attend, due to a slight indisposition. After an enjoyable evening spent in discussing matters pertaining to politics and *belle-lettres,* the guests bade their charming host and hostess goodnight. Light refreshments (liquid) were served.

Among recent luncheon guests at the Broadway and 115th st. cafeteria were a jolly group of visiting literati: Mr. Allen Tate, Mr. Jas. Laughlin IV, Mr. M. D. Zabel, Mr. Arthur Mizener, Mr. A. J. M. Smith, Mr. Cleanth Brooks, Jr., and Mr. Weldon Kees.

Norris, I meant to write a long account of last night's party; but I've decided it can be treated better verbally. Thanks a lot for sending the mail on.* We enjoyed your letter and hope you'll write again before we leave. We'll be here until the 24th; then a day in New Haven, a day or two in Pittsburgh before Chicago and Denver.

I enclose some literature. The Guggenheim galleries, with the exception of a few Legers, Gris, and Picasso, is very bad—but a wonderful place physically.

Yours
Weldon

W. H. Auden wears a powder blue necktie with a dark green sweater, but his profile is nice.

The "literature" that he sent along consisted of a brochure from the

---

*What we got checks with the list in your letter. [W. K.]

"first public exhibition in New York City of one representative part of the Solomon R. Guggenheim Collection of Non-objective Paintings."

Kees got several letters from Norris Getty while they were traveling. In one dated September 20, 1940, Getty wrote: "Believe you're going to find Denver a little changed when you come back—a matter of something in the air, getting a little more intense day by day, so gradually you could almost fail to notice it. The churches are beginning to hold meetings on the consequences of a German victory. The newspapers carry a few more pictures every day of smiling stalwart young soldiers taking off gaily for camp." Whatever the state of international affairs—Paris had fallen to the Nazis and the British had been evacuated at Dunkirk—when they returned to Colorado, they found that their lives went on pretty much as before, in part because Weldon had a low draft number. On November 2, he wrote to a friend in Chicago, Robert D. Harper, "It may be that as the war drags on and with the probable further involvement of the United States, a good many of us will find it more and more difficult to write. I hope you saw my poem, *June, 1940* in the current [Sept./Oct. 1940] *Partisan Review*." He continues, "The general atmosphere of the Literary Life in NY was much as I expected; I could live in it but I don't think I could write in it." In *June, 1940* Kees had written:

> . . . I am alone in a worn-out town in wartime,
> Thinking of those who were trapped by hysteria once before.

He concluded:

> It is summer again, the evening is warm and silent.
> The windows are dark and the mountains are miles away
> And the men who were haters of war are mounting the platforms.
> An idiot wind is blowing; the conscience dies.

Like many other Americans at the time, Kees did not want the country to become involved in "another European war." Though he considered himself a conscientious objector, he did not change his draft registration nor take any official action. He continued to write and to talk of writing. He thought of himself as a solitary worker, but in fact he needed a circle for support and during the fall and winter he sought sympathetic associates. A letter to Johnson on March 24,

1941, about hearing Thomas Mann lecture was like a report of the local Guild of Writers.

> Dear Maurice,
>
> Ann went to Wyoming to visit her parents; they wrote her she'd better come because her grandmother has been behaving very strangely ever since she was hit by that truck in Long Beach; she goes around turning on water faucets, wandering away and forgetting to turn them off; sometimes she does the same with the gas. She doesn't seem to know who all the members of the family are and is most of the time under the impression that she is back in Long Beach, which I consider a very dangerous fixation.
>
> I went down to Colorado Springs this weekend. Thomas Mann was speaking on "The Making of *The Magic Mountain*." It was the same old stuff: all the remarks on Wagner and Goethe and Nietzsche were worked in. I went with some friends of mine down there who study with Boardman Robinson: a bald young man from California who used to live in Europe with Anne Parrish (a relative) and whose sister was Alfred Young Fisher's first wife and who went to Princeton; his girl, who is very blonde and wears shell-rimmed glasses and whose father is librarian of the Grosvenor Library; and the bald young man's roommate, who draws a lot like Wm. Blake, is a biologist and an authority on the bloodstream of the horned toad, and earns his living by playing guitar for square dances, which the people out here are taking to in great numbers these days . . . We sat on the stage just back of Mann. His dinner jacket was made from very thin material and you could see the outlines of his suspender buttons and the spikes in the buckle on the strap of his vest. After the speech, just as he was going out the exit, a woman was saying to a friend, not knowing that he was near, "I thought it was quite charming." Mann turned and bowed very low. Later I saw him out in the hall autographing copies of *This Peace* and $1.89 editions of *The Magic Mountain*.
>
> We went to a party afterward. It was in a stable that a young artist and his new wife had converted into a home and studio. Everyone said that if you told the draft board you were a bedwetter you were a cinch for Class 3d. The stove in the middle of the room was very hot and when the door was left open a cold draft blew on one. Several

artists got quite drunk and played calypso records and someone knocked one of Otis Dozier's prints off the wall. There were about twenty artists there. Later in the evening, when the drinks got stronger as the grapefruit juice began to give out, someone tried to seduce the host's wife. I left about two. They say it got better after that. [. . .]"

Just before O'Brien died, he wrote me that he wanted to reprint "The Life of the Mind" in this year's *Best Short Stories.* The book was completed before his death; I haven't heard whether Houghton Mifflin is going to find someone to continue editing future volumes or not. Klaus Mann [Thomas Mann's son] took a couple of stories for *Decision* and I had a lot of work reviewing books after the [Kenneth] Fearing one appeared, [in *Poetry,* January 1939]. None of them have come out yet. Knopf will publish the new novel, a chapter of which you read this Fall, if and when I complete it; at least my agent and Knopf are now haggling over details in the contract.

On May 12, 1941, he wrote to Maurice Johnson:

I was thunderstruck a few weeks back to get a fan letter from Malcolm Cowley, commenting on "The Evening of the 4th of July" and a poem in particular. This week he has an article in the *Sat Review of Lit* [May 3, 1941] in which he definitely takes on the press agent role. I don't know what to make of it.

We feel more and more exiled here; rather, exile in reverse: almost everyone we've liked here has moved away. Gilbert Neiman and his wife, for instance, after living in New Orleans, are in Los Angeles, hobnobbing with such strange figures as Man Ray, Frieda Lawrence, [Hilaire] Hiler, and John Barrymore. Laughlin was out here for the ski tournament; be glad you didn't go to Harvard. He's as peculiar a person as I've ever known. We were eating dinner in a place where the walls are covered with stuffed animals, skins, animal heads, etc., and Jay kept staring at the head of a buffalo over us. After a very long silence, he said, "Gee, don't buffalo have little eyes?" I hear from Rexroth that he's now in San Francisco.

In his essay, "What Poets Are Saying," Malcolm Cowley identified Weldon Kees as among a half-dozen promising new poets. He observed the sharp division in Kees's world between ordinary experience and subterranean terror. Cowley wrote: "Kees ought to be published more widely." In him, he wrote, one can see "death intruding suddenly in the midst of petty affairs. . . . [He] will write a sort of fugue in which visions of destruction, expressed in dignified blank verse, are interrupted by the deliberately trivial remarks of Bones and Sambo." It was gratifying to have Cowley say in public what he had said in the private letter to Kees. When Kees's review of James T. Farrell's novel, *Father and Son,* appeared in *Partisan Review* (May–June 1941), he got a letter from Farrell telling him, "My publisher thought that it was the most intelligent review that was written about the book" (May 18, 1941). In spite of Kees's reservations about naturalism in fiction, he and Farrell remained friends.

And then, in June 1941, Kees learned to his astonishment that Edward J. O'Brien had dedicated his 1941 volume of *Best Short Stories* to him. In those days, these annual volumes attracted considerable attention; and since O'Brien had died before this volume appeared, his final dedication seemed especially significant. Kees's hometown papers commented on it and observed rather snidely that Kees had "yet to appear in the name magazines." Like Sarah Kees, local journalists did not distinguish between Weldon's kind of writing and Bess Streeter Aldrich's popular fiction. On June 15, the *Nebraska State Journal* said of him:

> So far, the young writer has had more renown than receipts. He has been accepted generally by the "little magazines," as against the conservative, slick, quality magazines. That may be partly Kees' fault. His talent is sound, Mr. Wimberly reiterates, dependable, real, and, moreover, brilliant.

> But he is an intellectual, who refuses to compromise with art as he understands it. He'll stick like a burr to his ideals of writing and consider their cold perfection more satisfying than a certified check. Kees has strong convictions, which probably will get in the way of sales. He's young too.

Weldon was on a crest, as he should have been. O'Brien's public endorsement had given him and his reputation a real boost. It was summer, and for the moment the dragons of depression had withdrawn. Continuing to work on the academic novel, *Fall Quarter,* he

also considered the possibility of publishing a volume of his verse, and
he began preparing an edition of Thomas Beddoes's poems. Beddoes
interested Kees not only because he was a good poet but because he
was a suicide. In his letters to Fort Huachuca, Arizona, where Norris
Getty was posted as a second lieutenant, Kees gossiped about the
national literary scene like the insider that he clearly wanted to be.
One, dated August 22, 1941, reads:

> It's been a strange week; Laughlin blew in from the East on Saturday,
> and Maurice Johnson was here yesterday, returning with his folks
> from a trip West. We went to a party a girl-friend of Laughlin's gave,
> but I'll leave that for Ann to write about, since she handles mob-
> scenes much better than I'm able to. Jay seems interested in the Bed-
> does, but is definitely going to do Herrick in 1942. Maybe 1943 for
> Beddoes, he will let me know. The Poet of the Month for next year
> will include that justly admired artist, Hildegarde Flanner; so you can
> see what joys we're in for. Hildegarde, according to Jay, is being used
> for bait . . . Jay had just come from Olivet College and the writers'
> conference there. Glenway Wescott had a nervous breakdown and
> didn't show up; neither did Katherine Anne Porter, who was adding
> final touches to her novel and couldn't make it. All these absences
> made Wystan Hugh Auden very unhappy because he didn't like the
> rest of the staff, and he spent most of his time playing "Indian Love
> Call" on a piano in one of the dormitories. When he wasn't playing
> "Indian Love Call" he was playing *Carmen,* singing all parts.

Both Weldon and Ann wrote to Norris Getty in camp, Ann upon
Weldon's urging. A friend of theirs recalls now that Ann "was a quiet,
rather withdrawn person with a pretty, 'faded' face—small features,
and quick perceptive eyes. She would often let the conversation roll
along around her, but she was now and then given to bursts of enthusiasm." She and Weldon appeared to be two of a kind: sensitive,
verbal, satiric, aware of nightmare. Indeed some people came to think
that Ann was so totally dependent on her husband that she had little
character of her own, and certainly her letters were so like Weldon's in
both style and tone as to be practically indistinguishable from his.

In September 1941, Ann and Weldon Kees went to New York City for
a second visit. A month later, on October 14, he described that scene
in a letter to Maurice Johnson:

7. Jay Laughlin, about 1942, in
mountain hut above Ashcroft, Colorado. Photograph courtesy of
James Laughlin IV

8. Weldon Kees, about 1940. Photograph courtesy of the Heritage Room, Bennett Martin Public Library

9. Weldon Kees, June 1941. Photograph courtesy of Nancy Johnson

10. L. C. Wimberly, editor, and Fred Christensen, associate editor, in office of the *Prairie Schooner,* about 1948. Photograph courtesy of Photographic Productions, University of Nebraska

11. Yaddo, Saratoga Springs, New York. Photograph courtesy of The Corporation of Yaddo

12. Guests at Yaddo, August 1942. Kees had left in July. Back, left to right: Newton Arvin, Nicholas Marsicano, Nathan Asch, Philip Rahv, Michael Seide, Karol Rathaus, Carson McCullers, Malcolm Cowley, unknown, Langston Hughes, Kenneth Fearing, unknown, Leonard Ehrlich, Jean Liberte. Front, left to right: Mrs. Asch, Frances Mingorance, Merle Marsicano, Katherine Anne Porter, Helena Kuo, Juan Mingorance, Nathalie Rahv, director Elizabeth Ames. Photograph courtesy of collection of George S. Bolster, photographer, Saratoga Springs, New York, and courtesy of The Corporation of Yaddo

Dear Maurice, Malcolm Cowley, just back from Washington, says that
Archibald MacLeish has his fingers in so many pies he is growing
several new ones. . . . Bruce Bliven bought an electrical horse which
promptly gave him a fistula. . . . Josephine Herbst says she is going to
start using her still on her Bucks County farm now that the new tax
on liquor has gone into effect [. . .] Oscar Williams now parts his hair
on the side. When Ivan Goll saw the new coiffure for the first time the
other night, he said, "Oscar, you have become a romantic." . . . Gene
Derwood read us a poem dedicated to George Barker—a rather horrible thing—and after she had finished and there was quite a silence,
she said "You know, that's about the smashing of the atom." . . .
Kenneth Patchen likes to buy toy mice for his cat . . . Muriel Rukeyser
is the most formidable-looking girl in the village . . . Horace Gregory
has a green corduroy vest with silver buttons . . . Carson McCullers
got that nipple-cutting business [in an episode in *Reflections in a
Golden Eye* (1941)] from autobiographical sources . . . Jim Farrell is
in Hollywood . . . William Carlos Williams has quit Jas. Laughlin
the 4th.

I was delighted, of course, that you liked *Fall Quarter* so much, and I
share your preferences for Derlin, Elliott Eliot and little Raymond
[characters in the novel]. It was grand of you to read it for me just
now, when your life must be pretty hectic. If you have any after-
thoughts on the book, I wish you'd write me at Denver about them.
All of your corrections were good ones—some I'm ashamed not to
have caught after so many drafts—and I'll take care of them. I want to
get the final draft to Knopf in a month or so and I hope they'll bring it
out in the early Spring. The ms. arrived in good shape yesterday.

And let us know about you and the Army. This is disturbing: I
thought you were exempt.

Yours,
Weldon

New York City
New Haven, Conn.
(NY, New Haven + Hartford)

In the fall of 1941, while Weldon was still living in Denver, the Colt
Press of San Francisco accepted his first volume of verse. "The coming

avant-garde press seems to be the Colt Press in San Francisco," he
wrote to Getty on September 30. Weldon wrote to Maurice Johnson
about it in November: "In the East, both Horace Gregory and my
agent, Mavis McIntosh, said not to submit my poems to Knopf, but
to The Colt Press. They had the most convincing reasons in the world.
So it has gone to them, been accepted, will earn me an advance, and
will be published next year, probably in the late Spring or the early
Fall, after they publish the collected poems of Edmund Wilson and a
book by Hugh MacDiarmid."

Unfortunately, this volume did not appear until nearly two years later,
in 1943, after delays that drove him nearly to distraction. Its title, *The
Last Man,* was taken from Thomas L. Beddoes. Also in the fall of
1941 he completed his novel, *Fall Quarter,* and sent it to Maurice
Johnson for review and criticism. Confident of Norris Getty's friendship, he then shipped it to him in Ft. Huachuca, Arizona. In a kind of
part payment, on October 28 he gave Norris a full account of an
evening he and Ann had spent with William Carlos Williams in New
Jersey:

> Awfully glad to have your letter, and especially pleased that you liked
> the Joyce poem ["Variations on a Theme by Joyce," *The Last Man,*
> 1943]. I haven't sent it out anyplace yet; wanted to get your im-
> primatur on it first. I'll let you know as to its fate.
>
> A gloomy little man from the Railway Express people has just gone
> out carrying the MS. of *Fall Quarter:* I hope it reaches you soon. It
> would be fine if it would arrive in time for you to cope with it over the
> weekend. I know you're rushed like everything, but I'll be awfully
> grateful for any and all reactions and suggestions.
>
> Maybe you'd like to hear about our evening with Dr. Williams. For us
> it was some kind of a high. Somehow or other I'd managed to pick up
> all the wrong impressions of what he's actually like. Well, to get to
> Rutherford, you take a bus east of Bdway on 43d Street, and that late
> afternoon it was drizzling and gray and we rode downtown and
> through one of the tunnels to New Jersey and emerged into the drab
> spaces of Weekawken, Union City, and I don't know what other
> towns. And between the towns would be vast stretches of New Jersey
> marshes, wet and empty. The ride takes about forty minutes and we

found Rutherford to be not unlike Hastings, Nebraska, slightly less flat, however; and we walked up the hill and were directed the wrong way four times by Rutherfordites. Williams lives in a big white house, very ordinary and comfortable inside except for things you wouldn't be apt to find in the home of a middlewestern physician: prints on the wall by [Charles] Sheeler and [Charles] Demuth and E. E. Cummings and books everywhere. Williams is charming, a little shy at first, decidedly boyish and with a rare kind of sweetness, and his wife is still pretty, though less likeable than the doctor. (She was telling us at dinner about how WCW used to ask people out, writers, and they would come and stay for weeks. "One time Bill asked Max Bodenheim to come here because he was broke and he showed up with his arm in a sling; we found out later nothing was wrong with it, he just wanted to get out of work. The first night we had dinner, I served carrots, and Max looked at them and said, 'Carrots, eh? I don't like carrots, Florence. In the future, while I'm here, you won't serve them.' So after that, I had them for dinner every night." She laughed and Williams said, "Poor Max. God help us." After dinner we had some drinks and Williams said he had been reading [my poem] "Henry James at Newport" [*Poetry*, October 1941] and would I read it for him? Of course I would. And after I had read it, he took the magazine from me; one particular line—*Remember the detached, the casually disqualified*—had caught his fancy, and he kept reading it over and over aloud, saying, "That's good! That's it! There's a line!" So I got *him* to read some things—"The Yachts" and "The Sea Elephant" and "On the Road to the Contagious Hospital" and some others and he was in fine form, especially on "The Sea Elephant." His voice is really not good, too high and nasal, but he reads marvellously, stressing the flat and anti-poetic qualities. And he seemed pleased by the choices I'd made for him to read. Mrs. Williams said, "I always try to get Bill to read some of the more lyrical ones, but he won't do it." Williams laughed and didn't say anything. Sometime during the evening I mentioned *The Knife of the Times* and how much I liked it and how I'd tried to buy it and couldn't, and Wms said, "Jesus, I've got a hell a lot of those babies up in the attic!" So we went up in the attic and everything was a mess. He had a hard time finding the books, but he did, finally, finding along the way some other things he said he'd been trying to find for years, and obviously pleased that he had. There was a fine photograph of an old lady sitting on a porch, which hung on the wall, and he said, "That's Emily Dickinson; you know, my English grandmother." . . . Walking down to our bus with us late that evening, we saw the bus coming and the three of us ran for it (me clutching the book he had given me with something he'd written in it for me) and he said, "You read better than I do! Gee, it's swell you came over." It was raining again and we had to hurry; the bus was waiting. "So long. Goodbye. Write!"

And sometime I want to talk with you and fill in the gaps.

Yours,
Weldon

28 October 1941

Abrupt ending caused by the return of Mrs. Billings from lunch, wanting to use the machine. I wanted to write about Cheever and some other people; I guess it'll have to wait until next time—have to get to work.

As Norris Getty served as editor for Weldon, Weldon served as literary agent for Norris. He sent Norris's poems to magazines, and when he placed some with *Poetry* he was as elated as though they had been his own. As one of his friends said, years later, he had an "exceptional generosity of spirit, the all-too-rare ability to take pleasure in the abilities and successes of others." His Denver friends recall him, a generation later, with affection and respect. Robert D. Harper, who knew him then, found that Kees had "an incisive critical mind and extremely personal views on modern writers, views that usually differed sharply from those that I had absorbed over the [previous] two years from the [University of] Chicago English faculty. For example, he had a low opinion of John Steinbeck, whose *Grapes of Wrath* was the most discussed novel of 1939." On February 18, 1940, he wrote to Harper:

> The modern novel seems to me in a very bad way—too much journalism, padding, artiness instead of art, and a staggering lack of irony, wit, and objectivity in the treatment of characters. This is especially true of the Americans. Isherwood, Evelyn Waugh, and almost any decent French novelist have more idea of the craft than Vardis Fisher,

> John Steinbeck, and such white boars as we raise in this country. The only book I've read in some time is Motherlant's *Les Célibataires,* which is almost too shrewdly packed with excellent observation. But I like him almost as well as Radiguet or Hemingway.

Kees's views were clearly "advanced"; he felt himself to be independent of received opinion. But though his ideas were unconventional, Harper reports that

> Weldon Kees, at least during his Denver years, lived a life quite typical of middleclass America. On the street he would be taken for a young business or professional man, which, in terms of his library position, he was indeed. His home was an attractive studio apartment remodeled from the third story of a nineteenth century mansion on Capitol Hill. Ann seemed happy to contribute to the family income through her job in a downtown office. I thought of this marriage as one of the more harmonious ones among my acquaintances, although there were no children nor any talk of future children.[2]

It was about this time that Kees wrote his most frequently quoted poem—"For my Daughter." The poem was published by John Crowe Ransom in the spring 1940 issue of the prestigious *Kenyon Review.*

> Looking into my daughter's eyes I read
>   Beneath the innocence of morning flesh
> Concealed, hintings of death she does not heed.
>   Coldest of winds have blown this hair, and mesh
> Of seaweed snarled these miniatures of hands;
>   The night's slow poison, tolerant and bland,
> Has moved her blood. Parched years that I have seen
>   That may be hers appear: foul, lingering
> Death in certain war, the slim legs green.
>   Or, fed on hate, she relishes the sting
> Of others' agony; perhaps the cruel
>   Bride of a syphilitic or a fool.
> These speculations sour in the sun.
>   I have no daughter. I desire none.

Supported by editors, friends, and his wife, Kees was astonished at the cool reception his novel, *Fall Quarter,* got from Mavis McIntosh; and

he did not anticipate the further trouble that he was to have with it.
The year 1941 had been triumphant, and near the end of it, on
December 4, he wrote to Norris Getty:

> I'm trying for a Guggenheim. I hadn't thought of doing so for years;
> but when I was in New York, talking with weird Oscar Williams one
> afternoon, he asked if I had thought of applying. I said I hadn't
> because I had had no book published. Oscar said that was no longer a
> consideration; but, since the deadline was only a few days off, I had
> better go to their offices and get an application. So a day or so later I
> went down to 551 Fifth Avenue, and some woman refugee (a lieder
> singer, I think) was worrying Mr. Moe's secretary, and the secretary
> kept calling on the telephone to someone or other and saying, "This is
> the John Simon Guggenheim Memorial Foundation." She had always
> to repeat it a couple of times; no one ever seemed to catch on right
> away. Seems she wanted to find out the name of some song that Paul
> Robeson sang—a tune that had been written by "one of our Fellows."
> After a while Mr. Moe came out and looked at me and asked what
> could he do. I told him, got an application, and he said since I was
> from out of town I could have two more weeks beyond the deadline.
> So [Allen] Tate said he'd recommend me; and Cowley said he'd like
> to; and I also got Mari [Sandoz] and John Crowe Ransom and James
> Farrell and Horace Gregory. Farrell was in Hollywood (where he did
> not last long adapting *Common Clay* for 20th-Century Fox) but Hor-
> tense [Farrell] said it would be all right. So when I got back I took a
> couple of days filling out all kinds of forms and now I am waiting.
> They make their decisions in March, I think.

> Which brings me to Cheever. Carson McCullers was staying at the
> Brevoort and John Cheever said he had seen her, that she too was
> trying for a Guggenheim. "Poor girl," John said, "she's so innocent, so
> totally lost. She doesn't know who to get to recommend her. All she
> has so far are Henry Seidel Canby and Thomas Mann. . . . As I may
> have written you, Cheever has an arrangement with *The New Yorker*
> whereby he gets something like two thousand a year and has to turn
> in so many stories a year—ten or twelve. He has been trying to finish
> a novel for no one knows how many years and is always behind on
> the stories. He and his wife (the daughter of a dean or something at
> Yale and a former student of Horace Gregory's at Sarah Lawrence)

have an apartment on 8th Street and John writes in a room above a restaurant named The Black Cat on Broadway. He does not value his stories highly and when Ann and Josephine Herbst and I kept telling him he could have a swell volume of short stories he kept shaking his head and saying they were not much. At one time, several years ago, he got in quite a jam because Simon & Schuster had advanced him several hundred dollars on a novel and when he turned it in they didn't like it and asked for their money. He didn't have it and finally got Childs of *Modern Age* to put up the money; so now Modern Age will be his publisher if he ever finishes this book he's working on. Other people in New York say they think him incapable of writing a novel; but I wouldn't be surprised if he'd fool them.

The Mrs. Cyril Connolly episode doesn't sound so exciting in retrospect. It was just astonishing to find her in the Village, separated from Connolly, apparently doing nothing, and running around with Clement Greenberg. Wish we could talk.

In spite of the war, Kees remained absorbed in his own affairs. When *Fall Quarter* was rejected by Knopf, he was overwhelmed, as perhaps he should not have been, since Miss McIntosh had suggested earlier that she was puzzled by it. Now she wrote that she had found the novel "was curiously monotonous in tone and lacked the depth, and for that matter, the breadth of story that I had hoped it would have, judging by the first section that we saw." Paul Hoffman, the editor at Knopf, said, "What promised in that first version to be a tart, amusing yard—and with real verisimilitude—becomes increasingly a caricature which we found unconvincing in the extreme" (quoted to Norris Getty, January 3, 1942). On the same day, Kees wrote, almost frantically, to Maurice Johnson, "Can you help me to discover what type of mind is operating here? I'm just bowled over; I feel as though I'd just told my favorite joke and no one even smiled."

In retrospect, the judgments are understandable. Kees's talent was essentially imagistic, in that he captured the tone of a moment and the atmosphere of a single occasion in short forms—poems, sketches, brief narratives. He concerned himself with the interior life, the response of a single person to a private world. Kees dealt with states of being, not with process. When O'Brien dedicated *Best Short Stories of*

1941 to Kees, Professor Wimberly told the *Nebraska State Journal,* "It
is possible Kees' ability as a reviewer and critic is superior to his
capability as a fiction writer" (June 15, 1941). That is, he was more
analytic than empathetic. Weldon Kees clearly had a gift for friendship and earned the lasting loyalty, the continuing love, of numerous
men and women, but on paper his sympathies were restricted and his
human curiosity limited. The poems and sketches present moments on
the edge of nightmare, the realistic detail masking a profound terror.

Indeed it is this combination of naturalistic detail and suggestive association that brought some of Kees's readers to associate him with
surrealism. On January 31, 1942, Ann Kees wrote to Norris Getty
that "a reviewer in the [New York] *Times* has coupled Weldon's name
with Parker Tyler's as a surrealist poet. They are both searching for a
magnet to draw their poems together, he says." A few days earlier, on
January 27, Weldon told Maurice Johnson:

> I don't have any of the [surrealistic] symptoms you mentioned in your
> note. But there is *one* thing that rather disturbs me: a number of very
> peculiar-looking insects keep crawling over the face of my watch. Do
> you think this means anything?
>
> I saw that thing in the *Times,* too. That my name was coupled with
> Parker Tyler's amused me as much as it will probably infuriate him.
> The one and only time I ever saw Parker, he and Gordon Sylander
> were preparing to go to a surrealist party; and Parker said, "Do you
> know anything about the surrealist movement, Mr. Kees?" I said I'd
> heard a little about it.
>
> I suppose you know that the *Southern Review* is folding up. I have
> become less and less patient with its air, or the air of its regular crew,
> rather, of "You be my Charlie McCarthy and I'll be yours;" but it's
> too bad it must go. I suppose others will follow. I hear from N.Y. that
> the *Partisan Review* boys are all mixed up and can't agree on any-
> thing. I also expect Van Wyck Brooks to come out for Mary B. Eddy
> any day now. I suppose the academic boys are pleased by his recent
> strategies. The world of beautiful letters have never seemed more dis-
> mal to me.
>
> I sent *Fall Quarter* to Colt. I'll let you know what happens there.

The anonymous reviewer may have been right. Like Parker Tyler, Kees was a shrewd critic of the movies, an art that exploits the kaleidoscopic association of seemingly unrelated images. In his poetry and prose, Kees characteristically used montage, unifying bits of experiences within a single sensibility. He worked in spurts, not on a continuous, heroic scale. In the early forties, he was not able to acknowledge the nature of his gifts and thus gave himself pain in attempting a sustained narrative. In time he stopped trying to write in forms uncongenial to his talents.

Kees complained all spring that he suffered from writer's block, but he composed introspective poems that he sent off to Getty for criticism. He wrote to Johnson on March 12, 1942:

> "Yesterday I saw a man sitting in a barber's chair looking out at the street through an old-fashioned spyglass of the type employed by mariners; and today two weird-looking women, waiting for the streetlights to change, were speaking in loud voices as I came up. "You're not going to kiss her, are you?" one of them said. "Of course I'm going to kiss her!" the other said with resolution. I don't know whether she did or not. [. . .] I think I get duller every day. I have written less in the last three or four months than I have during such a period in years. A few poems and reviews, and that's all. "When in doubt, do nothing."—Marcus Aurelius. I am in doubt.
>
> I hope this finds you still out of the army.

James T. Farrell's advice was different from Marcus Aurelius's. On March 26, Farrell wrote: "Keep working. It is very necessary that writers keep working. We are being drowned in banality, Philistinism, etc. Writers must go on, in the face of it, oppose it, and set an example. In New York here, it is possibly harder to do this than it might be in Denver." Farrell repeated his opinion on April 13: "It is a duty of serious writers to go on at all costs in order to set up some standard against the bilge that is swamping us." Weldon's depression, resulting from the war and the rejection of his novel, was intensified by a rejection of his application for a Guggenheim Fellowship. Perhaps he should have expected nothing else. As he himself had noted when he applied, his volume of verse had not yet been published.

But late in April he heard that he had been invited to spend the summer months at Yaddo, an artists' colony at Saratoga Springs, New York, where artists assembled, about twenty at a time. "I'm going to Yaddo for the summer," he wrote Norris on May 2.

> Cheever pulled wires; Cowley pulled wires, and so I got an invitation. Mr. Wyer very decently granted me a leave [from the library] and I expect to go early in June if the draft board leaves me alone. Which reminds me: I had a long letter from Dale [Smith], now in San Diego, warningly admonishing against being a conchie [conscientious objector]. He speaks of the war as "the struggle," and seems to be in quite a mellow mood. But I suppose you, also, have heard from him.
>
> Sometime when you're in need of some good escape reading you might look into the works of an author who has been pleasing Ann & me very much indeed. The name is Raymond Chandler; he writes very marvelous mystery stories and does the best job of dissecting Southern California of anyone I've yet encountered. The books are called *The Big Sleep* and *Farewell, My Lovely.* I understand all the camp libraries are more than heavily stocked with detective stories, so Ft. Huachuca might have these.
>
> I believe you owe me a letter. Ann sends her best.

Kees was, by all reports, an extremely competent librarian, and, as head of an interlibrary bibliographical center, he had a responsible job. But at Yaddo, on leave from his library work, he was in his element. Ann remained in Denver, occasionally going home to Wyoming. Weldon's gossipy accounts of Life Among the Writers is recorded in letters to both Maurice Johnson and Norris Getty. His equilibrium restored, he found that he could write both poems and fiction. On June 15 he wrote to Norris from Saratoga Springs:

> The stories you hear [. . .] William Carlos Williams has had a bad winter. He's been trying to get to work on this long poem, "Paterson," but he doesn't seem to be able to get going. He told me a wonderful story about Richard Johns, who used to edit *Pagany.* Johns [. . .] is now married, inherited a great deal of money, has a country house and has become fascinated by gardening. The Dr. ran into him one time and Johns urged him to stop off and see him if he was ever in

their part of the county. Well, Mrs. Williams and the Dr. *did* happen
to be up that way one Sunday: so they drove out to see Johns' place. It
was, it seems, a magnificent place, but there was something strange
about it: when the Dr. knocked at the door there was no answer, &
the door was ajar. He opened the door and yelled, but the house
seemed deserted. He and Mrs. Williams went inside: there were cocktail glasses turned over, with spiderwebs in them; the beds were un-
made, soiled clothing littered the floors: in the kitchen the sink was
full of unwashed dishes and rusty knives; in the icebox they found
butter turning green. Williams could hear something dripping in the
basement and when he went down found it half flooded. He discovered a faucet running and turned it off. On the second floor things
were in about the same kind of a mess. They prowled around the
house, rather prepared to come upon a corpse or two. No one, dead
or alive, was about, and they searched the entire house. Finally they
left, and some weeks later he happened to run on to Johns in New
York. It turned out that Johns had had a party at his house and
someone decided it would be a perfectly marvelous idea to drive up to
the Cape and continue the party from there. That's what they did. The
party went on for a month. No one had thought anything untoward
had taken place.

News gleaned in New York: Robert Cantwell has had an acute nervous breakdown, brought on, apparently, by overwork for Henry Luce
and worry over his inability to finish the novel he's been trying to
bring to an end for years. Cheever has been drafted, hated to go; is in
some camp in either South or North Carolina. I talked to his wife
over the phone and she gave me his address but I seem to have lost it.
Jas. Laughlin IV was turned down by the Army, his enemies say
because of the psychoanalysts' reports on him. His wife is alleged
already pregnant. Horace Gregory is taking a year's leave of absence
from his teaching job at Sarah Lawrence and his place is being taken
by Katherine Anne Porter, who is now in Reno getting her 5th divorce; her novel is still unfinished. Which I don't suppose qualifies as
news. Horace and Marya and the children may come out to Colorado
for the year; their plans are not definitely set. He has two prose books
nearly finished and has contracted for a book on Kafka. You remember Gerald Sykes' work in the old Caravans? He has a novel with

Simon & Schuster which is coming out soon. Tate was let out at Princeton & has gone back to the South. Kenneth Fearing has taken over Cantwell's job on *Time*. Harold Rosenberg is living in Cooperstown, N.Y., some 80 miles from here; I may go over to see him if I have any money left at the end of July. I was in New York a week; it was hot as hell and I was only too glad to get down here, where life is a little less intense, and as yet not very real & earnest.

Alfred Young Fisher is here: is 40, looks younger: a swell guy to drink with and talk to, looks Princeton but absolutely no side, has had a weird life in Paris & Dijon & Switzerland & Wyoming & Hollywood; once free-lanced for the movies while living on $40 a month; had a tragic breakup with his first wife; now teaches at Smith. (Sorry if that sounds like one of O. Williams' contributor's notes [in one of his anthologies].) Fisher likes jazz and I play things like "What Is This Thing Called Love?" and "St. Louis Blues" on the Steinway concert grand in the music room for him; for Fisher & for a non-objective painter who admires Fats Waller. Last night we found an album of Bix Beiderbecke records buried among Bach and Shostakovitch and all were dutifully played. Alfred Fisher & Newton Arvin (also teaches at Smith) want me for the next librarian at Smith, since their present librarian, an old lady, is about to retire. (I feel somehow that nothing will come of this.)

Alfred Kazin is here, and Michael Seide, whose stories you may have seen in the *Southern Review;* both nice guys, and bright. [. . .]

Back home in Denver, he was still full of Yaddo when he wrote to Getty on September 5:

I had forgotten that I was going to send you a letter on the Saratoga bars. Two blocks of Commercial Street, in the downtown district, are lined with whorehouses; since people develop thirsts along with erections, there are bars sprinkled amongst them. The [Nathan] Aschs and David Diamond and Al Fisher and I went to the Hilltop, one of the most lively bars, one night and drank beer and played the jukebox, which was of the automatic hostess type, untouched, it would seem, by the Effort. All the whores on Commercial Street are negresses, and they wander in and out between assignations for a quick drink. David knew the place and its lore forward and backward. He invited one tall, very light negress named Ginger over to have a drink with us; and she told David later that she certainly did go for Al Fisher. And a few nights later Al took his two dollars and paid her a visit. But not, not, mind you, before he had tried to talk himself on the free list. (We all got a little tired of Al before the season ended). Then the day after, David brought Al a cigar that Ginger had given him to give to Al. Evidently he had made the little bell ring. Al smoked it after dinner, but reported it a rather poor weed. But he took the butt up to his room with him.

In the bar of the Worden Hotel, where Cheever, it was said, practically lived for a time, and where one might run into Frank Sullivan, which was all right, or Monty Woolley, which was anything but right, the tone was much different. The smot [*sic*] Saratoga set, the men who play the horses, the corpulent ladies from Bensonhurst and Manhattan—mothers of wealthy Saratoga physicians, most of them, the people taking the cure, students from Skidmore College—those were the clientele. Overheard there (a plump peroxide blonde, who worked at one of the Aryan whorehouses, and who was usually with her Lesbian girl-friend): "Now that this war's on and men are being killed and everything—hell, I aint dietin'."

Smiley's is a dive on the way to town, across from the racetrack. Smiley always had a rather dirty match in his mouth, and an equally dirty hard straw hat on the back of his head. He was given to reminiscences of his days in the sport world. And when you would come in, there Smiley would be, needing a shave and drawing a short beer, and would say to you, "I will be approaching you in a moment." There was always some hard-faced man, connected with racing, on the verge of passing out, in Smiley's.

Wish I could see you and tell you all about Yaddo and my summer. The whole thing needs oral treatment, really, or, short of that, a book about the length of one of Henry James's later novels. Since your card holds out some hope of your getting to Denver again, perhaps I may have the pleasure of subjecting you to some total-recall.

I went through quite a siege with *The Last Man*. The proofs came late in June, as I think I wrote you, and went back to Roth. Then I heard nothing from him. [Philip] Rahv arrived early in July, with the disconcerting news that the Colt Press had gone "bankrupt." This term was a bit ill-advised. It developed later that there was very little money and that Roth was then planning on pulling in his ears a bit and would concentrate on smaller books only. But I still heard nothing. The summer passed that way. Then last week I had a letter from him, saying that my book would escape the deluge. I still do not know exactly what was going on or what is up now, and hesitate to hazard any guesses. The way things stand now, the book is all ready for the presses and should be out within a reasonable time, possibly late this month. Jane Grabhorn, who was Roth's partner, is now working at the Grabhorn Press, and the book will be printed when her brother-in-law decides that she has worked long enough so that he can no longer get out of doing a little printing for them. Roth is off for Alaska this week; I don't know what takes him there. The last twist of the knife, maybe.

At Yaddo I completed a long story about Hollywood, a shorter story, and some poems. I also picked up a new agent, Russell & Volkening, whom I think you know once wrote me, some years back, when they were just getting started, wanting to handle me. They seem to go in for screwballs: they handle Wyndham Lewis and Henry Miller and Eudora Welty, and like writers to be a bit off-the-beam. Time will tell what they're really like; but they do have senses of humor and they do like *Fall Quarter,* which they have now at Scribner's, and they do write every time anything happens. Miss McIntosh had her points, but none of these.

You make me ashamed that I've done nothing about those Beddoes pieces. I mean now to try to get someone interested in bringing them out.

Kees wrote to Malcolm Cowley of his plans for a proposed anthology of satiric verse, confident that Cowley would give him a sympathetic ear. In an attempt to establish some sense of community, he wrote to other literary friends. He commended Horace Gregory for some recently published poems and asked him for advice about his proposed volume of satiric verse. He sent Allen Tate some of his poetry and asked for information about the Colt Press and for comments on his anthology. Distressed at the delay in publication of *The Last Man,* he

got in touch with Edmund Wilson, who was bringing out a volume
with the Colt Press.

"God knows when my book will be out," he wrote Norris Getty on
November 7.

> They keep piddling around. Now they say "before Christmas." They
> have just succeeded in getting Edmund Wilson's *Notebooks of Night*
> bound and out; it was printed last Spring, I believe . . . I've written no
> fiction in months; just don't seem to have the vocation any more. Or
> perhaps a clue may be found in this passage, from Hemingway's intro-
> duction to his anthology of war stories: "The only true writing that
> came through during the (last) war was in poetry. One reason for this
> is that poets are not arrested as quickly as prose writers would be if
> they wrote critically since the latter's meaning, if they are good writ-
> ers, is too uncomfortably clear."

In the same letter Kees sent Getty a poem for editing that revealed his
state of mind. It begins:

> The stoned dogs crawl back through the blood,
> Through the conquered weather, through the wet silk light,
> To disenchanted masters who are not quite dead.
>
> Like severed heads of history
> They gasp in the square, in the alleys of dusk,
> Explanations are posted on the shattered walls.

The poem ends:

> . . . Down the street the lights go dead.
> One waits, one waits. And then the guns sound on another hill.
> [*Partisan Review,* Summer 1944]

In the late fall and early winter Kees seemed on a high that drove him
to feverish activity. It was not uniformly productive. The prospect of
military service distressed him and the world he rushed in was collaps-
ing. "The period during which one waits for the Army to gobble one
up seems to divide itself up neatly between the terrifying and the full,"
he wrote to Newton Arvin at Smith College on November 28, 1942.

Weldon's terror was shared by Ann—indeed she seems to have come

close to a breakdown by January. To her Denver friends she gave no
hint of her tension, but the mysterious dogs of Weldon's poem appear
in a letter she wrote to Norris Getty:

> January 26, 1943
>
> Dear Norris:
>
> Is it significant, I wonder, that I am afraid of the dogs? My fear has no
> significance, but the dogs are important. They are acting strangely and
> I feel that if I knew the reason a great many things would be
> explained.
>
> No that's not right. Just because I got drunk with a mystic Saturday
> night, do I have to be a goddam chameleon? Besides she isn't afraid of
> anything she just worries about the state of the Mortal Soul and she
> has explained how it cannot possibly be honorable to commit suicide.
>
> It has been over an hour since I first heard them barking and I can still
> hear them. I wish they would go away. I wanted to go to the market to
> buy the porkchops and turn in a pound of fat and I can't until the
> dogs go away.
>
> I heard them first when I was washing the dishes in the kitchen and I
> thought to myself facetiously that someone must have thrown some
> horsemeat in the garbage can and the dogs didn't approve. Later
> when I was sweeping the floor I thought perhaps there were some
> gypsies going down the alley on the lookout for an unlocked back
> door. But then I remembered there aren't gypsies anymore, just a few
> gypsies' grandsons who are in the army. After awhile I realized the
> barking was still running in the back of my mind and I went to all the
> windows to look for the dogs, but I couldn't see them.
>
> When I took the garbage down I looked down the street and saw the
> dogs in formation at the corner. It was a formation, I am sure. They
> turned and wheeled as birds do, in the sun. First they stood in a circle,
> facing each other, no one of them being in the center. Then the big
> police dog broke away and ran to the middle of the street. They
> waited for a signal, then ran after him to the opposite corner, where
> they stood in lines of twos and threes. They never stopped barking.
> There must be fifteen of them, all brightly burnished except for the

dull black police dog. I could distinguish one chow. The rest looked like mutts. Suddenly they deployed in a solid band to take their places on the corner where the bus stops. The police dog jumped one of the small bright dogs and the others barked while he heaved ridiculously. An old man in decent black stopped and watched him closely. Then when the dog had finished, he took out his white handkerchief and carefully wiped his mouth as one would after eating something juicy.

When I came back around the corner of the house, the dogs had moved again and were apparently gathered on the vacant lot by the big red house on the corner. I could see one of them now and again. They had never ceased their barking. A little boy went by and he stopped to count them, his finger pointing. An officer went by in a big yellow car and he craned his neck to watch. The bus went down the street, but the passengers had their heads turned the other way to avoid the sun. The barking became more frantic, and it sounded as if there might, at last, be a fight. This lasted only a few seconds, then one of the yellow mutts ran across the street on three legs. He stood on the corner a long time, watching the others. Finally he limped down the street. I thought then that they would surely break up. But they haven't. They are still barking monotonously. Occasionally there is a brief silence, then it begins all over again. And I am afraid to go down to the market after the porkchops until they go away. They have ignored the people on the streets, but they seem to be intolerably evil.

* * *

What is it, I wonder, that is of such worldshaking importance that even the AP cannot reveal it until eight o'clock tonight? They might, of course, announce the end of the world. I doubt if anyone would turn a hair. Dave Rose and Judy Garland are separated but hope to compose their differences. The army wife killed herself and her husband because she was afraid he would leave her to go overseas while she was having a baby. The latest RAF fraud is revealed. I enclose that, it's too good to miss. Perhaps your local papers won't carry the story. 5 bellboys at the Shirley-Savoy (2 for the price of 1) and two residents of the hotel are being prosecuted for spreading vd among the soldiers. The two residents apparently did the spreading; the bellboys were listed in the newspaper as procurers.

The mystic is Jean Hanson (now Johnson, she married a soldier last October). She came over about 8 Saturday night and promised to have hysterics, but they never developed. She visits the Catholic Church every day and finds it significant that the Church is never empty. She lights a candle when she has a dime. One cannot honorably commit suicide, because the Soul is the only thing that is important, and if you commit suicide you admit that the short span of human life is important to you. She thinks a great deal about what will happen to her after death. [. . .]

Weldon has had a strange communication from the Manpower Division of the Selective Service. Please advise us which draft district you are registered in, and your home address. The comm. was addressed to Weldon at the library and had his name spelled Keyes. We can't help wondering. I suppose we never will know. I am going to try to get one of the men at the office who knows somebody who knows somebody, to help us find out.

I was about to mail the letter when I discovered it had no ending—not even a polite yours very truly. That discouraged me entirely so it has been gathering dust for two days. Weldon thought I made up the part about the dogs, but I didn't. I haven't that much imagination. Finally, late in the afternoon, they went away and I was able to go to the store. The vacant lot where they had been looked trampled as a battlefield would, and there was a nervous little fox terrier running back and forth frantically to sniff out what had happened that afternoon. Occasionally I see one of the dogs that was there and it is rather shocking, like seeing one of your friends who only the night before had been engaged in mystic rites. [. . .]

Weldon appended a postscript to this letter, but he did not comment on Ann's dogs, and in the winter correspondence, one cannot detect any particular estrangement. Kees reported his frenzy of activity to Newton Arvin: "Some kind of whirlwind started blowing, and when it finally died down after a few weeks, I discovered that I had written ten poems, seven of which I think are good ones. Such a thing has never happened to me before, and I don't expect it to happen again." He secured leave of absence from his library job and determined to go to New York. "I have a job to finish before the Army gets me, and

[am] coming back to New York to work on it and await the draft there." The "job" was his edition of satiric verse. The Keeses Denver apartment was disturbed. "And now I sit in a room that looks as though a real whirlwind has struck it. I'm trying to pack; I am surrounded by string and boxes and suitcases and piles of books and suitcases and brimming wastebaskets," he wrote Arvin on February 21, 1943. Ann stood to one side. Weldon had decided that she was not to accompany him and her great distress must have pained him. But his letter to Norris announcing their separation was without explanation. For years both Weldon and Ann had been on the most intimate terms with Norris; and when they lived in Denver, they saw one another almost daily, but Weldon's announcement is enigmatic, sudden, and unforeseen:

> 22 February 1943
>
> Dear Norris, Awfully glad to have your card, and I think I can understand the way you've been feeling. I have been in a similar fix for a long time; Rat's Alley was never like this.
>
> Ann and I are separating: that is one item.* Her address will be 418 E. Center, Douglas, Wyoming; I wish you'd write her. I am going back to New York and will try to finish up a thing or two before being drafted. You can reach me % Russell and Volkening, 522 Fifth Avenue, New York City; and I hope very much that you will send me a note at that address very soon. I wish awfully, Norris, that you would holler for a leave and come back to N.Y. for a while. I'd love to see you again; was dreadfully sorry I missed you this summer.
>
> Can't seem to write any more.

In March 1943, Weldon Kees went to New York, by himself, to make his way in the writers' trade. At twenty-nine, he felt himself ready for the big time. He was going it alone.

---

*Please say nothing of this. [W. K.]

Immediately after arriving in New York, Weldon Kees reported his reactions to the city. He wrote on March 10, 1943 to Maurice Johnson, using his agent's office as a return address:

> Dear Maurice, It's a changed world: the Albert Hotel has been taken over by the Army, the Brevoort is crammed with refugees, and the other hotels I called were jammed. I wound up at the Chelsea, a fine place indeed; but no good as a permanent thing, at three dollars a day. I'm now somewhat settled in an apartment on East 30th Street, but the Russell and Volkening address is still best.
>
> I've been busy seeing publishers about the anthology. Scribner's (which means handle-bar mustached John Hall Wheelock and Maxwell Perkins, who wears his hat in the office and is quite deaf but enormously likeable, and who is the subject of a forthcoming *New Yorker* profile by Malcolm Cowley) is now considering it, after I was rebuffed by Harcourt. Then several other houses are expressing some interest. But almost all publishers are avid for books which can be turned over quickly and from which they can get immediate profits. Publishing has by now been almost completely Hollywoodized; but I hope this anthology will not have to be set aside until after the war.
>
> Recent draftees: Stanley Kunitz and Clem Greenberg.* [Kenneth] Rex-

* On March 21, Kees wrote to Norris Getty: "Clement Greenberg was drafted last month; the *Partisan Review* boys have had one communication from him since he arrived in a camp somewhere. It was a postal card, and on it was written: 'Save yourselves.' "

74

roth is in a Federal prison as a C.O.; I don't know details but wish I did. Kazin is working for the *New Republic* on a part-time basis; couldn't work in the same office with [Bruce] Blivin. Kazin will be inducted the first of May. Jim Farrell has been told by his physician that he must quit, among other things, smoking and drinking, or face the consequences. As a result, he has acquired a strange new humility.—I wanted to talk with E. Wilson about the Colt Press horror and called him up the other day. He wasn't in, but La [Mary] McCarthy was; and I'm to have dinner with them at their place tomorrow night. I'm looking forward to it; but it is true that so many people whose work one admires are fundamentally dispiriting to meet.

A long letter from Getty, finally. He is in a bad way, poor guy. The letter was full of blacker horrors than Mr. Faulkner usually provides. Thank your stars that you are not in a post like his. And let me thank mine that I am still a civilian, though one lives from day to day now more than ever.

I have been urged by various people to try to get a job with the O.W.I., but after a party I went to last night, at which there were several employees of that outfit, I think I ought to say no thank you. The staff is largely made up of homosexuals and former contributors to *transition* (or, former contributors, homosexual, to *transition*) who speculate on whether their psychiatrists are *really* doing them any good. [. . .] It looks to me like the Writers Project *cum* speedup *cum* missionary zeal. And more.

Please write. And let me know if there is anything I can take care of for you back here.

Edmund Wilson and Mary McCarthy were two of the most formidable of New York literary figures. Wilson had been famous for twenty years as a critic of the first importance; and though he lived in and out of New York and commanded universal respect, he was not part of the local internecine quarrels. Like Kees, he stood a bit apart. The *Partisan Review* group found him "too much in the American grain to serve now as an exemplar of the type" of critic they aspired to be. "Perhaps Delmore Schwartz was right in a way," one of the *PR* editors wrote later; "the intellectual, in popular journalistic references, was so often labeled the New York Intellectual because New York itself was a kind of foreign city—'the last outpost of Europe'—and the intellectual life was really alien to our native habits and traditions."

Weldon Kees was no "intellectual"—that is, he did not have a philosophical turn of mind nor did he prefer ideas to experience. If he had to choose between argument—intellectual gymnastics for their own sake—and gossip, he chose gossip. The New York–Europeans' search for pure essence, for concepts within which experience might be pigeonholed, was foreign to his way of thinking, as ultimately it was to Edmund Wilson. Both Kees and Wilson were outsiders and they did not engage in the ferocious competition for place characteristic of New York literary circles, at least not overtly. Mary McCarthy was much more competitive. She had learned to enter a man's world and to hold her own there. William Barrett of the *Partisan Review* wrote later, "I remember being at some party or other, sitting beside two older men who suddenly froze as she entered the room." A gifted satirist, she had "that impeccable syntax with which she might lash out in print at any time."[1] She did not frighten Kees, perhaps because he did not enter the New York fray. He continued to see Edmund Wilson for the next years, and his respect for him remained high, however ironically he wrote about him to his friends. Wilson and Mary McCarthy, his wife, are described in a letter to Maurice Johnson in March 1943:

> Dear Maurice,
>
> The evening I spent with Mary and Edmund Wilson was one of the pleasantest I've had in a long time. And I was a little alarmed, too, what with Newton Arvin's letter, what with the story Alfred Kazin had told me about the evening *he'd* had with them, and what with all the other stories I'd heard about both of them.—It was snowing as I got off the bus at Union Square and walked east on 15th street. When I rang the bell, "the electric clicking began—with its quick and ready profusion, plucking distinctly the string of excitement which was still capable of vibrating in my breast at the prospect of meeting new people in Greenwich Village."*—I had gone inside and had begun to climb the rather rickety stairway when the front door opened and I

---

* *I Thought of Daisy,* by E. Wilson, Charles Scribner's Sons, 1929 [W. K.].

heard my name called. It was Wilson, easily recognizable in the glum light of the hallway, his hat and overcoat snow-covered; he looked up at me and said, "What are you doing in town, Weldon? Awfully glad you're here, awfully glad you could come." And I passed some pleasantry, and we shook hands and went up the stairs together.—Mary came to the door, very dark, very young-looking, wearing a green wool dress, and said (to Wilson) "Hello, darling," and he said, "Hello dear"; and we were introduced and very soon were drinking old-fashioneds and I was being introduced to Edmund's eighteen-year old daughter (by what wife, I don't know) whose name is Rosamond and who resembles her father very much. And then Edmund said he thought he'd better shave, and took his drink in the bathroom with him and talked occasionally through the door while Mary and I talked about Graham Greene and Eric Ambler and Raymond Chandler.

It was a very fine evening, and the meal was good; and I found Wilson completely and marvelously articulate—no pauses or lapses or stutterings at all—and to me, at least, he exhibited no evidence of that "touchiness," about which I had heard so much. We talked a great deal about satirical poetry—he kept asking me, "Are you using this?" (naming some poem) and I was using them all, which may have piqued him a little; then finally he thought of a poem of Arthur Waley's that I had forgotten, and, I think, felt better.—Their little four-year old son had to go to the bathroom, and after he had attended to his small need, he came happily out of the john completely naked and romped around the room with elation. Mary finally succeeded in getting him into his pajamas, remarking, as she did so, that she had inadvertently bought girl's pajamas for him instead of boy's. When he wanted to know what the difference was, she gave a very neat explanation.—And now Edmund has gone to Red Bank, where his mother is very ill; and a couple of nights ago I was at the Rahvs for dinner, and later Lionel Abel came over, and a little later, Mary. Afterwards, as Mary and I left together, we discovered we were starving, and went down to the diner on 8th st. and ate hamburgers and played the juke-box (while we were there, one of the coffee boilers blew up) and she told me about how she had lost God (a Catholic one) when she was twelve years old. And about a story she wants to write called "4F."

No more paper. Write.

In Kees's accounts, Manhattan sounds no larger than Lincoln or Denver; all writers seemed to know each other and they were all of one, advanced kind. From the letters we learn how the rising generation lived, the kinds of parties they went to, their troubles with jobs, their relationships with one another—at least as all this appeared to a newcomer. A glimpse is provided by Weldon's letter to Maurice Johnson on May 3, 1943:

> Dear Maurice, Your letter has just come, and while waiting for Henry Volkening to come back from what seems to me an inordinately long lunch, I'll make use of this rather poor typewriter to answer your letter.
>
> I sort of envy you $164 a month and such quarters, as the Lazy U Motel in Laramie. I have been looking around for some sort of job to tide me over until the Army communicates with me, and have discovered what I should have known: that 3A men are about as popular as lepers. One is looked at as already in khaki. Yet there is a possibility that I may get a job on *Time,* where Princetonian T. S. Matthews appears to be less exacting on the draft status matter than most people. I'll probably know definitely this week.
>
> Which reminds me of E. Wilson. He got on a train going to New Jersey a few days ago, quite drunk, and ran into Matthews, who he has never much liked since their *New Republic* days together. He picked some sort of a fight with him, told him he had sold his soul to Henry Luce, and I gather they nearly came to blows. This is a good example of Edmund's absent-mindedness, or something, because Mary has been looking for a job and hoped to get one on *Time;* and Matthews was the person who could have given her one . . . The Wilsons are most appallingly broke at present, and I believe Edmund is going back to the Cape, and Mary is going to stay in town, if she can get a job.
>
> I went through ten days of terrible worry when a publisher lost both the ms. of the anthology and the novel. Someone thought they had

been returned to R&V by messenger; other records showed they had come back by express. Well, they didn't show up; then finally it was discovered that they had been missent to someone in California—a man who had submitted a work entitled *A History of the Chamberpot in the Anglo-Saxon World.* Honest.

Everyone I know of who has been called up by the draft lately has been rejected. William Phillips because he didn't exhibit any reflexes in one leg, and Alfred Kazin, who was turned down yesterday, for some minor ailment.

Louise Bogan says she would rather be a scrubwoman than a book reviewer, but the $20 a week *The New Yorker* pays her is too good to throw up. But she talks about going to Spokane. Theodore Roethke has written the following couplet:

Stephen Spender
Has no gender.

William March lives in a swank Central Park West apartment and has cocktail parties with strong martinis and uninteresting guests. Mari Sandoz has been bogged down and isn't writing; she lives in the Village and says bad things about the Knopfs, undoubtedly justified. Walter Quirt took me to a cocktail party at the Museum of Modern Art for Mitchell Wilder, the director of the Taylor Museum in Colorado Springs. I had done an immense amount of work for him on his forthcoming book on Spanish religious art, but had never met him until then. The place was full of Gaylorsville, Conn.: Peter Blum and Robert Coates, Cowley and Stuart Davis.

I wish I could write you about a taxicab ride away from a party a few nights ago, packed in with Matta, Dwight Macdonald, Lionel Abel and the girl he lives with. But the business about Matta is hardly fit for the mails.—I enclose a new poem instead.—Good luck.

With the help of Malcolm Cowley, Weldon got a job on the editorial staff of *Time* in May 1943. A letter to Maurice Johnson on May 18 was written on the magazine's letterhead paper:

Dear Maurice, Lean, gangling Weldon Kees is now working for Time, Inc., is a book-reviewer, works with other Time book-reviewers Nigel Dennis, Harvey Breit, Whittaker Chambers.

To drop the manner, which is with me a good deal these days, I might say that I find all of this pretty fantastic, but by no means unpleasant. T. S. Matthews turned me over to Wilder Hobson, who is editing the so-called "cultural departments" on the magazine. They liked the first review I did for them, and now I am on the payroll at an amazing salary—more money than I ever expected to make. And the arrangement is good in lots of other ways: for the time being I work at home and only go up to the 29th floor of the Time and Life Building twice a week—once to attend a conference, and the other time to turn in my copy. This happy set-up may not continue for long, since I may be shifted to another department. I dont find Books a bad place to be at all, though.

One thing I have learned: you can tell nothing of what people are actually on the magazine from looking at the masthead. Walker Evans, for instance, is doing movies; James Stern, art. One bumps into such people as Howard Moss and Reuel Denney. The place itself reminds me a little of a college dormitory: people are always wandering around the halls, dropping into one's office to talk.

* * *

Saw the Wilsons the other night before they left for the Cape. Edmund is going to do a book on Poe next. *The Shock of Recognition* has been postponed, but will be out early in June. I may do it for *Time*.

I've got a piece to finish that is troubling me and must get back to it; but I wanted you to know how things whirl here. I enjoyed yr account of the Lazy U enormously; do let me have the latest on it, and you.

Yours ever,
Weldon

Russell & Volkening address still safest.
Did you ever read Kenneth Burke's *The White Oxen?* As I recall, the U. of Wyoming Library has it. There are two or three very good stories in it.

Perhaps because it paid well—Kees drew $100 a week—*Time* was able to retain a number of promising young writers, some of them on the political left. Robert Cantwell, the books editor of whom Kees

wrote rather bitterly in the following letter, had come to New York
from the state of Washington as a free-lance writer in 1929. Author of
novels, biographies, and histories, he eventually became senior editor
of *Sports Illustrated*. Whittaker Chambers later became the celebrated
accuser of Alger Hiss and wrote the best-selling autobiographical *Witness* (1952).

> Sunday [June 1943]
>
> Dear Maurice, Since Whittaker Chambers got out of the hospital and
> returned to *Time* my life has been a far happier one. Cantwell
> bumbled on Books pretty badly. Things got to the point where Matthews bawled him out for rewriting our copy.—My last experience
> with Cantwell was the worst. I had done a piece on Lin Yutang [the
> Chinese man of letters], and he and I were going over it. A strange
> light came into Cantwell's eyes. "We ought to see Lin Yutang," he
> said. "Maybe there's a new angle there." The next thing I knew I was
> in a taxicab with Cantwell; we were headed for the Lin Yutang apartment, somewhere in the swank Gracie Square neighborhood. Dr. Lin
> wasn't home, but one of his three daughters was. She said papa would
> be home around six. As we left, I was instructed by Cantwell to call
> him up and make a lunch date for Thursday with him. I did. Then the
> next day Cantwell called up to say that he had been transferred to *Life*
> and was leaving for Albany immediately to do a story on Gov. Dewey.—So I was stuck for the lunch with Dr. Lin, and without Cantwell.
> I managed to talk Harvey Breit and Nigel Dennis and Chambers to go
> along. We met Dr. Lin at the English grill of Rockafeller Center. He
> bounces and pounds on the table, and is very glib indeed. Said he:
> "Damn it, mother-love is not a matter of ovaries." Other Lin Yutang
> gems: "Karl Marx was a moron." "If World War III comes, I'll go to
> Africa and talk to the monkeys." He also spoke disapprovingly of
> Picasso, Hemingway and Proust—L.Y. seems to be a follower of the
> current Brooks-MacLeish* line.
>
> I'm off Books for two weeks and am writing the music department
> while Winthrop Sargeant is on his vacation. I find it a very welcome

---

*Rumors reach New York that MacLeish thinks he is going to be the next Secretary
of State. Another rumor is that he no longer is invited to the White House, and is
apparently on Eleanor's black list. [W. K.]

change not to have to read a couple of bad books every week, and hope I will be switched to some other department permanently. Books leaves one scarcely any time to read anything one wants to, though writing book reviews for Chambers is a real pleasure. He wants things to be lively (see the reviews in the next week's issue of *McSorley's Wonderful Saloon* and *Judah P. Benjamin,* which Chambers and Harvey and I were responsible for) and the reviews in following issues. No more Cantwellian ponderousness.

I'll send along an example of *Time* checking copy, since it might interest you. (Please return.) The piece I'm enclosing was edited (badly, I think) after this draft, by Matthews. Usually he improves things.

Wish I could see you. Why don't you take a leave and come back here? Ann and I are together again and have a remarkably cool apartment on lower Fifth Avenue & 10th street. Last week I had my blood test and am wondering what will happen next. Ann is working a few days a week for Jim Farrell.

Do you want any more little magazines? *View* has 8 poems by e.e. cummings. *Furioso* has a new issue. The new *Partisan Review* (out in a few days) will have a study of Evelyn Waugh by Nigel Dennis.

Kees's casual announcement that Ann had joined him in New York leaves their relationship unexplained. "So much to say," he wrote to Getty on March 21, 1943, "and, as you once said, some things just don't get into letters." Winfield Townley Scott, the poet and literary editor of the *Providence Journal,* was "shocked by the rudeness with which Weldon treated his wife"[2] when they visited him in Rhode Island some years later; but neither in the letters nor in the poems does this harshness appear. "Ann sends regards," Weldon writes regularly to their friends; and if she or any woman is spoken of in the poetry, it is with distant civility. But of course the Kees poems are not ordinarily autobiographical, however subjective they may be.

Kees's job on *Time* did not last. "There was quite a purge on *Time,*" he wrote to Malcolm Cowley on Sept. 15, 1943. "I felt like hell about it the first day; since then I've felt better than I have in months. Just being away from Whittaker Chambers makes one feel like a new man.

But the job was a godsend for a while." In September he got another piece of news that he accepted as good. He was discovered to be "psychologically unfit for service," and was thus exempted from military service. On September 24, he wrote to Getty: "I went up to Grand Central Palace and was lovingly placed in classification 4F. (What is psychological classification 72B?; that's what *I'm* in.)" Classification 72B did not exist. Kees had it wrong, and it is now impossible to determine the exact cause of his exemption. Was he diagnosed a manic-depressive? In any case Kees now felt free, free to live his own life as he was able. He seemed untroubled that he should continue his private pursuits while his friends were confined in the military. As usual, Kees was self-absorbed.

In the very same week that he was rejected by the draft, Kees's handsome, long-delayed volume of verse, *The Last Man,* finally arrived in New York. In a letter to Norris Getty on October 9, 1943, he got around to the reception of the book after describing his recent past as a writer for *Time.*

> Dear Norris, "A letter," says Laura Riding, "must be composed in leisure. Its wrongness must have the authoritative formality of a premeditated crime. A letter written under stress and because its astonished author could not help writing it is an act of insanity. The mails are full of helpless insanity . . ."
>
> Rather than perpetrate an outright act of madness, I have waited until now to begin this letter, though I can hardly pretend that these recent days have not been without stress. Both Ann & I have been looking for jobs, at the same time searching for an apartment; and a few days ago my folks arrived for a week's visit. When I have nothing better to do, I write reviews.
>
> Did I write you that *Time* and I came to the parting of the ways? It is difficult to figure out why big organizations do anything that they do; Jim Agee believes that the people at the top are as bewildered as the people at the bottom. And perhaps a good Kafkaesque story might be written in which this very point could be explored. What if K. got to the Castle and found the hierarchy just as baffled as he had been? — Somehow, though, I don't like to dwell on Mr. Luce in these terms. Even though Elsa Maxwell's column portrays him as a man with a

"deep moral sense." —I used to race around from one projection room to another, from one on West 55th (very comfortable leather chairs) to another in the RCA Building, and on to the RKO Building—oh, hell, they *all* have lovely chairs; if only the pictures were up to the chairs—and one day I saw three features and two of them had both Noah Beery, Jr. and Diana Barrymore. Seeing pictures all day left no time for writing in the Time & Life Building; so I wrote my reviews at home at night. We were ostensibly working a five-day week; it seemed to me I was always working seven, and always going to screenings on what were hopefully referred to as "weekends." And my movie reviews did not please Mr. Whittaker Chambers, my editor. He had liked the book reviews. "Our readers," said he, "don't want to hear you groan." —As yet, *Time* has not found a cinema critic that thoroughly pleases. It is believed there that books, art, and a few other things may be written for a "limited" body of readers. In the case of moving pictures, though—well, *everybody* goes to movies. Consequently, a more popular approach. So the entire staff of the magazine is ransacked in order to locate this richly-desired individual with the man-on-the-street approach. I believe in one year there were seven switches on this job. —When I was to be inducted into the armed forces, I was given $400 severance pay, and I can't say it made me unhappy. —Or perhaps I was just part of the purge. They have fired about eight or ten writers this month, and some weird doings go on there. I heard yesterday that Luce, who ordinarily sits in his office on the 31st floor, dreaming perhaps of China and Episcopalianism, has come down to edit the magazine himself; Matthews has apparently been demoted. The arteries are hardening; there is much worry about the deterioration of the magazine. —Oh yes, another thing. So long as nothing is said to one about the quality of one's work, one is safe. At the sound of the question (from one of the Senior Editors): "Are you happy here?" you know that your goose is cooked. A friend of mine, who worked on *Time* several years ago, was called into [Manfred] Gottfried's office one day. Said Gottfried [the managing editor]: "I'm sorry, Sidney, but we have reluctantly come to the conclusion that you don't have that intangible something that makes a *Time* writer." Said Sidney: "Well, we can't discuss intangibles, can we?"

Then there's the story of the man on *Fortune* who was sent out to do a long piece on the Union Pacific R.R. He went west, rode on cabooses, tramped the rails, sold tickets, sat in the President's office, examined hotboxes, fired the engine, talked to railroad workers all down the line. For two months he saw everything there was to see concerning the U.P. At the end of this investigation he returned to his office on the 30th floor of the T&L Building. He had some hundred books on railroads, stacks of handouts from the U.P., piles of notes he had made himself. All these he carefully arranged on his desk. They almost covered its surface. —And every day he came down to work; other members of the staff, walking past his office, would glance in and see him sitting at his desk, slumped down in his chair, his arms folded, *staring* bewildered at this mass of stuff. Every day they went by, looked in; they never saw him move. They never saw him writing. It went on like that for weeks. Every day he came in, sat at his desk and stared for six or seven hours, and, at the end of the day, put on his hat and coat and went home. One morning, at the end of the third week, he suddenly jumped up from his chair, shrieking fiendishly, picked up everything on his desk and threw it out of the window. They took him off to Bellevue.

* * *

What you wrote about *The Last Man* could only give me great pleasure. And there's no one I'd rather please. There are naturally some things in the book that I no longer like. That you approve of *Fugue* and *When the Lease Is Up* is something I was particularly glad to know about, because I felt a little queasy about those two. Sometime, if you care to, you might let me know of any particular words, lines and effects that displease you, with suggestions for revision. I think a writer gets blind to certain things after a poem is frozen in type: he may admire his worst faults and underrate some merits. This may sound foolish, but what I have always tried to do is to write the kind of poetry I like to read: an impossible task one sometimes, through luck, manages to do. Or thinks one does —I must say I feel too little sense of "belonging" with my immediate contemporaries, with the exception of four or five guys. It's so easy, don't you think, to feel a sense of identification with the men of the Pound-Eliot generation, or even the Hart Crane–Tate–Horace Gregory generation, rather than the present gang, with its Rukeysers and Shapiros and John Frederick Nimses.

Your letter about the book came on a day when I needed it badly. I had just gone over to see the editors of *Common Sense* about an article on Randolph Bourne I'm writing for them, and Dick Rovere showed me Babette Deutsch's review of *The Last Man,* which will come out in the magazine's next issue. It was in an omnibus review that included the new O. Williams anthology, a Tom Boggs anthology, and a few other books. After much praise of Boggs poetry and the work of one Lenore G. Marshall, she turned in a displeased report on *The Last Man.* It appears that while there "is no denying my competence," what impressed her was the fact that I had read a great many books and was much-traveled. No individual or original response, etc. The poems also depressed her.

Wish you could get back here on a leave. We'd love to see you. Tomorrow we're moving to a very nice apartment indeed (129 East 10th Street); write us there from now on.

Ann sends her best; congratulations on your promotion; let us hear from you often; let me know if there's anything in the way of books, magazines or anything else I might pick up for you here. I asked the *New Republic* to send you a copy of this week's *NR* that carries a review of mine. [. . .]

In the fall of 1943, Kees began writing continuity for newsreels. "I'm working for Paramount Pictures—making newsreels," he wrote to Jay Laughlin on November 30. "It's a good job, though I must say it's taking up far too much time." A week later, on December 2 at 4:00 A.M., he noted to Norris Getty that he was "just back from a 19-hour stretch on the newsreel." But such long working hours were unusual; many weeks were easy and short. His account to Maurice Johnson of how newsreels were made is now of some historic interest.

December 16, 1943

Dear Maurice,

That was an awfully good letter of yours about letters, and we were grateful to have the letter and clipping regarding the activities of the large cat in Roselle that gave Mr. Leach so much trouble.

Now:

EDMUND WILSON AND OTHERS:

/\/\/\Edmund was in one of his grumpier moods. Ann had never met
the author of *Axel's Castle* and other works before and was a little
shocked at his lack of amiability. This was a few evenings ago at the
Rahv's. There were two people there whose names I didn't at first
catch (one of them turned out to be Philip Blair Rice, managing editor
of the *Kenyon Review*) and I spent the first half-hour deliriously trying
to figure out, from things that were said, who they were. Wilson
evidently had the same trouble: he kept calling Rice "Mr. Wheelwright"; finally he said, "You *are* Philip Wheelwright, aren't you?"
This may have had something to do with Rice's sotto voce remark to
me: "I think everyone in New York is crazy." This was said, as I recall,
at some point between Mary McCarthy's explanation of who the real
heroine of *The Golden Bowl* is (I never found out: Natalie Rahv was
telling me, rather irritably, what all was wrong with Dwight Macdonald) and an argument about the proper way to pronounce Randall
Jarrell's last name. (Accent on the last syllable, says Edmund Wilson,
adding that Jarrell is "essentially an adolescent and only interesting in
his poetry when he is working off his infantile obsessions." In connec-
tion with this, you once mentioned the bevy of bears that turn up in
Jarrell's work. I think now that these are all, to the last one, teddy
bears.)—The Wilsons have just moved back into town from the Cape
and Edmund begins as [Clifton] Fadiman's successor either this week
or next. He said he was going to write more about little-known
books. But he didn't want to talk about his job much and kept asking
me to tell him about my experiences on *Time*. "What about Cantwell?" he kept insisting; later on he revealed that he has been working
on a piece showing how Luce ruins promising writers—a thesis one
should have little trouble in proving. —The Wilsons went home
(Gramercy Park) before we did; we left with Rice and the man whose
name I hadn't caught. I suggested we go someplace in the Village and
have a sandwich; Rice had to go home; so the nameless man (who
had bothered me all evening because he so closely resembled that
bundle of horrors, Robert Paul Smith) accompanied us. Somehow I
had picked up the information that he lived in Philadelphia and
taught there, and I asked him what he taught. "I used to be head of

the Romance Languages Department at Haverford until this Spring; my wife was going to have a baby in five months and one day she shot herself," he said. Now he spends every Tuesday evening with Wystan Hugh Auden, who is in a bad way himself. Isherwood is in Hollywood translating the *Gita;* but what he *really* wants to do is to write a novel about Hollywood. "Christopher," said our new friend, "was fascinated by *The Last Tycoon*."

NOTES ON THE MAKING OF NEWSREELS:

/\/\/\Most of the time we sit in one of the two little showrooms and look at film that comes in. The make-up staff and several cutters, usually. There is the stuff that our own cameramen make, film from rotapool, newsreels from England and Russia and Australia and Canada and South America, captured film from the Germans and the Japanese. On Mondays and Thursdays most of the actual work is done. With the cutters we decide what scenes we are going to use; film is cut; other film is pulled out of library material sometimes for other scenes that are thought worth including; by one o'clock in the afternoon, ordinarily, one newsreel story has been completely edited and cut. A title is written and printed, the announcer is called to report at a certain time, the sound men go to work fitting music to the film and putting in effects, the writer sits in front of a little meter that ticks off footage and, with a copy of the scene list (which looks like this one below), writes what the announcer will say.

1. TITLE IN THE CLEAR: GLUE FOR VICTORY:	5 ft.
2. General view of old horses	6 ft.
3. Close up of bottle of glue	11 ft.
4. Hand pours bottle of glue on enemy alien	16 ft.

etc., for anywhere from 60 feet to 700 feet.

By that time the chief editor has set a time for the synchronization, and this is usually about an hour or two after the scene list has been typed up by the cutters. At that time the writer takes his lines up to the studio; the announcer is there, a projectionist, and the sound crew. The writer and announcer go over the lines as the film is run, and the sound men rehearse the music and effects. When all are satisfied that everything jells, a preliminary take is made, a bell rings, and most of the staff come up to hear the playback. Revisions are made in the lines and music and effects and the announcer is instructed to put more feeling into a certain passage, or his pronunciation of some word is questioned. After everyone is satisfied (the most difficult matter is the one of timing) two master takes are made and these are sent down to the laboratory to be printed. The announcer, I ought to add, never looks at the screen while he's enthusiastically describing what goes on: he keeps his eyes on the lines that have been written for him and speaks only when cued by the writer (some announcers like to be cued by a sweeping motion of the fingers and some by being tapped on the shoulder.) Everything clear now?

On Tuesdays I get out the reels in Portuguese and Spanish. Mr. Pardo, the Spanish announcer, and Mr. Feldman, the Portuguese announcer who doesn't use that name on his title credits, make Tuesdays fascinating if often exhausting. It is wonderful how many devices can be employed in cueing languages one barely understands.

REQUEST:

If you can send more letters from soldiers, I wish you would. Jim Agee and I are thinking of editing a book of letters, all kinds of letters. I think such a book, if carefully edited and cut with an eye to surprise, would make most current fiction look even duller than its worst detractors say it is. All letters would be ones never before published— letters one and one's friends have received, letters found on the street and in library books, a vast catchall for some of the marvelous things that should be printed. I'd be grateful for anything at all you'd send. Do you still have that fantastic letter of recommendation from Stepanek? We'd have to change names in many cases, of course. And would you object to having some of your own letters included? — When our plans are more definite, I'll let you know. We don't plan to put in much work on this project unless we can get an advance from a publisher that will pay a good typist's wages for a couple of months. And though Jim and I agree, I think, pretty much on the sort of thing to include, I wonder how this projected collaboration will work out.

COMING!

NOTES ON FILM CRITICS, or, MANNY FARBER AND JAMES AGEE, TOGETHER AND APART.

Write. Ann sends her best.

Kees enjoyed making newsreels for Paramount Pictures, movie buff that he was; and he stayed with it until late 1947. Ann got an editorial job on the magazine *Antiques*. They had found the congenial environment that Weldon had searched for since undergraduate days, and they felt themselves to be living among the advanced writers of their time, as indeed they were. But though he encouraged friends to write reviews of his book and notices of his poems, he did not play the standard New York game of success. Norman Podhoretz, who became precociously successful when named editor of *Commentary* at age thirty, has given an account of "making it" in his autobiographical volume of that name. It was a game that Kees elected not to play.

For many New York Intellectuals with whom Kees was now associated, the road to success was clearly marked, and Podhoretz was explicit about its signs. He wrote:

> *Partisan Review* and *The New Yorker,* so opposed in most other respects, had one important thing in common: they were both magazines with a (justified) reputation for being very hard to crack. To write for *Partisan Review,* it was supposed, one had to be formidably intelligent, conversant with impossibly difficult books, and full of deep thought; to write for *The New Yorker,* it was conversely imagined, one had to be graceful, witty, and charmingly casual about one's learning. Each magazine represented the quintessence of a different species of sophistication: *Partisan Review* was the arbiter and embodiment of intellectual sophistication, and *The New Yorker* was the arbiter and embodiment of worldly sophistication.[3]

In the forties Weldon Kees published in both *Partisan Review* and *The New Yorker,* and he was on more or less intimate terms with the New York Intellectuals. Indeed Philip Rahv, founding editor of *Partisan Review,* consulted him about Henry James as he compiled his collection of James novellas in 1944, before Henry James became fully fashionable. But Kees had only a peripheral part in the urban ambition for place. He "belonged to no group, was part of no movement, created no stirs," a friend remembered later. "He was not a legend, like Jim Agee."[4] He wanted to be accepted, but on his own terms; and he would not tailor his work to fashionable critical judgments. He was thus in the circle but not really of it.

Kees's interest in writing fiction did not revive in New York, even though his agent continued to try to sell *Fall Quarter*. Since publishers sometimes accepted a first novel if its author seemed about to produce other, salable books, Kees constructed a synopsis for a new novel, as a kind of bait. This "plot" contains sequences inspired by the cinema and reveals his continued fascination with the buried life. It was signed and dated February 21, 1944:

> *Synopsis of an Untitled Novel by Weldon Kees*
>
> Carl Ellis, a young scholar at somewhat loose ends, comes upon a volume of poems by a writer named Fredric Shore Strandquist. Fascinated by his work, which is little known, Ellis attempts to find out something about Strandquist, with a view to writing about him, but meets with small success. All he is able to dig up are a few reviews of his book. The publisher who brought out the volume is dead, and his small press no longer in existence. After following several roads that turn out to be blind alleys, Ellis discovers that Strandquist's family lives on Long Island, and goes out to see them.
>
> They are people of wealth who are little inclined to give Ellis much information about Fredric, a black sheep; but what Ellis learns—that they have not seen Fredric for some fifteen years and that they are not sure (or willing to tell) whether he is dead or alive—greatly excites his curiosity. The outcome of this meeting is a private conversation with Fredric's uncle, who tells Ellis that he himself is most interested in learning what happened to Fredric, and feels Ellis out on the possibility of Ellis undertaking an investigation. The few facts Ellis has learned are of such interest—the uncle shows him several letters and photographs of Fredric and hints darkly about various misdeeds of his—that when the uncle offers to pay him a good salary and his expenses to conduct this search, he accepts at once.
>
> The story from then on will deal with the progress of Ellis's search (which takes him to Chicago, San Francisco, Hollywood, Denver, and several small places in the middlewest and, finally, back to New York again), in the course of which he comes in contact with many people

Strandquist has known, including two of his wives and several mistresses. He learns that Strandquist twice changed his name, is a bigamist, may be a murderer, and worked at a variety of occupations, at some times making fantastically large salaries and at other times living in great poverty. The more material Ellis assembles, the more confused he becomes as to what sort of a man Strandquist was: he seems to have been capable of many changes of character and personality. Ellis's quest is further complicated by the fact that he suspects various persons who knew Strandquist of lying to protect themselves.

Ellis's discovery that Strandquist is still alive, and his meeting with him forms the climax of the book, with Strandquist's personality at last fully clarified for the reader, if not for the man who has searched for him—for Ellis has seen and heard too much and knows that the task of fully discovering and understanding another human being—at least this one—is an impossibility. A moving picture version would of necessity, I should think, concentrate on the shock effect of Strandquist's appearance and the contrast between his expected personality and "real" one. The whole work, I hope, will have the same kind of chase excitement supplied by Greene and Hitchcock.

Kees had admired *Citizen Kane* when he saw the Orson Welles film in Denver soon after it was first released, and this synopsis is clearly indebted to it. It may be that his disposition to fiction was used up by his involvement with newsreels. In any event Kees never mentioned this project again; and as he wrote to Getty in November 1942, he seemed to have lost his vocation to fiction. If his stories had received the praise from editors that his poems received regularly, he might have developed that side of his talent.

During the war years the Keeses continued their literary life, though Weldon wrote less than in the years before he came to New York. In a letter to Robert Harper after his first encounter with "the Literary Life in NY," he said, "I could live in it but I don't think I could write in it" (November 2, 1940). A letter written to Maurice Johnson on April 1, 1944, describes the life that Kees and his literary friends knew during the war years in New York.

1 April 1944

Dear Maurice, Outside, in the courtyard, a man in a gray hat and gray topcoat has been standing for a long time now making little marks on a piece of paper. Ann says it is a map. Maybe so. He keeps looking in windows. A survey, no doubt. The Lenten bells of the neighborhood have been ringing like mad ever since we got up.

We got up with slight hangovers. Yesterday, after work, we went to a cocktail party at Dwight Macdonald's. There was quite a mob and lots of noise; when Harold Rosenberg arrived, he said it sounded like an auction sale. "What," asked Harold, "am I offered for this worthless political idea?" —I suppose you have read about Jim Farrell's latest turmoil. The cops have been investigating *Studs Lonigan:* they had the impression that it was concerned with the Wayne Lonergan case.* And, even when it had been pointed out to them, by [James] Henle of Vanguard, that this could not possibly be so, since it was published in 1935, they were still not unsuspicious. Mary McCarthy told me at the party that Jim had written to Edmund, asking him for a statement. Edmund didn't think any statement was necessary, since there had been no ban, only a little snooping around, and didn't write anything. He could have written: "Studs Lonigan and Wayne Lonergan are not the same," I suppose. But he wrote nothing, and now Jim is sore at him. —What, by the way, do you think of Wilson's pieces in *The New Yorker?* This is certainly criticism, especially after Mr. Fadiman; but they seem fearfully uneven in merit. The piece on Evelyn Waugh, for example, with its astonishing admission that he had never read anything of Waugh's until a year ago.

After Dwight's party, we had dinner at a Mexican place and saw a French movie with Raimu, *Heart of Paris:* none too good; and wound up at George's, a night club in the Village, which, before the war, was almost exclusively patronized by painters. We ran into Herb Bernstein there, the brother of William Poster, the chap who reviewed *The Last*

---

*This was a celebrated murder case of 1943. A socialite was found dead in her Manhattan townhouse. Her husband, an RCAF aircraftman in training, was accused of her murder, tried in the newspapers as well as in the courts, and convicted.

Man for the *NR*. Herb and Willie lead mysterious lives: even their closest friends have never seen the place where they live, their address being carefully guarded. They can only be reached by calling Herb's mistress, a girl named Evelyn who takes pictures in uptown nightclubs. Willie once worked in the postoffice and Herb taught philosophy at Columbia, but now neither of them seem to work or to have worked at anything for years. Where their money comes from is something no one knows. It is rumored that they own a couple of apartment houses. Neither of them like to get above 14th Street and they rarely see daylight, I gather. —Herb was in a strange mood and revealed that he plans to take trumpet lessons from Frankie Newton. Frankie is supposed to be playing at George's (although he wasn't there last night) but his interest in music, so Herb informed us, is on the wane: he's now taking drawing lessons from someone on 57th Street and is distressed when one attempts to talk to him about anything else but Art. Herb said that life had been looking up for his (Herb's) set of late because recently they had managed to get their hands on a really splendid new shipment of "tea": he reeked of it. People kept socking it in on the dancefloor. The guitar player looked something like Hot Lips Page. Herb said, "My wife's up at the bar; I'll get her." We had never met her, though we had heard of Dorothy, who is still in love with him and won't give him a divorce. We liked her better than Evelyn, and it was a bad moment when I asked her where she lived and Herb said, "Thirteenth Street," and she corrected him, "Twelfth." A friend of theirs came up who has some money in a new musical called *Allah Be Praised;* he said it was flopping in its tryout in Philadelphia and they had removed Ned Sparks from the cast because he was no good. For a man whose show was doing so poorly he seemed remarkably well pleased with things.

We had gone to listen to the music, but the music wasn't any good.

What do you think the post-war world will be like?

It was Herb who threw Alfred Kazin out of the Bernstein home years ago. It was Herb and Willie who introduced Alfred to literature years before that, when, I gather, Alfred was fourteen or fifteen and then bent on a career as a concert violinist. (Alfred still extracts neurosis-inviting sounds from a fiddle; there are no aural effects quite like

those produced by a combination composed of Alfred, violin, and
Saul Bellow & Isaac Rosenfeld, recorders. Have you ever heard a *New
Republic* editor play a recorder?) —And now Alfred's paranoia has
come in to its full flower. No one knows where he is. He lined up
three jobs a few weeks ago—a teaching job at Black Mountain, another at Swarthmore, and another which he created for himself by
talking the Rockefeller Foundation into sending him to England to
investigate the Army's educational program abroad. Now he's going
to England—if he can get a passport. His wound, his rectal wound,
has healed. He has quit his job at *Fortune.* No one knows where he is.
Even Isaac Rosenfeld, his closest friend, doesn't know where he is; but
he thinks he is hiding out in a hotel in town somewhere. Meanwhile,
he has not yet returned *I Thought of Daisy,* which he borrowed eight
months ago.

Yes, I put together a new collection of poems. It's called *The Fall of
the Magicians,* and is just the size for Laughlin's POET OF THE
MONTH series (soon to be changed, one hears, to POET OF THE BI-
MONTH). So I sent it to Jay and he's had it for a long while, and I
can't get any word from him.

Getty is somewhere in the South Pacific. [. . .]

Five months later, on September 2, Kees was still full of gossip in
another letter to Maurice Johnson:

You asked about Jim Farrell. I think it was early this summer that they
moved to Pleasantville, no doubt because there young Kevin would
have a lawn on which to romp. And probably, too, there will be bird-
baths for him to overturn, flower beds to destroy, and lots of nice fresh
air in which he can scream and fly into irritable temper-tantrums. —
The only word I have had from him—if it could be called a word—
came a day or so ago in the form of a copy of his piece on Hollywood
in *The Saturday Review's* 20 years of Henry Canby issue. I had already read it; so I gave it to a colleague at Paramount who said he
didn't think it was very good.

As a matter of fact, the only thing I've heard about Jim lately was
from William March. He used to see quite a lot of Hortense and Jim.
It seems that last spring Jim called Bill on the phone and asked him if

he could hurry over to their apartment and take Hortense to the hospital. She had broken her arm. So Bill rushed over, struggled with her to carry her down the stairs, got a taxi, and delivered her to the hospital. (Why Jim couldn't have done this is one of the less clear parts of this story. I think there was some sort of explanation, but I can't remember what it was; I do remember that it sounded unconvincing.) —Some weeks later Bill was at a party and had a conversation with that person who he referred to as "that creepy individual, Kyle Crichton," during the course of which he told Crichton what an unnerving time he had had of it getting Hortense Farrell to the hospital. Just at this moment Hortense herself appeared at the party, and Kyle Crichton immediately boomed at her, "Hello Hortense! Bill March here was just telling me what a hell of a time you gave him with your broken arm!" At this, Hortense wheeled away in anger; and Bill hasn't seen the Farrells since. Doesn't seem to be minding it too much, either.

March fancies himself a graphologist and I must say he does a good act. He was over here the other night with some other people, and did a rather amazing job on twenty or thirty examples of handwriting I got out for him. I happened to find an old appeal for support for the Partisan Review, signed by Edmund Wilson, Allen Tate, John Dewey, Louise Bogan, Sidney Hook, John Dos Passos, and Katherine Anne Porter. He took one look at it and said, "Hook seems to be the only normal person here." He said some astonishing things about Wilson and Tate, and then suddenly seemed appalled by what he had revealed. "For God's sakes; don't *ever* repeat what I've said!" he cautioned. —March has been working with psychoanalysts for years, and his jargon is almost certainly psychoanalytic.

You asked also about [James] Agee, and it was on Agee's spidery signature that Bill did one of his sharpest jobs. The [Manny] Farbers, who were here, too, seemed most impressed. —Agee is on his vacation now, but usually he writes the movie reviews for *Time*. He has a remarkable facility with words, but I think that Manny, a more clumsy writer, *sees* more and has keener insights. He also is free of sentimentality—Jim is full of it—and has none of Jim's need for self-abasement. But to write intelligently at all about films these days, and

do it week after week, and keep one's sanity, is quite a trick. I know I
couldn't begin to do it. [. . .]

But making newsreels was also demanding. One for Paramount on the
battle of Iwo Jima sent him home sick. "I haven't been to work for
almost a week," he wrote to Maurice Johnson on March 20, 1945. "It
was the full reel on Iwo Jima that laid me out. Worked from nine in
the morning until six the next morning. Knocked me flat for two
days." James Agee called it "one of the best and most terrible of war
films" in the March 24 issue of *The Nation:*

> The Paramount newsreel issue about Iwo Jima subjects the tremen-
> dous material recorded by Navy and Marine Corps and Coast Guard
> camera men to an unusually intelligent job of editing, writing, and
> soundtracking. [. . .]
>
> The Fox version of the same battle—the only other version I could
> find—drew on the same stock, and is interesting to compare with the
> Paramount. In one way it is to its credit that it is much less noisy and
> much less calculated to excite; it is in other words less rhetorical, and
> the temptations to rhetoric must be strong in handling such material,
> and usually result in falseness. But in this Paramount issue it seems to
> me that rhetoric was used well, to construct as well as might be in ten
> hours' work and in ten minutes on the screen an image of one of the
> most terrible battles in history. And that is not to mention plain sense:
> the coherent shape of violence in the Paramount version, which moves
> from air to sea to land; its intact, climactic use of the footage exposed
> through a tank-slit, which in the Fox version is chopped along
> through the picture; and its use of the recorded dialogue, which Fox
> didn't even touch. The Fox version does on the other hand have two
> shots—a magically sinister slashing of quicksilvery water along the
> sand, and a heartrending picture of a wounded Marine, crawling
> toward help with the scuttling motions of a damaged insect—which I
> am amazed to see omitted from a piece of work so astute as
> Paramount's.

When at last the war was over, Ann and Weldon Kees, no less than
Norris Getty and Maurice Johnson, hoped for a return to stability. In
the fall of 1945, Ann and Weldon had to move from their tiny St.

Marks Place apartment, the leaseholder having returned from her
wartime factory work. Janet Richards, then married to Manny Farber,
the film critic, remembers the Kees's New York life: "They lived on the
East Side, in St. Mark's Place, a decayingly elegant cul de sac, with
mossy houses from the Eighties and a silvery atmosphere of intangible
regret and faded dreams." Like their earlier place in Denver, this one,
described below by Janet Richards, had style.

> It was truly small, that apartment, having one little room with an
> alcove just big enough for a little Jacobean dining table. There was a
> kitchen that was only a short hallway between the alcove and the
> bathroom and, like me, Ann washed the dishes in the bathroom sink.
> In the living room there were two single beds, covered with faded
> brocades, one against a wall, the other in the middle of the room,
> since there was no other place for it. In the windows that looked out
> onto St. Mark's Place, were trailing vines and ferns, and all of the
> furniture, the chairs, bookcases, little chests and tiny tables were relics
> of the 18th century, inconspicuously maintaining their unalterable
> perfection of design. On the floor was an ancient Oriental rug.
>
> The rooms had very high ceilings, and the walls were panelled with a
> graying wood, perhaps walnut.
>
> Upstairs lived Harold Rosenberg, and he and his wife, and sometimes
> their pretty little baby, were often at the Kees when we were.[5]

Janet Richards recalls how Kees appeared to his contemporaries in
those New York days:

> Weldon's conversation, like his poetry, was apt to consist of apparent
> irrelevancies, for example, he might quote the opinions of a science
> writer for *Time* magazine dated in May, 1937, which he had read
> while waiting in his dentist's office. I never heard him refer to, or reply
> to, a profundity. Instead, Weldon could bring all his trivia together
> during an evening, and on the way home you felt that you had just
> glimpsed the grave. For my own part, I did not share his belief that if
> life had ever had any goodness or meaning that day was long past;
> and I always, with dread, felt that the grave I kept seeing after being
> with him was not my own nor even the Universal Grave, but
> Weldon's. [. . .]

It sounds as if I am describing a Nebraskan Strindberg, or a man who suffered like the pathetic English poet William Cowper, who wrote that he "lay down in despair and rose up in horror." But actually Weldon as a social being was not even one of one's moody friends, he was funny, joking and always in good spirits. He had, however, a touch-me-not quality, an implicit faith in his friends' respect for his desire that they not come too near. He and I were very close and loving friends in New York, yet when we met again for the first time in five years, we did not even take each other's hands, let alone kiss.[6]

With the help of another friend, Howard Nemerov, not yet the acclaimed poet that he was to become in later years, they found a satisfactory new place to live at 227 East 25th Street. On Thanksgiving Day, 1945, Kees wrote to Maurice Johnson that they were "very glad to be out of the cold."

Dear Maurice, We might very easily be living in a Flatbush warehouse by now had not Howard Nemerov tipped us off to this place. He got out of the army, after having flown successively for the C.R.A.F., the R.A.F., and the A.A.F., and came back to Manhattan with his new English bride to land in this block, the noisiest in town, next to Mulberry Street during a gang-fight. So here we are, with our Flents, our frayed nerves, our new Hans Knoll furniture, none too securely held up by floors that look as though a herd of large, solid-hoof herbivorous mammals had once used them for hourly stampedes; but very glad to be out of the cold we are.

A couple of weeks ago we went to a remarkable cocktail party given by Henry James, Jr. He is a pale, none too bright young man with the high-domed forehead of his granduncle; and, at his father's town house in the East 70's, said next to nothing as his co-host, Bill Roth (who published my book of poems) and tweedy, whitehaired, balding Gorham Munson spoke of Cantwell, who has vanished from the Luce organization and whose present whereabouts remain a mystery. The ancestral oil paintings glistened from the walls of the upstairs rooms where women came and went, speaking in low tones of Prentice-Hall's trade department, for it is there that Henry James, Jr. and Munson are employed, and it is there that Roth, somewhat bewildered, finds himself ensconced as Publicity Manager after a few years with Mr. Elmer

Davis's group [in the Office of War Information]. But there was nothing said of the author of *The Golden Bowl* until after Henry James, Sr. [the host's father] arrived ("got a drink for the old man?": pepper and salt hair: dried-up: Atchison, Kansas Kiwanis Club vice-president: ill-fitting Finchley worsted double-breasted) and was being talked to by a Southern gentleman of declining years and [with] the mouth of F. M. Ford: "Quite a boom he's having. I hear there was once a whole set of his books . . . someone brought out another little volume . . . Now even Kip Fadiman is taking him up." Clement Greenberg came with a girl whose upper gums showed marvelously plain when she smiled widely.

————————

Please tell me more about River House. We have always intended to go to Bucks County for a weekend, and may do so soon.

We have a gift here for you. If you'll send me your wife's address, I'll get it off. —Your note about your marriage reached me on the same day I learned that Manny and Janet Farber had separated, an event that distressed us considerably. I wish you all the best with your marriage.

Altogether, 1946 would be a good year for Kees. "I'm still at Paramount News," he wrote to Getty on July 23. "Have had several raises and I still find it as good a way of making a living as any I know of. It continues strenuous. The week we got out a full reel on the Bikini tests, I was here until 7:30 in the morning; the next makeup day I was here until 5:00." An undated letter to his parents concerns this 1946 production:

"When we devote an entire reel to one 'story' I'm elected to write it. You can't get any coordination or over-all treatment to such a reel unless one person conceives and writes the whole thing. The last reel with the Bikini underwater tests and the Japanese films turned out amazingly well; it is no doubt one of the best newsreels ever released. Its power and relation to the current world crisis is so marked that the state department ordered prints to be rushed abroad; they will be screened in Moscow and at the Paris Peace Conference."[7]

Kees was having some success with the publication of his verse too. The trouble that his first volume of poetry had cost him seemed to belong to the past. He wrote to Johnson on May 12 about his second volume, *The Fall of the Magicians,* but first there was a juicy tidbit to share:

> I suppose the oddest bit of news I can bring you is the story about Auden's sex life. According to a source I have always found reliable, W. H. has been sleeping with the wife of a little-known book-reviewer named Klonsky or Kloski or something of the sort. Before consummating their passion, a conversation between the couple had reference to Auden's heterosexual purity; he told the girl never to mention this matter to anyone, i.e., that he had slept with her, because "no one would believe it anyway." But everyone does. Everyone, that is, except Allen Tate.
>
> Tate won't believe, either, that Randall Jarrell has been excommunicated by the *Partisan Review* boys. He says it's just because Jarrell doesn't like to see anyone and stays in his loft on Hudson Street—where he lives with a man who writes textbooks on radio engineering—writing poems and reading [Georg] Groddeck [the psychoanalyst]. Evidently that bear in the cave metaphor of Jarrell's comes right from the heart.
>
> Tate is now working as an editor for Holt, which has brought about a strange situation for me. For six months I've been sending my new book of poems around. I probably went about it wrong, sending it to all sorts of unlikely places. Suddenly two houses wanted it—Reynal & Hitchcock and Holt. Reynal is going to do it, but don't hold your breath: it will probably come out this winter. Meantime the feud between the firms continues. Both of them want to publish poetry on a wider scale. Tate is sore that R&H are publishing Denis Devlin, Reed Whittemore and me; and R&H are sore that Tate got Howard Nemerov. Watch the best seller lists. [. . .]

For *The Fall of the Magicians,* Kees gathered twenty-six new poems and reprinted thirteen others from *The Last Man.* On July 23, he wrote to Getty that

> the scene in poetry publishing has taken on more glowing hues. This is due somewhat to Tate. He got fed up with the town of Sewanee and also needed to make some more money; so he took a job with Henry Holt when they agreed to let him wave a free hand in the stratosphere

of belles lettres. This move coincided with a move on the part of
Reynal & Hitchcock, where Albert Erskine was pointing out to his
colleagues that Stinky Shapiro had taken them out of a red ink as far
as verse is concerned. Suddenly there were two houses "vitally" "interested" in "poetry." (As I write this, I have a sinking feeling that this
all means next to nothing.) What has actually occurred is this: Tate
wanted my new book of poems for Holt, and so did Reynal & Hitchcock. Tate didn't appear on the scene quite soon enough; so R&H got
it and it should be coming out sometime this winter. Erskine does
such a good job of designing that I'm pleased they're doing it. Hell,
I'm terribly happy it's coming out at all. . . . [. . .]

The references to Tate give me an opportunity for a smooth transition
to the news of his friend, Thomas Stearns Eliot. I suppose you've read
that Eliot is over here in this country. Just *what* he's doing here I don't
know. He came down here to see Dwight Macdonald—we're living in
Dwight's apartment for the summer while he's on the Cape—but all
D. had to say about Eliot was that he was a devotee of *Politics*
[Macdonald's periodical] and that he looked very old and worn down.
Apparently Dwight spent the entire evening delivering a lecture. . . .
Tate spent a good deal of time with Eliot and took him down one
evening to see Djuna Barnes (a meeting to tear old men away from
their chimney corners, I should think), but I haven't seen Tate since.
Eliot's journey has had very little mention in the press. I expected, at
the very least, an interview in one of the Episcopalian organs.

Now we track back a bit to a reference in the preceding paragraph,
just like in a Conrad novel. We're subletting Dwight's apartment to
get away from our little 25th street noisebox: in the summertime it
combines some of the poorer features of Grand Central Station, Eb-
betts Field, Bellevue and the Chautauqua Bell Ringers. Here we have
wonderful quiet, a Steinway grand, tropical fish, a fine library (a bit
topheavy on Marxism) and five times the room. All this will end in
September and we hope we'll be able to find something else instead of
returning to 25th Street.

I wish I could tell you about my painting, but I don't think I'd have
any luck, even if I tried. It is all abstract and probably too derivative
of Picasso, so far. You'll see what I've done when you get back here,

which I hope will be soon. What have you heard from the Harvard Graduate School?

I've seen something of Randall Jarrell lately. He is rather oddly childish at times: once, in a restaurant, he became abnormally tickled over one item on the menu, "Turkey Wing Au Jus." The thing that rather puts one off about him is his way of hoarding his wit for his writing. But I feel very warm towards him: he took a couple of my poems for *The Nation,* and I just finished a review of Hoffman & Allen's *The Little Magazine* for that publication. Have you seen the book? I thought it was cretinous. The subject needed "inside" treatment, which those boys couldn't supply. It does have, though, some of the most wonderful unconscious humor I've run into, outside of small-town journalism. You're mentioned, by the way. Look yourself up in the index.

Reynal and Hitchcock brought out *The Fall of the Magicians* promptly, in the spring of 1947. It was dedicated "To Ann." In 1945, Kees had entered a version of it in a Houghton Mifflin competition, and though it did not win a prize, the readers had been astute. "This is intellectual art with a strange emotional impact characteristic of some contemporary painting," one of the judges wrote on July 3, 1945, in a letter forwarded to Kees. "I find in it brutality and violence and salt. He has real vitality and a surgical way with a satirical scalpel." In May 1944, Kees had, in fact, taken up painting and was working at it regularly, aware that artistic frontiers were with the New York Abstract Expressionists.

In working with film and painting, Kees's commitment to visual arts grew. Determined as always to go his own way, he did not plot his career with an eye toward "making it" in the New York manner; and when he and Ann moved to Brooklyn in the fall of 1946, they might have gone into outer darkness as far as ambitious young New Yorkers were concerned. They did not isolate themselves, of course, and they continued to see their friends and to report on their activities. But their circle widened now to include not only the New York Intellectuals, many of them associated with *Partisan Review,* but also artists of the New York School, just then coming into prominence.

On June 5, 1944, Ann reported to Norris Getty that Weldon had "lately taken up painting," and a month later, on July 14, Kees told Maurice Johnson that he did "mostly abstract things. [. . .] it's wonderfully satisfying." In the next two years, he devoted increasing time to painting, but he continued to write. "I paint every day, and have been writing more than I have in years," he wrote Getty on February 16, 1947. He worked hard, with mixed success: "What a lot of junk one has to erupt to get, on a good day, a couple of lines or a passage of painting that one can contemplate without disgust."

Through painting Kees associated with artists who thought of themselves as "advanced." When in November 1946 Byron Browne, one of the Abstractionists, exhibited at the Kootz Gallery, Kees wrote an introduction to his catalog to explain what the new painters were up to. He said that Browne was "among the American painters working in an international style." Kees understood that the center of the art world had moved from Paris to New York. He said these artists took "a delight in the physical qualities of paint and texture that had never been more arresting than in these new canvases. Scratched, glazed, sanded, scumbled [sic], their surfaces are marked by a grainy sensuous, heroic character."[1] When he saw the essay in proof, Browne in a note on October 23, 1946 told Weldon that he thought these words "an honest summation" of what he was trying to do.

Once more Weldon Kees found himself where the action was. If the painters did not totally accept him as one of themselves, perhaps it was because he was a writer before he was a painter, and they saw him moving in on their terrain. But they repeatedly turned to him for help with letters and manifestoes. He knew them all: William Baziotes, Fritz Bultman, Adolph Gottlieb, Hans Hofmann, Willem de Kooning, Karl Knaths, Robert Motherwell, Jackson Pollock, Mark Rothko. And he went to their Manhattan parties though he and Ann had moved to Brooklyn. Kees's preoccupation with painters and painting is clear in a letter to Norris Getty on November 13, 1946:

> Dear Norris, [. . .]
>
> [Samuel] Kootz had a party for Byron Browne at his apartment last night. It was remarkable chiefly for the remarks for Victor Wolfson, who had just bought a *collage* of Susie Fruylinghuysen's and was lengthily defending her for simply refining, in her fixated but rather charming way, certain early works of Picasso & Braque. "Repose!" he kept insisting. "That's what I want, and she's got it." Since Miss F. is not one of Kootz's painters, Kootz did not take kindly to this attitude at all. There was a rather sleek man who kept talking about how good Katherine Dunham is, and a lot of those odd-looking women (who are the wives of painters or Great Collectors) whose names you never catch as the introductions are inarticulate.
>
> Now that the truck strike is over and our furniture has dribbled in, the apartment has become very pleasant. However, Lovely Rose, our colored handywoman, has succeeded in doing something very odd to the floors in the process of scrubbing them. In one corner, disgusting whitish spots have appeared—the wooden equivalent of some loathsome skin ailment.
>
> I've done an enormous number of paintings since you were here, but I'm afraid not many of them are very good. I'm embarking, though, on a lot of new departures, if I can ever manage them the way they should be managed. [. . .]

The Fall of the Magicians was published in May 1947. It was widely reviewed, and Kees was mentioned in the national press as one of the leading poets of his generation, grouped with Randall Jarrell, Robert Lowell, John Frederick Nims, Elizabeth Bishop, and Karl Shapiro. When *Furioso*, an enterprising little magazine, established a Poetry

Book Club in 1947, its editors selected *The Fall of the Magicians* as
their first offering. Its second selection was by Howard Nemerov. Kees
continued to send manuscript poems to Norris Getty for comment,
including a troublesome one called "The Furies." He and Ann spent
their summer weeks on Cape Cod, in a Provincetown artists' colony
where writers, painters, and musicians gathered. (This so stimulated
them that they returned in 1948 and again, spectacularly, in 1949.)

In the fall of 1947 Kees quit his job at Paramount, hoping to support
himself by free-lancing and filmmaking. Ann kept her editorial job at
Antiques. His health was uneven but not life-threatening, his illnesses
of the sort often associated with stress: skin rashes, headaches, incip-
ient stomach ulcers. Ann was hardly stronger. In reply to an October
30 letter from Getty with an account of literary life at Harvard and
Stephen Spender's lecturing manner—"so plainly sincere and likable
that you somehow want to believe in him"—Kees wrote on November
16 of his own poems, his editors, his health, and of literary parties
and the Abstract Expressionists as well:

> I'm going to try to stay away from a regular job as long as I can,
> unless something so tempting that I can't resist it comes along. I paint
> every day, and have been writing more than I have in years. And
> money has been coming in, sometimes in surprising amounts. *The
> Tiger's Eye* took "The Furies," and paid me $96 for it! —Have you
> seen that magazine, by the way? All that potatoes and no meat. [. . .]

> Have I written you that they [the editors of the *Partisan Review*] want
> to kiss and make up after all these years? I had a letter from William
> Phillips, the only one of the four editors with whom I've had any
> friendly social dealings in some years, asking for something. I sent
> them those three [poems] you just had, and "Interregnum," the war
> poem you liked—previously entitled "Poem," because I couldn't think
> of a title at the time. If they take any of these I shall be vastly
> surprised; but if they want to be friendly, I'll try to cajole my hostility
> a little. [. . .]

> The party Frank Taylor threw for Spender had a peculiar, undefinable
> and traumatic quality of horror that I shall not soon forget.* The

---

* At one point, late in the evening, Spender was sitting out in the hallway, quite
alone, on the cooling radiator, his head in his hands. [W. K.]

main idea seemed to be to pack every available square foot of the Taylor house with people, and the more celebrities the better. The house is not small, as Village houses go. There were people there you never expected to see, like Graham Greene, looking like a pasty elderly edition of one of his weaker heroes; and people you thought were permanently settled in sanataria, like Jean Stafford, looking more ravaged and nervous than you had thought possible; and people you thought were in Europe, like Janet Flanner; and people who did not quite seem to fit in to a party for Stephen Spender, like Clifton Fadiman and Max Lerner. And then all the old familiar sights at parties like that: Allen Tate getting drunk and H. R. Hays giving his facial tics a furious and unremitting workout. —I don't know what it was about that party, but everyone was so *nervous*. Everyone's nervousness got on everyone else's nerves; after a while I began to think I was in worse shape than anyone there, but on reflection I don't see how this could be true.—When Ann was upstairs talking to Frank Taylor's wife, Mrs. Taylor was holding a bottle of some patent medicine. After a lengthy conversation she said, "I've got to take this medicine down to Miss Flanner. On the label it describes what it will relieve, among other things flatulence, and that's what Miss Flanner is suffering from." —I got to talking to Peter deVries, who is now on *The New Yorker,* in charge of poetry. But he said the poetry side of things did not really intrigue him very much; it was the gag writing he liked better; he has been working as a gag writer for the cartoonists, all of whom, it develops, have run out of ideas and are being fed gags by such as Peter. The only one who still uses his own brain is Alan Dunn. —Well, there was a lot more about that party, but writing about it is beginning to bring it back in all its full-blown hideousness; so forgive me if I cut myself off. —When people left, they said, What a lovely party! Thank you so much. See you soon.

A couple of days ago, when I was uptown, I was waiting on the corner of Sixth Avenue and Forty-Fifth Street for the lights to change when I became aware of the familiarity of the fat neck on the man in front of me. It was Edmund Wilson all right, and I walked part way across town with him, to the *New Yorker.* He has gotten fatter and much older, but was in one of his rare moods of affability, and kept telling me I ought to resurrect that old project of mine for an anthology of satirical poetry. I asked him if he had read [Lionel] Trilling's novel, [*The Middle of the Journey*], remembering that he and Trilling don't get along, or at any rate, that Edmund is not fond of Trilling. "Dreadful! Shocking!" he began to mutter in that Princeton–Reginald Owen accent of his. "One of the worst novels I ever tried to read! Just skipped through the last part, simply couldn't face it, etc., etc." —I sort of liked the book, myself, even though Ann is in large agreement with Wilson. I suppose the fact that I once knew Whittaker Chambers pretty well, who is the obvious model for one of the characters, can explain a lot of the fascination I felt for the novel. [. . .]

Last month I thought I had an ulcer. As it turned out, I didn't, and so far as I know, haven't; but it is no fun even having the idea. My stomach has been more or less on the fritz ever since my days on *Time*—that great despoiler of bodies & souls; things finally got to the point where I went to the doctor, who sent me to an x-ray man. It was a bad day. They don't let you eat any breakfast or drink any water, and it takes all day. Most of the time I sat around in an unpleasant little room, dressed only in one of those white Dr. Kildare gowns (it wouldn't fasten properly in the back) talking to other patients who kept drifting in and out. They all seemed to have far more horrible things wrong with their stomachs than I had; one man, it had just been discovered, had a stomach that was upside down; it was moving up into his diaphragm and he bled a lot. He told me he hadn't had anything to eat in three days, which made my own miseries seem very piddling indeed. —Every so often I would have to drink some barium and they would take pictures; then I would come back in the room and wait until the time came for me to drink more barium and stretch out on the table. There was nothing to read in the room except for a forbidding textbook on ailments of an incredibly distasteful nature (with many illustrations), and a copy of *Goodbye, Mr. Chips*. I read half of *Goodbye, Mr. Chips* that afternoon, while there were no fellow sufferers around to talk with; I can report that it is very poor reading, at least under those circumstances.

I am supposed to relax, and every so often I take a teaspoonful of some evil-looking black medicine. They tell me that my stomach is an organically sound organ, but I wonder. I worry about how to relax. The doctor couldn't tell me. [. . .]

> Perhaps I wrote you that Sam Kootz is getting out a book, with examples by all of his artists; and he has asked various writers to write poems or prose pieces or articles for each artist. I did one on Motherwell, but [Robert] Goldwater, the new editor of the *Magazine of Art,* wanted it for that publication. [. . .]

The piece on Robert Motherwell appeared in the March 1948 issue of *Magazine of Art.* Kees wrote:

> The beliefs to which the most advanced painters of our own time give their allegiance were foreshadowed by Flaubert, who, interrupting himself from his torments with the world-haunted manuscript of Madame Bovary, parted company with his own century to set down this unfulfilled desire: "What I should like to write is a book about nothing at all, a book which would exist by virtue of the mere internal strength of its style, as the earth holds itself unsupported in the air. . . ."

> "A book which would exist by virtue of the mere internal strength of its style. . . ." This is the literary equivalent of the canvases of Robert Motherwell. He has pushed the major emphasis of abstract painting to one kind of Ultima Thule. [. . .]

> In Motherwell [. . .] a new kind of subject matter becomes manifest. It is paint itself. The paintings are quite simply "about" paint. Fathered, curiously enough, in view of his most recent work, by Mondrian and continuously nourished by Picasso, from whom Motherwell "lifts" objects and passages with complete acknowledgment (and in a manner far more likable and disarming than do those painters who are merely under the influence of some particular period of the Spaniard), Motherwell assumes the full consequences of the furthest tendency of abstract art. His circular forms are not oranges or abstractions of oranges, heads or abstractions of heads; his rectangles, blots, blurs and brushstrokes assert nothing but their own existence, their own identity and individuality. They are objects from their own world, and that world is the world of paint. Motherwell's insistence upon this concentration and definition is as fierce as Céline's insistence of hell on earth or the insistence of the air on its own transparency (pp. 87–88).

While painting and writing, Kees continued his association with the New York Intellectuals. The painters were not such good talkers as the writers. No one was more full of talk than Kees, as this letter to Norris Getty shows:

4 March 1948

Dear Norris, First, Mary McCarthy's story I promised you. You may have heard [. . .] that Spender lined up a lot of people for a poetry conference at Sarah Lawrence a few weeks back. Don't ask me what the purpose of it was; but the undeclared intent was apparently to include throngs of people who know nothing about poetry, whatever their other abilities in the literary world may be (William Phillips, Lionel Trilling, etc.), academics like Donald Stauffer and Norman Holmes Pearson, poets who have not written any poetry for years (Louise Bogan, Robert Fitzgerald, etc.), poets who don't write much poetry (Marianne Moore), and characters such as Mary McCarthy, who don't seem to fit into any of my classifications. I seem to have left out the [Horace] Gregorys, Karl Shapiro (who sent regrets by telegram; said he had "neuralgia of the knee") Auden (who sent similar regrets: "neuralgia of the back"); Mary said that F. O. Matthiessen also wired he couldn't make it; she thought he was suffering from neuralgia of the brain. —All this is introductory. The affair went on for two days, and some of the people stayed in the dormitories overnight. One was Marianne Moore. She went upstairs early; and Mary was sent up by someone to tell her not to worry about getting up for breakfast: they would send her something on a tray. When Mary knocked at the door, Miss M. answered it in a state of dishabille; she wore only a pair of old pink bloomers and a little white shirtwaist. She seemed to want to talk and, a bizarre figure in this costume, which she did not bother to cover, she discussed various topics of the hour with Mary for quite some time. Mary says Miss Moore has two words that she uses continually; one of them is "generous" and the other is "courageous" and she uses both of them with a steady undercurrent of maliciousness: "Wasn't it *generous* of President Taylor to make that fine introduction for Mr. Spender?" "Wasn't it *courageous* of poor Louise Bogan to come way out here from 168th Street, the poor dear?" etc., etc. —Well, next day, Mary was talking to Spender, who had with him a new autograph book Ruthven Todd had given him. He was very happy with this possession and had been going around getting the poets and non-poets to write little inscriptions in it for him. Some of them had even written poems therein. "And I want you to see the nice thing Marianne Moore wrote in my book," said the author of *Ruins and Visions*. He showed it to her. "To courageous Mr. Spender," Miss Moore had written in her rather spidery hand. Spender was terribly pleased by it.

There seem to be an awful lot of parties around here lately. Sunday we went to one someone threw for Jean Malaquais, who just got back from Europe. It throbbed with people from splinter Marxist outfits, Sidney Hooks, Dwight Macdonalds, etc., and turned up an intense and rather handsome little man who turned out to be Michael Fraenkel, the guy Henry Miller exchanged so many letters with on *Hamlet*. He seized my hand with marked avidity and told me that that review I did in the *Times* on Miller was just the ticket, which rather took me aback, since I had thought that he and Miller were still bosom pals. Not at all, said Fraenkel: Miller's old cronies think he is a sell-out and getting terribly stuffy to boot. —We wrenched ourselves away from this party (the liquor was beginning to run out and the hostess, whom Malaquais says was "some sort of an activist," was getting very nervous) and went on to another one at George Davis's. Here one entered another world: smooth publishers' young men, Nancy Walker, Josephine Prémice, Truman Capote, Dawn Powell, several very creepy fairies, and an appalling woman left over from *Nightwood*. Capote said to me, "Why don't you want to be a *success?* I can tell from the way you act you don't want to be a success. You're like Newton Arvin. Why, you're a much better poet than that old Robert Lowell. I just feel terrible. Nobody likes my novel that I want to have like it. All the wrong people are praising it. I just got back from Haiti. In San Francisco I stayed with the Saroyans—" In a large cage by the piano, Davis's green parrot stirred uneasily, and Oliver Smith went over and said something to it in consoling tones.

Have you seen [Leslie] Fiedler's [disparaging] remarks on Frost in the current *PR*? Now we're beginning to get someplace.

Bought a record player finally. It's one of those table models in a very simple cabinet of light wood that Victor made up particularly for dealers. Seems to me superior to Magnavox. Maybe you've seen it. A couple of days after I got it, *The Nation* came out with one of those pieces [Bernard] Haggin does now and then on phonographs; he picked it as one of the best. I was lucky to get a slightly used one at about half-price. Anxious to have you hear it. Now we're spending money like drunken sailors on albums. The Lee Wiley album of Harold Arlen songs is one of my most cherished acquisitions; have you heard it?

Wrote a new poem about Robinson the other day and will send it to you very shortly; I'm a little blank about it at the moment. —That's a beautiful poem of W. C. Williams in the last *PR*. I also liked a new long one by William Plomer in *New Writing*. [. . .].

Hope you can get down during Spring vacation. Are you still interested in renting a house this summer? We'd still like to. If you're agreeable, I'll get busy on it as soon as the weather gets decent enough to look around on weekends.

Do you know of a decent translation of Propertius? The one I'm reading is not so good.

Three weeks later, on March 22, 1948, Kees wrote that *"The New Yorker* took 'Aspects of Robinson' like a shot." This was a poem that readers of Weldon Kees have come to think of as prototypical. "Robinson" concerns a modern, urban professional whose emotional life is "dry as a winter leaf." It is one of Kees's most frequently cited pieces.

Kees began to make plans for summer on Cape Cod with Norris Getty. Getty, now a graduate student in the classics at Harvard, reported on literary and academic life in Cambridge; and he shared Kees's enthusiasm for popular music. Kees had taught himself to play barrel house piano in the manner of Jelly Roll Morton while still a boy and had always played as opportunity presented itself. For example, he told Johnson that during a party at "Jim Agee's brother-in-law's" he had participated in a "jam session featuring Wilder Hobson on trombone. We scored our greatest triumph in our rendition of 'The Sheik of Araby,' 'Sweet Lorraine,' and 'Tea for Two'" (March 20, 1948). But he had not had access to a piano regularly until the sum-

mer of 1946, when he and Ann briefly occupied the Dwight Macdonald apartment while the Macdonalds were in Europe. Kees made
good use of their Steinway. After he bought the record player in
March 1948, he began collecting records in earnest, reviving an enthusiasm that became almost an obsession. His article, "Muskrat
Ramble: Popular and Unpopular Music," defending both pure and
commercial jazz, appeared in *Partisan Review* in May, 1948. In it,
Kees tried to distinguish between the meritorious and the meretricious
in popular culture, and the essay has subsequently been anthologized.

The spring of 1948 was full of poetry, painting, and jazz, and summer
in Provincetown was all that they hoped for. Weldon wrote to Maurice
Johnson from there on July 22:

> Dear Maurice, We live here in a state of almost uninterrupted sloth;
> occasionally Norris or I totter over to the piano (a very poor one) to
> play "Nice Work If You Can Get It" or "Someone to Watch Over
> Me," or we walk across the dunes to swim and beachcomb, or Ann
> and I go down to the Tennis Club to play ping pong. The beaches are
> wonderful and we have all, at one time or another, suffered from
> ultra-violet poisoning.

> I've done some painting and writing. One of the poems I wrote up
> here has been taken by *The New Yorker*. But the long poem goes
> slowly. I rather thought that would be the case.

> The big news here is the folding of Kootz's gallery. It has put his
> painters, most of whom are up here, in a bad spot; and the 57th street
> scene in general has them rather jittery. Several other galleries are
> closing up, among them Julian Levy's. None of Kootz's printers, so far
> as I know, have found other galleries yet; but they were left rather
> high & dry, since his closing came at a time when a lot of the dealers
> are out of New York, and a time when decisions are not quickly
> arrived at.

> Provincetown seems less crowded than during other seasons I've been
> up here. A number of Provincetown regulars, like some of the *Partisan
> Review* people, Lloyd Frankenberg, Bert Wolfe, are elsewhere; and the
> merchants complain that business is poor. Most of the night clubs are
> deserted: and from the quality of their entertainers, well deserve to be.

> On the bureau: a huge seashell that looks like Paul Klee had a hand in
> its design, an odd cork object, a piece of driftwood shaped like a
> dolphin, a stone with a pattern out of [Jean] Arp, a number of dried
> starfish. [. . .]

Back in Brooklyn in the fall, Kees wrote another chatty letter to
Johnson, touching on present projects and summer memories:

> 11 October 1948

> Dear Maurice, Meant to write you before this. I had a pretty good
> painting streak there for a while, a little later a better streak for
> poems, my folks paid us a visit (they travel like Cecil Beaton or Dos
> Passos these days), somebody called and wanted to know whether I
> wanted to go to South America to write a documentary movie (I
> didn't very much), I went to Philadelphia in connection with another
> film I may write, spent the last three days preparing materials for a
> Guggenheim. Maybe I stand a better chance than I did when I applied
> in 1942. Considering all the time it takes—my bibliography was a
> nightmare to compile—they ought to give everybody $2500 just for
> all this trouble. I would take it without a qualm.

> Some sort of a high point of this summer was one afternoon when we
> drove down to Wellfleet to have cocktails with Edmund Wilson and
> his new wife. We went with a girl we know and her mother. The
> mother is a very old friend of Edmund's who chatters incessantly and
> who is married to a very nice guy who is (a) Ernest Hemingway's
> oldest friend, (b) John Dos Passos' brother-in-law (they were living in
> Dos Passos' house in Provincetown), (c) an old friend of Wilson. The
> Wilson household is odd. There is the new wife, who is attractive and
> nice and has a Russian accent; her son by a previous marriage;
> Rosalind, Edmund's daughter by his first marriage; Reuel, Mary Mc-
> Carthy's offspring; a baby by the *new* wife; two dogs. There was also
> Waldo Frank and his wife and *their* baby. Waldo fed his baby a
> teaspoonful of tom collins. I was surprised to see Waldo Frank at
> Edmund Wilson's, but summertime brings on a lot of strange confron-
> tations. —Wilson turned to me at one point in the afternoon and
> announced that he had written a lot of satirical poems that he thought
> were very good but that no one would print them. He said he had sent
> them everywhere; all the little magazines had rejected them. He was a

little grumpy about *that,* but not so much about other things: we got to talking of Thornton Wilder's new book [*The Ides of March*] and I mentioned that Norris Getty had pointed out to me that the versions of Catullus which Wilder prints are frequently corrupt. Norris then took this up as Edmund got very excited about the matter, went out to his library and brought out several editions of Catullus, along with *The Ides of March*. He and Norris had quite a discussion about the poems. Norris told me later he was a little dubious about Wilson's Latin. [. . .]

Best to you and Nan. Hope to see you when you come down in November. I am standing first on one foot and then the other waiting for one of the 57th Street gallery boys to come over and look at my paintings to decide if he wants to give me a show. I have got to have a show because I have room for no more canvases in the closet.

Yrs ever,
Weldon

This summer we got to know a very good abstract painter named Fritz Bultman, who has a very nice wife who comes from Hastings [Nebraska] and was once a burlesque queen. Doesn't look like it at all. [. . .]

Late in October 1948, Kees learned that he had been awarded the Oscar Blumenthall Prize by *Poetry* Magazine. "This prize," the editor wrote, "is in recognition of your group of Four Poems in the October 1947 issue and Four Poems in the August 1948 issue. Our check for $100 is enclosed."

• • •

In the late forties, though some galleries exhibited the work of the Abstractionist painters and the critics in the journals treated their work with cautious respect, the popular press looked with some disdain on pictures that had no recognizable subjects. The October 11, 1948, issue of *Life* carried an elaborate spread on the state of modern art. During the summer of 1948, the editors had assembled "fifteen distinguished critics and connoisseurs . . . to clarify the strange world of art today."[2] They decided that the cutting edge of contemporary art seemed to be with the Abstractionists, centered in New York. Kees and the New York painters tried to remain superior to all this talk, but they were in fact much concerned with their popular reputations. They observed that the scholar-critics had some points of agreement: though they could not agree on principles or on the merit of all the paintings, they seemed to agree that William Baziotes's painting, *The Dwarf,* was less successful than pictures by his contemporaries Willem de Kooning, Jackson Pollock, and Adolph Gottlieb. Baziotes was of course upset. Kees wrote to Norris Getty on October 11, 1948:

> Have you seen this week's *Life,* the one now on the stands? It's mostly on the round-table held early last summer on modern art. One of Bill's [William Baziotes's] paintings is reproduced, along with others by DeKooning, Pollock, etc. Clem Greenberg is much in evidence, also Meyer Schapiro; Greenberg pans Bill's painting, and there are other surprises. The whole thing goes on for an unbelievable length. Luce must have bought an Arp or something, to bring this on.
>
> We were invited up to the Baziotes last Friday night, the day this *Life* appeared. Bill made an act out of the whole thing—we hadn't seen the magazine—and before showing it to us went into a long story about what a fine buildup Clem had given him. They said we were their first guests since they got back from the Cape: they hadn't had anyone before because Bill was vomiting all the time. He got into such a state of worry over things that he finally had to go to the doctor. One time he was down to ninety-three cents. Still doesn't have a gallery. It's a damn shame.

Kees was elated when Lou Pollack gave him a one-man show in his new gallery, the Periodot, in November 1948. It attracted important critics and artists. The *New York Times* observed on November 5 that Kees "has already secured himself a place as one of the more conspicuous and interesting young American poets. In his painting Mr. Kees is still concerned with assimilating the idiom of a number of abstract painters—Browne, Baziotes, Pollock come to mind." The following spring Kees was asked to show his work in an exhibition of American Abstract Artists, and the Brooklyn Museum asked for a watercolor. "I believe that painting and writing complement one another," Kees told a reporter from the *Brooklyn Eagle* on November 7, after his first show opened. "Shifting from one to the other I don't get into the periods of absolute sterility that are often experienced by writers who just write, or painters who just paint." The majority of painters and writers, he said, "become narrower and narrower. They get over-specialized. They're in a trap and they can't get out."

In private both Hans Hofmann, the senior member of the New York School, and Clement Greenberg commended his painting. "Hofmann asked me to write a poem for the catalog of his Paris show," he wrote to Getty on November 27. "It will also have essays on his paintings by Tennessee Wms. and another guy. I do not like poems of celebration for occasions very much, but I think maybe this one is better than the one Auden did on T. S. E." Hofmann was pleased by the poem: "The poem is wonderful," he wrote Kees on November 30. "You are as great a poet as you are a painter. I found your exhibition fascinating. It's poetry in color. That it is—what painting should be."

After Kees's one-man show at the Periodot, ordinary life returned. Ann and Weldon both got colds and took to their beds; they bought discounted jazz records; they read and commented on books; Weldon wrote poems and painted. Hans and Miz Hofmann returned to New York from Paris, bringing their warm support. By January 26, 1949, Weldon was reporting to Norris that "All sorts of feelings of uncertainty and inadequacy [kept] playing hell" with him. He had a much greater need of public support than some persons around him seemed to understand.

In 1949, Weldon Kees found himself involved in the political life of New York. In March the National Council of the Arts, Sciences and Professions held a "Cultural and Scientific Conference for World Peace" at the Waldorf-Astoria Hotel. "The conference had little to do with either culture, science or peace but it was nevertheless of great significance," Dwight Macdonald wrote in his paper, *Politics* (Winter 1949). "It was strictly a Stalinoid affair: the NCASP is a Communist-front organization." Organizing themselves into a group called the Americans for Intellectual Freedom, the non-Communist left, chaired by Sidney Hook, the New York University philosopher, denounced the NCASP.

Kees was one of more than two hundred persons pledged to "the spirit of free inquiry and honest difference of opinion—the true hallmark of a gathering of intellectuals whose minds are not twisted into the straight-jacket of the Communist party line." Ever since his undergraduate days, Kees had been contemptuous of Communist orthodoxy, and he rather enjoyed this brouhaha with the Stalinists. F. O. Matthiessen drew his particular contempt, for he thought that as a gifted critic and superb literary historian Matthiessen should not submit to any party line.

Norris Getty had written about a Harvard forum—on the question "Is the Novel Dying?"—in which Matthiessen had taken a socialist position: "[Harry] Levin said the novel *was* dying—nowhere to go from Joyce, etc. FOM said novelists ought to write like Dreiser. C. M. Bowra said they ought to write like Dickens. A man with a French accent said they ought to write 'subjective epics.' Take your pick" (20 March 1949). Kees reacted to the forum in a letter to Getty on March 22, 1949:

> Dear Norris, Just had word from the good Guggenheim people that my "application for a Fellowship has not been granted." Called up Bill [Baziotes], who had put in for one, but his mail hadn't come yet. We still have money in the bank; so we go on in this way for a time yet, although that $2500 would certainly have been welcome.
>
> That session on "Is the Novel Dying?" sounds like a report on it for a *Partisan* [*Review*] Variety piece would be a dandy. Why don't you do it? Under a pseudonym, under the circumstances, I'd imagine. F. O. Mattetc. gets more tiresome by the minute. I see he is still right around the neck with the Party and is taking part in this conference at the Waldorf. I am working with Hook's committee and helping them out on newsreel publicity and things look interesting at the moment. Speaking of F.O.M., I was amusing myself the other night with a song for him (to be sung by the most unappealing of the seven dwarfs):
>
> Heigh-ho, F.O.,
> Though the lights are getting low,
> Still greet the dark
> With a C.P. lark
> That yet may crow. Heigh-ho!

> Heigh-ho, F.O.,
> And cheers for Uncle Joe!
> High Kremlin names
> Supplant H. James
> And rightly so! Heigh-ho!
>
> Heigh-ho, F.O.,
> One gets a steady glow
> From dying sparks
> Of a burned-out Marx
> In wastes of snow. Heigh-ho!

> I have more, but I'll spare you that. Eventually we segue into a chorus
> led by Paul Robeson singing a Marc Blitzstein arrangement (danced
> by Paul Draper) of *God Bless Czechoslovakia*.
>
> I think I wrote you that I'm having a painting in the American Ab-
> stract Artists show, opening next week. Of more interest is the fact
> that Clem G. [Greenberg], who has been painting for about twenty
> years off and on, is for the first time showing a painting. He is nervous
> as hell about it, naturally. We were over at his place a week or so ago
> and he showed us his most recent works. They show a strong influ-
> ence of Jackson Pollock. [. . .]

A month later, on April 11, Kees was still talking of politics in another
letter to Getty:

> Things have been a bit more lively than normally, what with all the
> excitement of the Waldorf Conference (Macdonald has a good ac-
> count of parts of it in the current *Politics*) and the opposition meet-
> ings; Rexroth was here, waiting for a boat to Europe, and put on a
> bang-up performance the night he came here to the apartment; Bob
> Lowry is just back from a year in Italy, with some rather gruesome
> accounts of the behavior of the artistic expatriates over there and in
> France (one of his main reasons for leaving New York was to escape
> the Truman Capote set; they were wherever he went in Europe, in full
> force); people in general here are behaving with greater wackiness
> than ever before in my experience.

On May 5, Weldon gave a detailed account of "the recent scandal at Yaddo" to Maurice Johnson. In those days of the Cold War, all aspects of life seemed inevitably politicized:

> It has been a strange winter and spring, with a number of odd or enlivening things going on. I single out the following as perhaps the outstanding ones:
>
> (1) The Yaddo Affair. In February, when that report on spies came out from General MacArthur's headquarters, with its allegations against Agnes Smedley, FBI agents descended upon Saratoga Springs and the Yaddo mansion. But Agnes Smedley, who had been living at Yaddo for four straight years, had left some weeks earlier. At the time of the FBI invasion, there were five guests spending part of the winter at Yaddo: Elizabeth Hardwick, Robert Lowell, Edward Mazell, James Ross* and a girl whose name escapes me. Hardwick and Lowell, whether correctly or not I still don't know, has become convinced that for years Mrs. [Elizabeth] Ames had been either a C.P. member or a completely malleable fellow traveler, and had been using Yaddo as a retreat for Communists. They raised quite a fuss; Lowell, who only a short time before had been elected to the Yaddo Board of Directors, called a meeting of the Board members who live in Saratoga and demanded Mrs. Ames' immediate resignation. Now, of course, the matter of Mrs. Ames' methods of administration has been a scandal for years, as anyone who has ever been to Yaddo is eager to go on about for hours, but the political charges had never before been raised with such heat. (One board member, a Wall Street man, who gets heart palpitations at the mention of the word "Communist," used to write to Mrs. Ames occasionally when he got reports of some well-known and bona fide Communist being at Yaddo. Mrs. Ames, I am told, always denies the charges: she once wrote this Wall St. man, when he inquired what Alfred Kantorowitz was doing there, that Kantorowitz was a "Jeffersonian Democrat." Since that time it has been learned that even then Kantorowitz was an OGPU [Soviet Intelligence] agent and is now running a school for American commissars in the Soviet Zone of Germany. There are other examples.) This is getting a little drawn-

---

*Ross, it is alleged, was a narcotics addict. He became so frightened about the FBI that he pulled out of Saratoga in a matter of minutes. [W. K.].

out. Anyway, there was hell popping in Saratoga and, later, in New York. A committee composed of Alfred Kazin, Eleanor Clark, John Cheever, Kappo Phelan and Harvey Breit sent a long report to about a hundred former Yaddo guests, asking that they rally to Mrs. Ames' support, and enclosing a statement they asked to be signed and sent to the Board. Meanwhile the Lowell faction was busy with more accusations. Last month a full board meeting was held in New York; among those voting for Mrs. Ames' dismissal were Newton Arvin, Louis Kronenberger and Granville Hicks. Malcolm Cowley was the Board member most vociferously supporting Mrs. Ames. (I have heard that the Kazin Committee was actually set up by Cowley, operating behind his (Cowley's) well-known Stalinist connections. I didn't sign Kazin's statement, since it seemed to me sycophantic in the extreme, and an all-out endorsement of Mrs. Ames' regime, which I don't feel it merits.) I have barely scratched the surface of this business, but I should add that Louis Kronenberger told me the other day that the Board finally decided to chastise Mrs. A., keep her on for the time being, and (a suggestion of Cowley's) turn the matter over to "an impartial board of investigation . . . perhaps the Carnegie Foundation." Kronenberger said he hoped the board of investigation didn't come back with the recommendation that the Yaddo station wagon needs a new tail-light.

(2) The Mary McCarthy–*Partisan Review* caper. You may have noticed that Mary's theatre pieces no longer appear in the *PR*. Her story "The Oasis" [a *roman à clef*] has the *PR* editors chewing the nap off the rug, and I must say I found the story a spiteful one, quite aside from the fact that it seemed to me an empty and badly-confirmed piece of work. Nor can I imagine it can have very much meaning to those who don't know Rahv, Phillips, Macdonald, etc. Did you read it?

(3) The Robert Lowell Affair. Shortly after the Waldorf conference, Lowell went insane. He had gone out to Chicago to see Tate, became wildly excited in Tate's apartment and was screaming obscenities out of the window when they sent for the wagon from the puzzle house. He is now in a sanatarium in Boston, being treated by Merrill Moore. Apparently paranoia plus a God complex. Lowell had been going

around New York threatening to "get" Jean Stafford, who, he said, represented "evil," and that he has been singled out by God to stamp her out.

I might go on, my index finger willing, with (4), (5), (6), etc., but perhaps these items will give you some sense of the literary atmosphere in the world's greatest city at this particular period of man's upward march.

Later

I'd like to see yr. baby, but can wait until the pulverized-spinach-spitting stage abates: I have enough trouble with Harold Rosenberg when he says some phrase like "purple passages." —My parents are going through a similar stage of the uprooting process that you write of yr. own parents. Mine have just sold the house and are *in* the midst of clearing out for Orlando. They have so much vigor and endurance and elation over travel that I feel, by comparison, like Tiresias around them. [. . .]

In spite of the curious atmosphere of late, I've had a fairly productive time since Provincetown. About twelve new poems—some of them moderately long. I *think* I have a new book almost ready, but can't tell until I begin arranging the poems to see if they add up to a unit. *The Fall of the Magicians* had a thematic unity, I think; but I am too close to these new poems to get any kind of an objective notion about them. I am going to see my editor at Harcourt soon to find out if they cd bring the book out in the Fall if I finish the book early this summer.* —Then I've furnished eight new canvases since my show, and have another one-man show schedule for next November. The Brooklyn Museum has a water color of mine in its International water color show that opened yesterday; and I think I sent you an announcement of the American Abstract Artists' show.

For some reason or other I seem to have a car. Bought a 1938 Plymouth from Mark Rothko for $175. It runs; though the interior of it must have been used exclusively for hauling porcupines and railroad spikes. Looks a little like an unmade bed in a Bowery fleabag. We

---

*The long poem I was working on came to nothing. I wrote a hundred lines before I called a halt. [W. K.].

> hope to drive up to Provincetown next week to look for a place to stay
> this summer. I am not too eager about Provincetown again, but don't
> know where else to go that wd. be much of an improvement.
>
> Write. And let me know what the Syracuse U. Press decides about yr.
> book. Best regards to you and Nancy from us.

In June 1949, Ann and Weldon Kees returned to Provincetown for the
summer. Getty's reports of forums at Harvard on topics as various as
the state of the contemporary novel and of values in the arts had
suggested to Kees that a series of forums on Cape Cod, where many
artists and intellectuals assembled, might be worth setting up.
"Dwight Macdonald suggests a panel for the Provincetown series of
evenings, with three or four analysts and psychiatrists who will be
staying on the upper Cape this summer; suggested topic (by Dwight):
'The Psychopathology of Vacations,'" Kees wrote to Getty on May
23, 1949. Kees planned to set up panels, discussions, lectures and
demonstrations in Gallery 200, and the more he worked on it, the
more elaborate the whole venture became. He wrote to Dwight Macdonald from Provincetown on June 22, 1949:

> Dear Dwight, The plans for the forums have been going along great
> guns since I last saw you. Meant to get some word off to you before
> this, but for the last three days Fritz Bultman and I have been spend-
> ing about 18 hours a day on the posters, publicity releases of various
> kinds, arrangements on seating, lining up sponsors, etc. You know
> how frantic this can be.
>
> We have run into a certain amount of hysteria of a sort we hadn't
> counted on. Somebody got a look at our program, saw the word
> "soviet" in the title of your talk, and the next thing we knew the
> rumor was all over town that "the Commies have taken over the
> building at 200 Commercial." It now develops that this all goes back
> to the height of the Wallace* activities last year, but the rumor is still
> very lively in these parts. I am releasing stories to the paper on the

---

*Henry Wallace ran for President as the candidate of the Progressive Party in 1948,
campaigning for closer cooperation with the U.S.S.R. and criticizing Harry
Truman's "get tough" policy with the Communists everywhere. Wallace said, "We
have no more in common with imperialist England than with Communist Russia."

entire series, the new gallery and the opening show tomorrow, and it should take care of these rumors once and for all. Apparently some of the talk was helped a bit by the fact that a lot of people here in town, due to the ever-present cultural lag, still think that you are a foaming Marxist. Do you still run into this sort of thing? Anyway, I had a long talk with one man here, who is still not convinced, after all I told him about your various changes in philosophies during the past five years, that you are not a Communist. (Incidentally, most Provincetownites do not make any very subtle distinction between a Stalinist and a Trotskyite.)

Anyway, on account of all this, I have had to go completely overboard on all publicity releases about you, for this locality, in order to make certain that your antistalinism matches mine. One particularly difficult occasion was the other night when the wife of the man who has rented the building went completely hysterical on us and tried to lay down an ultimatum that our forums were to be "absolutely devoid of all politics." I gathered she even wanted me to go back on our commitment with you to speak. Luckily, the man who *owns* the building seems a completely honest and ethical man—one of the few we have run into so far in our arrangements—but without his backing God knows what would have happened. There was a moment when I was just about ready to tell her that if you were not allowed to speak there would be no programs at all. All this has its hilarious aspects, but there were a couple of times when I failed to make them out clearly.

On the posters it seemed essential, because of the local practice here of regarding any mention of the word "soviet" as meaning pro-soviet, to explain your title a little. The copy now reads "'The Dream World of the Soviet Bureaucracy.' Speaker: Dwight Macdonald, editor *Politics*, on a new theory exposing the lies of the Russian dictatorship." I trust this is satisfactory to you and does not misrepresent anything. I truly regret the necessity for this at all.

I will have plenty of press releases on the whole series, a number of which have already gone out to the New York, Boston, and Cape papers, *Time, Newsweek, Nation, New Republic,* all the art magazines, etc. I want because of your talk, to see that releases get out to the *New Leader* and other such sheets. I will be grateful if you will

13. Weldon Kees, Provincetown,
1949. Poster by Fritz Bultman.
Photograph by Bill Witt. Pho-
tograph courtesy of the Heritage
Room, Bennett Martin Public
Library

14. Exhibition at 200 Commercial St., Provincetown, 1949. Judith Rothschild, Fritz Bultman, Weldon Kees. Paintings by Bultman, Pollock, Kees, Rothschild. Photograph by Bill Witt courtesy of the Heritage Room, Bennett Martin Public Library

15. Exhibition at 200 Commercial Street, Provincetown, 1949. Left to right: Hans Hofmann, Karl Knaths, Weldon Kees, Cecil Hemley, and Fritz Bultman. Paintings, left to right, by Hofmann, Roy Chaffee, Serge Chermayeff, three by Knaths, Bultman, and Jackson Pollock. Photograph by Bill Witt. Photograph courtesy of the Heritage Room, Bennett Martin Public Library

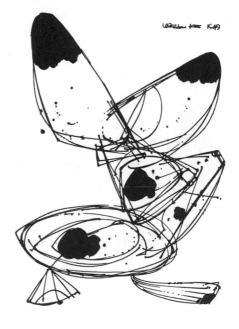

16. Painting by Weldon Kees, 1948. Photograph courtesy of the Heritage Room, Bennett Martin Public Library

17. Frontispiece for the *Partisan Review* (October 1949), commissioned by Clement Greenberg. Originally appeared in *Partisan Review,* vol. 16, no. 10 (1949). Photograph courtesy of the editors of *Partisan Review*

18. Anton Myrer, about 1975. Photograph courtesy of Anton Myrer

send me a list of ones you think should have news of our programs, along with their addresses. [. . .]

Official histories of the Provincetown art colony record the success of Forum 49, as it came to be called: "By the end of July there was no doubt that the first month of Forum '49 had been a success. With an admission fee of sixty cents, attendance had broken records even on hot and sultry nights. The admission charge barely covered basic expenses, but then these were kept to a minimum. Even the most celebrated speakers were paid only with a bottle of Scotch, but they were put up for the night by the artists and by their close friends. An added attraction was that the forums were always followed by lively parties, usually at Weathering Heights, with Weldon Kees playing jazz piano and uninhibited dancing until all hours."[3]

• • •

In the summer of 1949, Ann and Weldon Kees made several friends who were to be important to them for the rest of their lives. Since Weldon had admired Conrad Aiken's work for many years, he was delighted to become acquainted with him and his wife on the Cape. Also during this summer he and Ann met Anton Myrer and his wife, Judith Rothschild, the abstract painter. Tony Myrer was a fledgling novelist. Years later Myrer wrote:

> "Weldon was one of the last great romantics: he genuinely believed that sensibility and talent would receive due recognition with time, that beautiful and important moving pictures could still be made in Hollywood (I can still remember his great excitement after he'd been to an advance screening of *Sunset Boulevard* in New York City), that open-handed generosity of spirit was a vital necessity in a world of gentility and merit. He refused to ally himself with the intellectual Establishment of the Eastern academies the way Lowell and Berryman did, or play the Librarian-of-Congress power-broker game, as did Jarrell and Nemerov . . . and of course he paid for that, bitterly. He was a bundle of fascinating anomalies: his esthetic sensibilities were almost Proustian, and yet he loved to see himself as a 1930s tough guy, a kind of Zachary Scott–Barton MacLane blend. [Scott and MacLane were film actors.] He could—and did!—drink with the best of them, but his manners could be almost courtly on occasion; and he would not

stand for boorishness or bad manners. I was sitting beside him at the
opening night of the Provincetown Players' performance of Conrad
Aiken's *Mr. Arcularis,* when Dwight Macdonald began ridiculing the
play, and Weldon told him to shut up or he'd break a chair over his
head—and he would have, too. (Macdonald kept quiet the rest of the
evening.) And Weldon delivered what may well be the merited rebuke
of all time when the painter Mark Rothko, who is Jewish, said he
didn't feel anything when he saw the films of the Nazi death camps,
he didn't feel anything at all. There was a shocked little silence, and
then Weldon said: "What you mean, Mark, is that you're a moral
dwarf." He would not put up with bad manners—and he hated inhu-
manity . . . At times I think he saw himself as a kind of latter-day Ezra
Pound (whom he deeply admired for his poetry and critical bril-
liance)—lending critical assistance to aspiring writers, supporting local theater and printing projects, writing for amateur musicals, and so
on; keeping it all going in the face of this most violent and wasteful of
societies.[4]

Kees regarded the summer of 1949 as one of the high points of his life,
and subsequently he remembered it as one of Ann's happiest times
too. Judith Rothschild recalls that "When we met her, Ann had just
resigned from her job at *Antiques.* She seemed more a 'homebody'
than a career girl, and much that she did made me see her as a
Wisconsin farmer's wife rather than the wife of an artist." Judith
Rothschild recalls her appearance:

> Her face was white and her skin thin—like white tissue paper. She
> wore little make-up. Her eyes had a way of moving before her head
> (usually towards Weldon for corroboration), thus giving an impression
> of wistfulness. [. . .] Her clothes were practical and appropriate:
> slacks and shirts, that suit, nothing dressy or sexy that I recall—what
> the English call "country." In general her opinions seemed to be
> Weldon's. She had a few of her own. W. C. Fields was a real hero to
> her. And she was always vehement, even venomous about children.
> She said she hated them and this was always said with a force that
> seemed all the more strong because she so seldom expressed that sort
> of unilateral position.

Unlike Weldon, who often made a lasting impression on people of all kinds, Ann seemed strangely neutral. "From the very first summer we met I think we considered Ann to be a sort of mild, controlled alcoholic," Rothschild concludes. "By that I mean that she drank sometimes alone during the day for no particular reason."[5]

Ann and Weldon Kees stayed on in Provincetown into September, writing and painting and resting. On the 18th, he wrote to Norris:

> It's been beautiful here: a number of wonderful days of sun and some nights with fog out of [best-selling mystery stories by] E. P. Oppenheim, and at eleven at night you can walk through the town without seeing a soul. (I omit Harry Kemp, etc.) Played a couple of dances in Wellfleet with some local cats this month; and during the last week have produced two new paintings, two articles (one of which is supposed to be my opening piece in *The Nation,* supposedly Oct. 1 issue, but with them it's hard to tell), and yesterday we went to the lake in Wellfleet and had some first-rate swimming: water perfect and the leaves beginning to turn. —I spent an agonizing week trying to turn out a drawing for a *Partisan Review* frontispiece, which Clem had asked for; must have done 75 or so before I got one I liked. Went through two bottles of Higgins India ink, in the course of which I came through with some horrendous numbers. The drawing is supposed to be in the October *PR,* according to word from NY. Also, "Land's End" will be in the Oct. *Harper's;* "Round" and "Saratoga Ending" in the Fall *Furioso.*
>
> The latest is that Robert Lowell & Elizabeth Hardwick got joined in holy wedlock. We had a cocktail party last week (Hans,* the [Albert] Halpers, the Francis Biddles), and Mrs. B. says that Robert Lowell's mother is known to her and implied she's something of a fright. A Winslow and a psychiatric social worker. Biddle has been asked to defend the unfriendly Hollywood 10 if it gets to the Supreme Court, but he's still undecided†

---

* Miz [Hofmann] has gone to NY, I think to check up on how [Samuel] Kootz is doing. [W. K.].

† When the Committee on Un-American Activities of the U.S. House of Representatives held Hollywood hearings in 1947, ten persons refused to testify on the Constitutional grounds that anything they might say could incriminate them. They were indicted for contempt of Congress, convicted, and imprisoned.

Tony and Judith Myrer, who had gone back into the city promptly at
the end of August, scouted for a Manhattan apartment ahead of the
Keeses. "The Hudson St. place sounds encouraging," Kees wrote on
September 21, 1949. "Has Judith had any interesting dreams about
either it or the new owner? I am very discouraged indeed about my
own dream-life; only have repetitive and moth-eaten old dreams I've
been having for years, some of them so tiresome I'd give a good deal
not to have them any more."

• • •

During the summer Weldon Kees was asked to be Clement Greenberg's successor as art critic on *The Nation*. He accepted with a
certain reluctance. That summer Congressman George A. Dondero of
Michigan had got a good deal of mileage in the popular press by
linking "advanced art" with revolutionary, i.e., Communist, ideas. In
his *Nation* piece for October 1, 1949, Kees replied to Representative
Dondero, in the name of all artists:

> Look, Mr. Dondero, art is not a weapon, no matter how insistently
> you, the Nazis, and the Communists maintain that it is. Persons desir-
> ing to make weapons do not become artists—a very difficult, uneasy,
> and ambiguous proceeding—but engage instead in pamphleteering,
> speech-making, gunpowder manufacture, advertising, the designing of
> flame-throwers, and so on. The man who looks at a painting and
> inquires about the political opinions of the artist may be an idiot or
> merely tiresome; he is totally unconcerned with the nature of painting.
> As painters we have no concern with politics; as men we are in the
> midst of them. Our world entails a vast individual schizophrenia, and
> not to grasp this is to enter a community of dwarfs.

In New York the Keeses went to live on the lower East Side, for-
tuitously close to their new friends, Anton Myrer and Judith Rothschild. The Myrers and the Keeses were among the first of the literary-
art world to turn East Side warehouse lofts into studios. In the next
decade or two warehouse studios became fashionable, but in 1949
and 1950 the lofts were unpainted, unheated, nearly uninhabitable;
and the Keeses were miserable in theirs at 179 Stanton Street. Weldon
told Maurice Johnson about it:

6 December 1949

Dear Maurice, So we came back to New York, though I frequently wonder why, lived for several weeks in a flop on 14th Street, and finally found this place, which is on the lower East Side in the heart of the lox and bagel section. It is a loft almost fifty feet long, with thirteen windows, and was formerly a factory. The tenant immediately preceding us was a girl who worked as a designer—I am dim on the matter of just what she designed; but she left the place jammed with wire, gallons of an evil-smelling fluid, beds, tables, practically immovable cans of molding clay, God knows what else. We spent a week getting such items out of the place and down four flights. Then we put in part of a ceiling, built a kitchen (there were two washrooms previously), painted walls, ceilings, and floors, and converted some of the furniture she had left into more aesthetic objects. In all, it took us about six weeks. Now I am slowly, with little heart, I'm afraid, getting back to painting and writing. Since we furnish our own heat, by way of a temperamental kerosene stove, we have been in no danger thus far of heat blisters. We go around in layers of sweaters, looking swollen and clumsy. I find myself becoming more & more anti-social: it is an ordeal to get myself out of the house and there are fewer & fewer people I care about seeing. It may be the end of New York as a romantic idea. I would like to live in a warm place by the ocean and weave baskets or split kindling wood.

My manuscript of new poems was turned down by Harcourt (after they had kept it for four months) and has now been given the same treatment by Harper's. I gather that publishers are no longer even much interested in keeping up the old pretense of altruism on books of poetry. Nemerov is having a book published in February by Random House; I was told they wouldn't have done it except for a promise of more novels; his is about the only book of poems to be announced. I have even heard that Harcourt dusted off Robert Lowell, which I find very hard to believe. (He married Elizabeth Hardwick, perhaps you heard, then proceeded to go off his rocker again, and is in a sanitarium someplace uptown.)

My show was very well received, but I sold nothing at all. I guess people are mostly buying Ben Shahns and television sets.

What a gloomy communication! Where will it all end? When is yr.
Swift book coming out? Are things any cheerier in Syracuse?

After the Peridot gave Kees a second one-man exhibition, Lou Pollack
included Kees's paintings in group shows. One of his pictures was part
of the 1950 Whitney Annual, the exhibition that attempted to bring
together some of the most important work of the previous season.
Kees's piece was displayed in a prominent spot. Beginning in October
1949, his art criticism began to appear monthly for which he was
paid thirty-five dollars each. He also got contracts for making training
films for the Signal Corps. Things seemed to be going well; but
though the success of *The Fall of the Magicians* had been gratifying to
both publisher and author, his proposed new volume was rejected
rather harshly, first by Harcourt, Brace and then by Harper's. Myrer
thought that this was "a tremendous blow to him . . . I think he never
got over that."[6] During the winter of 1949–50, he produced poems
and paintings, though not in any great number; he suffered from
chronic depression and both he and Ann had a series of debilitating
illnesses. They began to think of escaping the cold and clutter of
Manhattan. They considered Florida, but California seemed the more
attractive. In the spring he visited Ezra Pound, incarcerated at St.
Elizabeth's Hospital in Washington D.C., as mentally incapable of
standing trial for treason. He described the visit, and his life in New
York, in a letter to Norris Getty on March 18, 1950:

> Dear Norris, I have a fearful hangover from too many of Conrad
> Aiken's orange blossoms, but will see if I can subdue this typewriter
> anyway. It's idiotic to try to keep up with Conrad's glass-lifting; he's
> such a rumpot of long-standing that I should know better. Although I
> must say that Ann has come through this morning with flying colors
> and says she's feeling no pain. The Aikens found a wonderful little
> apartment with a garden for $14 a month, the arrangements having
> been taken care of through a lady novelist, a nymphomaniac and a
> friend of theirs whose lovers are usually drawn from the ranks of
> longshoremen, truck drivers, plumbers, etc. One of her blacksmith
> friends ran down the apartment, and the Aikens plan to use it only
> occasionally, whenever they have enough money to come to town.
> Conrad got going on Malcolm Lowry last night. He turned up in
> Cambridge years ago, at the age of 18, with a suitcase full of dirty

socks and a ukelele, a great admirer of *Blue Voyage,* and already at that age a pronounced alcoholic. Lowry's father is a millionaire, and for years Aiken was hired by the old man to look after Lowry. The Aikens were with him in Mexico during the *Under the Volcano* period, and Conrad says that he is the original of the movie director character.

We saw *The Cocktail Party.* Our only visit to the theatre this year. I don't want to be too extreme, but I thought it was one of the worst plays ever to get on the boards. It's appallingly amateurish and redolent of corn. I can't recall anything worse by a previously first-rate writer. He *uses* everything, and uses everything badly; now, instead of Swift and the Elizabethans and the French symbolists, it's Chesterton, Shaw, Evelyn Waugh and Frederick Lonsdale. A sorry affair. And someone has just told me that the new Hemingway novel represents a similar comedown.

The winter seems to stretch on endlessly, and it's been a brutal one for us. The place never gets really warm, and for a while the stove went completely on the blink. For a couple of days we huddled around our electric heater and another one we borrowed from the Myers. We are thinking very seriously of taking off for Florida or Mexico next fall. Meanwhile I count the days until the 1st of June. Lately everything has got to be more and more of an effort (I suppose fighting the cold hasn't helped any) and I have one hell of a time grinding out the things I have to do: the *Nation* pieces hang over me like so many vultures, and I seem to be losing my touch on the film scripts: each one is like a trip to the dentist. The ms. of *A Late History* [his volume of verse] has just come back with a pleasant letter of rejection from Macmillan. So it goes.

I had to go to Washington for a couple of days on a script I was doing at the time. It turned out in typical army fashion: the woman who was supposed to be technical advisor on the film turned out to have had no advance warning of my visit, and also it developed that she was no longer technical advisor on the film, having been supplanted by a nurse stationed at Governor's Island. The trip was not a total loss by any means, though: I looked up Elizabeth Bishop, a very nice person, and she asked me if I'd like to see Pound. She had to go over to the hospital the next afternoon to take him some books from the Library of Congress. He receives visitors from 2 to 4 every afternoon, and Mrs. Pound, who lives in Washington, goes to see him daily. I found the experience somewhat inhuman, rather like visiting a museum, but certainly not an experience to have missed. He "receives" at the end of a corridor in the hospital, which is a pretty gloomy affair, with catatonics and dementia praecox cases slithering about; but he certainly keeps up a spirit. Very lively and brisk, and his eyes go through you like knives. He started out by talking about some new little magazine, *Imagi,* the young editor of which he seems to have under his thumb; and there were lots of references to "the Brits," "the yids" and "the estimable Stevens" and "the admirable Eliot." When Elizabeth, who had seen *The Cocktail Party* in New York, told him she thought it was pretty poor stuff, he seemed pleased. (Pound calls her 'Liz Bish," which she doesn't care for; nor does she care much for Pound, regarding him as a pretty dangerous character, through his influence—particularly the anti-semitism—on the young.) Sometimes he has a good deal of trouble remembering things, gets started on a story and lapses into something else that's pretty irrelevant. Just the method of the Cantos, I guess. There are even sentences that end "and . . ." But he's far from crazy, I'd say, though an egomaniac of the first water. The people who knew him back in 1912 say he's just the same as he's always been. I felt very curious when Elizabeth and Mrs. Pound and I left the hospital—Pound shooed us out promptly at four, so as "not to get anybody sore"—and we waited on the road for Mrs. Pound's bus to come along; it was an experience hard to grasp, and more "unreal" somehow than the mere previous knowledge of Pound's predicament. It was a cold day; we could see the Capitol dome in the distance; and there was Pound, waving goodbye to us from the window of his cell. [. . .]

In the spring of 1950, the Metropolitan Museum announced that it would mount a juried show in December to be called "American Painting Today—1950". The advanced painters thought that they were excluded, for the jury seemed rigged against abstractionists. Only "conservative"—that is, representational artists and critics—had been asked to serve on it. In an "open letter" to Roland L. Redmond, president of the Metropolitan Museum of Art, eighteen American artists, including Weldon Kees, jointly rejected the validity of the national jury and announced that they would refuse to submit their work to it. In the popular press they became identified as "the irascible 18."

Kees discussed the affair in the June 3, 1950, issue of *The Nation:*

> For years the Metropolitan Museum has been under attack for its lack of interest in contemporary art. Its cushy Hearn fund, bequeathed to it generations ago for purchasing work by living American artists, has been left in the vaults, most of it, and what little has been touched has been spent for paintings that might as well have been chosen by a committee of Congressmen or the ladies of the Elkhart Bide-a-Wee.

> The present director of the Metropolitan, Francis Henry Taylor, makes no secret of his hostility to advanced trends in contemporary art—he reached some sort of high in philistinism, where competition is keen, when he compared Picasso's *Guernica* to "The Charge of the Light Brigade" and remarked that Picasso "has only substituted Gertrude Stein for Florence Nightingale."

Kees continues:

> It has been suggested that this jury "may surprise us" by picking an adventurous and valuable show. I look forward to this with the same warm expectations that I have of the American Legion building a series of marble shrines honoring the memory of Randolph Bourne [the literary radical] or of Baudelaire being named the favorite poet of the Cicero, Illinois, junior high schools. Preparations for this endeavor have been under way for "nearly a year," says the Metropolitan; it is clear that the selection of a jury as humdrum as this must easily have consumed that long a period of time.

When the Metropolitan show finally opened later in the year, *Life* covered it rather fully and even pictured the "irascible 18" as a group. Kees was not included in the *Life* picture since he was in Provincetown when it was taken; he said later that he would not have cooperated even if he had been in Manhattan. Hans Hofmann also refused to join the group for the photograph. Miz Hofmann, his wife, wrote to Weldon in November that Hans had not wanted to interrupt his vacation even when *Life* offered to pay for his flight from the Cape. She

noted that Hans, Fritz Bultman, and Weldon Kees were the only members of the protesting group not in the picture.

• • •

For Ann and Weldon, Provincetown in 1950 was not what it had been
in 1949. When his friends, led by Fritz Bultman, proposed that something like Forum 49 be repeated in 1950, he declined to take responsibility, or even to have a prominent part in it. He did not have the
energy, or the spirit, to recreate the excitement of the previous summer; and he wanted to devote himself to his own painting and writing. The Provincetown group, without him, sponsored an exhibition
entitled "Post-Abstract Painting 1950: France, America." Kees was in
a productive period when he wrote to the Myrers from Provincetown
on July 19, 1950:

> Dear Judith & Tony, "The art of letter-writing is a lost art."—Eliz-
> abeth Barrett Browning, or was it Irita Van Doren? We live in confus-
> ing times. —Adolph [Gottlieb] & yrs truly squandered a quarter of a
> dollar to hear the forum at the Fart Association on "What is Realituh
> in Art Fer Muh?" with Morris "Satchelmouth" Davidson holding
> down the m.c. post the other night. Karl [Knaths] kept saying: "Kinda
> hard to get going . . ." Finally he swallowed practically an entire
> pitcher of water and came through nobly, if briefly. B[oris] Margo told
> about how he painted a picture of his mother—not a realistic job, but
> a painting that incorporated *all* the *emotional* tension of her *life*. I
> think I heard it before, somewhere, or maybe in a dream. Henry
> Botkin is a real smooth item who pokes himself in everybody's
> pigeonhole; you know, "I deeply admire the work of Miró, Klee,
> Matisse, Sassetta, Winslow Homer, Jake Glotz, Leonardo, Eddie Eu-
> ler, Raphael, and the old lady across the way who does those charm-
> ing paintings of nasturtiums; but these present-day doodlers shd. go
> back to the academy, which is the fount of all wisdom." And then a
> lot of malarkey about how he slaves over a painting for six weeks
> before he's pleased with it. He forgot to say that they all come out
> looking like Max Weber [The American Expressionist] with the last
> drop of sensitivity squeezed out. A good 25¢'s worth, I'd say. Wdn't
> have missed it for anything. [. . .]

A local spy reports that he met Norman Mailer at a party. The body

> of the evening was given over to listening to Mailer discuss the fas-
> cinating topic of the relationship of his work to that of Tolstoi &
> Dostoievsky. Mailer is of the opinion, it seems, that he is more in the
> tradition of T. than D. [. . .]
>
> I have been working like one possessed & have done a couple of new
> canvases since you were here. Hope this productivity keeps up; it
> makes all the difference between the manic & the depressive, as San-
> tayana once remarked to Bud Freeman.

Thirty-five artists exhibited in the Provincetown show, among them
sixteen of the eighteen artists who protested the Metropolitan jury. In
August 1950 a round table discussion, rather like those of Forum 49,
included Kees; Weldon and Tony Myrer had translated and edited the
remarks of Hans Hofmann, Hofmann's English being rather unsure.
The whole venture, exhibition and discussion, was felt to be a success,
but it was not covered by the metropolitan newspapers.

The summer went very well, and in August Norris Getty joined Ann
and Weldon. The three spent a good deal of time helping Tony Myrer
shape up his first novel, and they were delighted when Random House
took an interest in it. The book dealt with an art colony where
sunbathing and painting were the common activities, but it also considered the essential nature of human beings. Before it appeared in
1951, Ann and Weldon went through it several times, finally checking
its punctuation, spelling, and sentence structure in galley proof. Myrer
never forgot their generosity and in gratitude dedicated his second
published novel, *The Big War* (1957), to the memory of Weldon Kees.
On August 26, 1950, Kees wrote to Maurice Johnson:

> It's been a very productive summer for me. I've been working like hell,
> after a wretched winter, and have done some poems and finished six
> canvases. Am having another one-man show in New York in February.
> Trying to get enough paintings for it before we leave Provincetown.
> We're going to New York about the 12th of September for a couple of
> weeks and then plan to drive across the country and spend the winter
> in California, probably Monterey. My romance with New York City is
> over; last winter was the last straw. A nice place to visit, etc.
>
> You have owed me a letter for at least six months. Cat got your L. C.
> Smith? Our best to you and Nan and the daughters.

In leaving the East Coast in the fall of 1950, Weldon Kees was leaving a relatively secure place. He was withdrawing from an artistic community in which he had a real, though marginal, part. As poet, painter, critic, cultural middleman, and jack-of-all-artistic trades, he could not be quite of the group, any group; but he was there, nonetheless. If he had worked harder at it, he could surely have been nearer the center of things. His friend, Fritz Bultman, wrote of him later:

> He viewed his departure from New York as fleeing a stricken city—a city that he characterizes as "a dark and dreadful place." He said, "By the winter of 1949–1950 I would have settled for Atchison or Lone Pine, Ark., it had gotten that unappetizing." Weldon wanted the New World, the New Day that the mid and late 20th century cannot offer us. Totally American in his orientation, he could find no antidote in his interior history or nature to America the hustler, the wheeler-dealer. Yet his work needed these tensions and commitments. This duality between his own dedication and his disgust for a world "gone rotten" was both his goad and the seed of his end.[7]

The trip across the country in a new car, a 1946 Lincoln, was pleasant enough. The Keeses stopped in Lincoln on October 10 to see Professor L. C. Wimberly and in Douglas, Wyoming, to see Ann's family shortly thereafter; and then they came on to Los Angeles. There they stayed longer than they had planned—into early November—fascinated by the jazz to be heard in various clubs. Nesuhi Ertegun, whom they had met in New York through Manny Farber, the film and art critic, and his brother, Dr. Leslie Farber, the psychiatrist, showed them around. Ertegun was a professional student of jazz. He introduced his brother, Ahmet Ertegun, to it; and Ahmet became the great entrepreneur of popular music in the next generation, finally heading a series of large recording companies.

Since at least 1945, Weldon Kees had been committed to the study of popular music. He regarded Jelly Roll Morton with admiration almost to the point of veneration. In an essay-review for *The Nation* (March 24, 1951) he wrote that the "once-famous Creole singer, pianist, composer, arranger, bandleader, and self-styled 'originator of jazz' . . . stands in relationship to most other jazz artists as Bartók, Schoenberg, and Stravinsky relate to the raft of thin and derivative 'serious' men who thinly and derivatively follow in their wake. He was not only one of the best singers and pianists of a period when talent was prodigal but a composer and arranger of a far more impressive and original nature than any of his contemporaries—and there have been no successors" (283).

In the same essay, Kees defined the origins of jazz and identified some of its masters: "Ragtime, a mixture of folksong, banjo syncopation, and complex African rhythm, is the vigorous, intricate, highly accented pianism that preceded jazz and has permanently affected 'serious' Western music from Debussy to the present. In its classic phrase it was a product of a handful of devoted composers, both Negro and white, who touched off a nation-wide ragtime craze. The principal hotbeds of ragtime composers were mostly in the North—Sedalia, Missouri, St. Louis ('the capital'), New York, and Indianapolis." Long before they became fashionable, Kees championed "such composers as Scott Joplin, James Scott, Joseph Lamb, Jelly Roll Morton, and James P. Johnson, among dozens of others, who out of their bounteous and creative spirits have given us such enduring works as 'Maple Leaf Rag,' 'Grace and Beauty,' 'Sensation,' 'The Pearls,' and 'Carolina Shout'" (284).

When they planned their trip to the West Coast, Ann and Weldon had expected to settle in Monterey, near the Myrers. Tony and Judith Myrer had come on ahead from New York, but they had had car trouble in Albuquerque. When they finally settled in the wilds of the Big Sur, the Keeses moved on to the Bay Area, which was then "enjoying a glorious traditional jazz revival," according to Tony Myrer. In November the Keeses rented an apartment in Point Richmond, where Janet Richards, formerly married to Manny Farber, and her present husband, Charles Richards, visited them "in their grayed and splintery redwood aerie at the top of a hillside."[1] From there, "one could look west across the wide, pale blue misty bay to the white city."[2] Two years later, Weldon explained to Malcolm Cowley, a permanent fixture in the East Coast literary world, why they had left New York. On November 3, 1952, he wrote:

> We came out here almost two years ago & are glad we did. I was around San Francisco many years ago & loved it. New York got to be too much of a struggle, at least for me, and one that availeth close to naught. Mostly got tired of all the dirt and darkness, and getting burned pieces of the *Mirror* in my left eye everytime I went out of the house, and seeing so many people turning sad and/or crazy. Some of it had to do with the fact that we were living, if you can call it that, during the last winter there, in a loft on the lower East Side, poor as

hell, with a kerosene stove that only heated about a thirtieth of the room. We damn near froze.

But the cold and filth of New York City were only a memory when the Keeses found an apartment at Point Richmond. In the building were some young painters who participated in the most dramatic artistic movement of that time and place. According to Thomas Albright, in *Art in the San Francisco Bay Area, 1945–1980* (1985), they were "responding to the new energies that had [also] been stirring among artists in New York" (p. 19). They had been influenced by Clyfford Still, who was prominent in San Francisco in the late forties—his vigorously abstract paintings had challenged them all. The people with whom Kees now associated confronted Abstract Expressionism just as his earlier associates had. "Most of the younger artists who sought to free themselves from Still's influence gravitated . . . to the orbits of Hofmann and de Kooning," Albright has observed, for their "painting seemed more inclusive, more catholic in its sources, and thus more 'open' to development"[3] than Still's (p. 35). Kees, the friend of Hofmann and the New York School, was thus again at the center of creative life; and if he was delighted to find Hassell Smith, Ed Corbett, Robert McChesney, and others who were to leave a mark on their time, they must have been delighted to see him and to hear his reports of the East Coast. Kees wrote to Norris Getty about his good fortune in finding a community and about his increasing preoccupation with jazz—another art flourishing in the Bay area—and his continuing commitment to literature and publishing. He wrote to Getty on November 11, 1950:

> 204 Western Drive
> Richmond, California
>
> Dear Norris, We are sort of at loose ends for a time: waiting around for an apartment at the above address to become available. It *was* to have been ready for us around the 1st, but a strike of tile-layers has screwed things up but good. Perhaps a little detail would not be out of order. We got on to the apartment through a painter named Hassell Smith, a friend of Manny Farber's from fifteen years back (Manny, as you may or may not know, went to school in San Francisco); Hassell teaches at the California School of Fine Arts, which is the avant-garde

outpost here. He & his wife have been living on the top floor of the 3-story house at 204 Western Drive; another painter & *his* wife (the Robert McChesneys) live on the middle floor and are now buying the house; still another painter, & a damned good one, too, named Ed Corbett, lives in the basement. So you can see it's quite a hive of creators. The Smiths are moving to another place, in SF, but are being held up because the people whose apartment they are taking are building a house, now delayed because of the tile boys. When the Smiths finally are able to move, the McChesneys will move upstairs, and we will move into *their* place, which is very fine. A large L-shaped living room, a bedroom, kitchen, bath, and a room I can use as a studio. It is a few steps from a beach on the bay, the house is surrounded by eucalyptus trees, and it's about a half-hour drive from downtown SF. I am wild to get back to painting, have a lot of writing projects lined up, must be at this publicity work for *Botteghe Oscure* [the multilingual literary journal] (for which TSE [Eliot], [Thornton] Wilder, and E. [Edmund] Wilson have promised blurbs); but for a while we are doomed to life in a rather expensive motel where, at least, Ann is able to cook. After a while, restaurants lose their charm, if any. [. . .]

We went back to Los Angeles for a time, when we learned of the apartment difficulties—mostly to hear [Kid] Ory. (By the way, there is a new Ory album out, on Columbia, Album C-216, just issued last week, shd. be available in Boston by now.) I think I may have written you that we were lucky to have the guidance of Nesuhi Ertegun & his wife through the mazes of LA jazz activities; Nesuhi is the son of the former Turkish ambassador to the US and runs the Jazz Man Record Shop in Hollywood—a beautiful place that looks more like an interior decorator's office than what it is—and who issues Jazz Man records. His wife, Marili Morden, was the gal who talked Ory into coming out of retirement in the 30's & lined up the Ory job on the old Orson Welles show. They know everybody in jazz from years back; so we were able to meet everybody we wanted to, plus some we didn't. The best of the bunch, as human beings, are Joe Darensbourg, Ory's clarinetist, a wonderful person, and Joe Rushton, probably as good a white horn-blower extant, who is with Red Nichols. Nichols' band is extraordinary on things like "Riverboat Shuffle," "Chicago," "Ida,"

"Mama's Gone Goodbye"; but are also given to fancy Beiderbeckeian things like "In a Mist" and "Candlelights" (which they do well enough, but sometimes verge on the soupy side) and they try to do things like "High Society," which they have no tradition to fall back on. It is white jazz at its most intelligent—and Rushton is a bit better than that. (Rushton, by the way, is a Yale man, the black sheep of a "good" family, who bears a spookily-close resemblance to Chester Morris [the movie star]; he's enormously witty.) Ory is one of the most nervous characters I've come up against: a peasant with worries, rubs his face & eyes until you wonder how his skin takes it; all those gestures which from a distance look joyous are only (possibly) nervous tics. His eyes are in bad shape but he is too vain to wear glasses, and is said to be a worse driver than Hans Hofmann, which I find difficult to believe. Ory is also incredibly tight, and there are a raft of stories about his difficulties with musicians where moola is concerned. All of which has nothing to do with the fact that he is one of the great men of our time, along with Matisse and Schweitzer and Proust, and is playing breathtakingly. He and his boys are fed to the teeth with LA, and will probably be up here pretty soon, if their contract at Lyman's (on Vine St in Hollywood, where they now play) is not picked up again. [. . .]

California seems, if not to hold its own, to debase itself less frenetically than the East Coast. At least my central nervous system has responded to it rather nicely. And the jazz, some of the painting, the landscape, the temperature, have it all over the E. seaboard.

Ann sends her love. Write soon.

Kees was full of plans. He offered the Bay Area papers his journalistic services; and he reminded the New York papers that he could keep them informed of West Coast activities. Howard Devree, editor of the art pages of the *New York Times,* commissioned him to write a piece on the San Francisco Art Festival, which finally appeared December 31. He was paid $50 for that job. His friend, Wilder Hobson, now an editor on *Harper's Bazaar,* gave a sympathetic ear to a number of his suggestions. As he wrote to Hobson on November 14, 1950: "I have never found it difficult to be interested in more than one thing at the same time." Hearing that the State Department had allocated some

$21 million for the making of documentary movies about America to be distributed abroad, Kees proposed to Douglas MacAgy, president of the California School of Fine Arts, that they collaborate in making short films for the government, his experience with both newsreels and training films for the Department of Defense being rather extensive.

Before coming to the West Coast, Weldon and Ann had become involved in the American distribution of the international literary periodical, *Botteghe Oscure*. This semiannual volume was published from Rome in three, four, and five languages, beginning in 1948; and though its subscribers never numbered many more than five thousand, it presented such luminaries as Brecht, Camus, Auden, Alberto Moravia, Ignazio Silone, James Agee, R. P. Warren, and Dylan Thomas to an international audience. Weldon Kees's poetry appeared in its pages. *Botteghe Oscure* was sponsored and edited by Marguerite Caetani, a New England aristocrat by birth, a Roman aristocrat by marriage. It was said at the time that she was a Henry James heroine in the flesh. In September 1950, while Ann and Weldon Kees were still in Provincetown, Katherine Garrison Biddle, the sister of Marguerite Caetani, approached Weldon asking for advice about how to distribute *Botteghe Oscure* in the United States. The Keeses had become acquainted with Francis and Katherine Biddle through Conrad Aiken and Forum 49. Katherine Biddle thought Weldon's energetic commitment to all the arts, as proved in his Provincetown activities, could be turned to the journal's purposes. He agreed to help get it accepted in America, for he wanted to play on the national scene.

Though he did not want to live in New York City, Kees kept up with what was going on there. Lou Pollack, the director of the Peridot, wrote to him on November 19, 1950: "Alfred Barr [of the Museum of Modern Art] was in this past week and asked to see new works by you, Brooks & the Bourgeois sculpture . . . He told me (*but keep this strictly on the Q.T.*) that he is recommending purchase of work by you, Brooks & Bourgeois." On November 26, Weldon replied, "The intelligence about Alfred Barr's good work is . . . exhilarating, and I'm both keeping my fingers crossed and my lip buttoned." He went on to report on the Bay Area, as he saw it:

There's one hell of a lot of damned good painting going on out here; will probably do an article on some of the better painters here. Three or four of them certainly are ready for one-man shows in New York, and would make 57th Street sit up and take notice. Incidentally the painters here—or most of those I've met so far—are in general much better rounded people than their New York equivalents. Haven't met one yet who isn't a jazz fiend, for instance. Some of the painters who teach at the California School of Fine Arts, which is the hot bed of advanced painting here, have a splendid 7-piece Dixieland band. Can you imagine Motherwell playing the banjo on "Sister Kate" with Mark Rothko and his Hot Five?

Unfortunately for Kees, nothing came of the sale to the Museum of Modern Art. Pollack wrote on December 30: "Received a call from Barr last week. He was sending the work back from the Museum. Said he'd done his best but the committee didn't respond to purchase as much as he had. Well—better luck next time. Your show is scheduled from Jan. 29 to Febr. 24." Subsequently MOMA took a couple of his collages for its lending service, and Kees took this to be a vote of confidence in his work. A painting of his was included in the Whitney Annual (1950) and received favorable comment.

Kees kept up a correspondence with his New York friends, and their continuing affection for him and Ann is obvious in all of their letters. Hans Hofmann gave him one of his paintings, *Flight,* which he and his wife, Miz, shipped to California, presumably in payment for the poem that Weldon had written for the Hofmann Paris catalog. Willy Poster, a brilliant and eccentric free-lance literary journalist and now movie critic for the reborn *American Mercury,* wrote to the Keeses regularly and wittily of Manhattan life. Poster was a particular favorite of Ann's. He could always make her laugh. Ann did not often laugh aloud, her friends noted; and of all their witty friends, only Willie seemed able to send her into such gales as to be heard next door. Weldon wrote to Willie Poster and his new wife, Connie, in high spirits:

6 December 1950

Dear Willie & Connie, Sorry to be a bit slow in responding to yr. good communication of 19 Nov. —About [Sidney] Hook's request for

143

me to preside over a committee to bring Czechoslovakia to California. Tell him I shall be glad to serve, providing we can get Reinhold Niebuhr and Dwight Macdonald to act as joint sub-committee heads in charge of Spiritual Guidance and Native Etiquette. This is *essential.* Gov. Warren says the entire Czech population can easily be settled in Oakland without anyone noticing a thing (Warren promises his warmest support) and all are assured of immediate employment either in (a) the new Kaiser shipyards, (b) the woodwind section of Morton Gould's orchestra. Hope these plans will meet with Sidney's approval. No sacrifice is too great in these times of world stress. Rexroth has volunteered his services as director of the California-Czechoslovakia Cultural Committee for Adult Education, and will offer a course in mountain climbing, sacramental marriage, and the later works of Tu Fu.

I am sorry to have to refuse Paul Goodman's kind offer to sell his collected works; but I will buy the orgone box if it is a mahogony one and not too splintery. Please quote his *lowest* asking-price. They are very dear out here, and built in Early Mission style. Obviously these are out of the question.

I will be delighted to do a piece on the paintings of Gene Derwood; please relay this intelligence promptly to Oscar, s'il vous plait. By one of those strange turns of fate, *Good Housekeeping* has just asked me for precisely such an article.

[Anatole] Broyard's request that I introduce him to God is, I fear, a less easy one to grant. I have contacted Him, but He is very tied up these days—collaborating with Calas, He says, on something on Kierkegaard for the *Hudson Review.* Says can He put it off until the late Spring. Okay? [. . .]

* * * * * *

Thanks for the full report on the Whitney and all those kind words. I heard that Jas. Thrall Soby is doing a piece on it for the *Sat. Review of Litachoor* and is reproducing my painting therein, but will believe it when I see it. Makes one wonder what has happened to Loren McIver. —The NEW NEW *American Mercury* has not as yet made its appearance on San Francisco newsstands; shall keep looking. [. . .]

Various vistas opening up here. Hope all goes well and that the storm spared you both.

Kees was amused to find himself listed in the annual Christmas doggerel that Aline B. Louchheim wrote for the art section of the Sunday *New York Times* for December 24, 1950:

> With apologies to Frank Sullivan,
> This Christmas poetic
> Is for those persons called esthetic.
> Let angels sing a lusty "Noel"
> To Francis Taylor and Leon Kroll . . .
> . . .
> Watch the Yuletide fire blaze
> For Gordon Washburn and Bartlett Hayes,
> For Edie, Edgell and Weldon Kees,
> For generous and hard-working trustees. . . .

The Keeses seemed to be making a place for themselves on the West Coast. Weldon wrote to Norris on December 28:

> I have the best damned place to work in I've ever had—a moderate-sized room at the back of the house, with a crummy floor that I don't mind dripping painting onto & good space & light. Warmed up by doing a couple of Jelly Roll Morton album covers and then fought it out on canvas, letting Mr. Miro have it in the groin, and Mr. Matisse in the old kidney, and Mr. Picasso in the nose, and it was good & it was fine, and I said, "Daughter (name of one of the cats on the premises), Daughter, it is good and it is fine, and this will show Mister Dubuffet a thing or two, with the Flik Quick Drying Enamel singing off my brush the way only I can make it sing, and it is good and it is fine, Daughter." At this point the cat arched its tail & clawed at the back door to be let out. [. . .]
>
> We spent three days with Tony & Judith at their Big Sur estate just before moving in here. They have a fine bargain at $15 a month, but it *is* isolated as hell, and probably engenders one hell of a lot of paranoia. Also they are having terlet trouble; their can has the unnerving habit of flushing imperfectly and throwing one's excrement back at one. And it's a long drive for groceries, over one of God's more

hairraising stretch of mountain hairpin curves. But it is beautiful, certainly; and one afternoon Tony & I climbed down a mountain back of their house to the ocean and saw a sealion swimming (he looked us over very intently, swam under water, and came up for a closer look) and a huge rock covered with cormorants, all in profile & looking like society ladies in black at a swank opening. Tony is going ahead slowly on revisions, rather tired at this point with all the fiddling necessary & eager to get on to fresh work; but what he had done seemed okay. —The second day there, while we were just sitting down to breakfast, at about nine o'clock, Henry Miller's wife breezed in for a little visit. Since she had never given the Myrers the slightest attention before, she got a rather chilly reception from them. I gathered that I was supposed to say, "Gee, Mrs. M., I just can't wait to meet your hubby!" But I didn't. We also saw Gilbert Neiman's ex-wife, whom I think you once met, now married to a poet named Hugh O'Neill, a rather wet smack. No one seems to have had a look at the product of his pen; and he is said to spend a good deal of his time these days busy at the pottery wheel. And we had a good evening the night before we left at an Inn where I was taken to play the piano (pianos are scarce in that wild country) along with the [Harry] Links. I had seen him before the Myrers arrived, and liked him, also his wife, a nice Mexican gal. He is rather solid looking, dependable type, modest, probably a lot coursing around under the surface. Tony complained that he was behaving rather boorishly the last night we were there, but it didn't strike me particularly. I haven't read any of his novel.

Incidentally, I like to think that my own work at the keyboard has taken a sudden spurt of improvement, no doubt due to rather constant exposure to such as [Paul] Lingle, [John] Wittwer, [Burt] Bales, etc. Didn't I write you about Paul Lingle? We got quite friendly with him, went into the lesbian bar where he works, the Paper Doll, very often, sat down at the end of the bar with our ears right up against the piano. At his best, he is probably the most exciting pianist *I* ever heard, very influenced by Morton but swings more. He had been working at the Paper Doll for a year and a half when he was fired about a month ago. Told a rather confusing story (he is in a rather bad way some of the time, due to alcoholism & narcotics) about getting into a fight with a colored girl he said he had been living with; she stabbed him quite a lot (his arms & hands were covered with scars); then, later, she came in the joint one night with a couple of cops when he was working, intent on getting the keys to a car they'd been jointly purchasing. Paul swung into "When Irish Eyes Are Smiling" as a last resort aimed at the policemen, but they turned out to be Neapolitans. Caused such a furor that the Paper Doll management had to let him go. Such is Paul's story. Anyway, he's out, and for a while they had no pianist, then a replacement guy of no great shakes. However, Wittwer opened there last week and we went to his opening. Had never seen him plain before & went up and requested "Ragged but Right." Still playing, he turned around & said, "Who're you?" I told him my name. Wittwer said, "Oh, yeah, you're the author of *The Last Man* and *The Fall of the Magicians*." This is God's truth. After that set, he came around to the booth where we were sitting with Bill Roth & his wife; I asked him if it were true about the rumor that he'd recently been going to library school at Stanford. He said he'd thought of going to library school—"having always been something of a bookworm"—but finally decided against it, and was working in Seattle for a while as a single before the Paper Doll opening beckoned. Young guy, about our age. A remarkable performer, but doesn't have Lingle's lyric quality. However, he (Wittwer) is always, I gather, on the ball; when Lingle was in deep trouble, he could play abominably.

In January 1951, Weldon signed on with Gregory Bateson and Jurgen Ruesch, M.D., of the Langley Porter Clinic, University of California, to make some films on a grant from the U.S. Department of Health. Presumably he got this post with the help of Douglas MacAgy. Gregory Bateson was a peripatetic genius who had written a classic in theoretical ethnography, *Naven* (1936), but rather like Kees, he could not restrict himself to a single line of inquiry. Ruesch guided Bateson to psychiatric medicine, in which he was to make notable contributions, especially in schizophrenia. Kees worked very happily with the two scientists.

In that January, Louis Pollack mounted another one-man show for Weldon. He saw to it that Kees was also exhibited in a number of group shows, both in his own gallery and elsewhere. The show was well attended and got some comment in the press, but nothing was sold. As such things go, the cost of the show was not great, but it took six months for Weldon to repay Pollack's advances. The following month, while the New York show was still hung, Jermayne MacAgy, the acting director of the California Palace of the Legion of Honor, offered to have a one-man show of Kees paintings. "How would you like an exhibition here in the fall of paintings produced during 1951?" she wrote to him on February 27, 1951; and of course Weldon liked that very much. He thought the Palace the finest place to exhibit in San Francisco. They agreed upon October, to give Kees time to finish as many works as possible. He and Jerry MacAgy decided they would need some eighteen pictures for a good exhibition.

Weldon wrote of his life at this time to Fritz and Jeanne Bultman, who were spending the year in Rome, and Kees's letters to Norris Getty and Maurice Johnson continued, but by now he had another regular correspondent, Anton Myer. His letters to Tony Myer and Judith Rothschild give a picture of the Bay Region just before the Beat Generation of Ferlinghetti, Kerouac, City Lights Bookstore, and the street people. In San Francisco a group of writers clustered around Kenneth Rexroth, who tended to manage the literary scene; another group, mostly musicians, gathered around Turk Murphy, the jazz musician; and painters were associated with the MacAgys, at the San Francisco School of Art. In a loose and informal way, the Keeses participated in all three groups.

Ann and Weldon continued to help Tony Myer with his novel. When he discovered that he would have to pay for permission to quote the lyrics of the popular songs that he had incorporated in his text, he and Weldon were at first indignant; but, a moment later, they decided it would be fun to simulate lyrics. Still puzzled about a title for the novel, Weldon finally suggested *Evil under the Sun,* from Ecclesiastes 9:3: "This is an evil among all things that are done under the sun. . . ."

On February 24, 1951, Weldon wrote to the Myers:

> Dear Tony & Judith, I feel like writing a letter like arranging a kazoo chorus of *Tannenbaum* for Elsie Witherstine's* Blue Five: a very

---

*Elsie Witherstine was a "local" in Provincetown whom all the artists and writers knew.

rough day yesterday; but here goes. I may pick up a bit by paragraph two.

Which might as well concern yesterday as my original intention—to delineate my most recent theory of the second law of thermodynamics as expressed in the meeting of Erskine Tate, Teddy Weatherford, and Stomp Evans, particularly as expounded during the opening bars of *Stomp Off, Let's Go!* on the old Vocalion Label, recorded in 1926. It is curious, isn't it, as Edwin W. Heffelfinger, stormy petrel of bread mold scholars, once remarked to M. Rufus Bultitude, that Evans' name, or nickname, i.e. "Stomp," is the first word of the title of this tune; and that the word "stomp" is a dialect variant of "stump," which, in addition to its variety of meanings, may be used colloquially as a "dare" or challenge. All this strikes me as *no accident*. The rumored intelligence that Evans *may* have been temporarily suffering from schizophrenia during *the very time* that this particular recording was made strikes me as a matter of the deepest significance, and makes possible the following hypothesis: the title is a triple pun: Evans was indeed mentally ill or "off"; thus the title may be interpreted as meaning "Stomp" is "off," but this fact will not deter us (the musicians, members of Erskine Tate's band) from "going," i.e., playing; similarly, they are not "stumped" by this reversal or setback; the "stump," or capacity for being "stumped" is challenged (another interesting change, the subtlety for which I am indebted to "Murf" Roethacker) and they plan to "go" anyway. The exclamation point is not without interest.

I should have thought of that fearful song lyrics business; but I had not known that publishers kindly offer to let the writer cough up for permission fees. I knew *somebody* had to cough up; in my innocence I thought it would be the publisher. There was an angry, sensible, and admirable piece in the *Sat. Rev. of Literature* not so long ago by Melville Cane, a New York attorney and member of the board of Harcourt, Brace, going into this whole matter. He's apparently been fighting the lyrics permission fee racket for years, but not much luck. If you're interested, I'll try to run down that issue for you.

Rather slowly warming to the topic that grazed me briefly a few lines back. Got up at 6:30 yesterday a.m. to drive into S.F. Worked at the clinic during the morning on peripheral movie matters, in the afternoon to Marin County with Bateson to do some shooting. Rexroth is starting a series of Friday evening poetry readings at his house, and I was the opening gun. Ate dinner & went over there at eight, already a bit pooped; but as such things go it was a success—a capacity house, even though 50¢ admission was charged, to quote Kenneth, "to keep out the people who drop cigarette butts in the goldfish bowl." He had a reading a couple of years ago as a benefit for some hungry Japanese poets; didn't charge admission, just passed the box; people put in nickels, pennies, pants buttons, streetcar tokens, etc. —I tried the experiment of reading all four of the Robinson poems together, arranging them in a new order; so that they add up to a single poem, in a sense. Read about thirty poems. A good audience, better, I think, than you'd get in New York. Not so professionally "solemn" about Poetry, more alert, more ready to laugh at the satirical. Kenneth gave me the entire gate, less expenses for a jug of wine, thus, for me, combining pleasure with profit. And most welcome. [. . .]

The *Botteghe Oscure* caper, after months of diddling around on the part of all & sundry—mostly the Countess, T. S. Eliot & various other hands—finally struck me as dragging on rather too long, and I wrote Wallace Stevens & Charles Abbott (Director of Libraries at Buffalo) & Thornton Wilder for hurry-up blurbs on the magazine. Stevens & Abbott came through in record order with just the ticket; no word from Wilder, who seems to have got his lessons from the same correspondence course in letter-writing subscribed to by Karl "Let's-Get-Away-From-It-All-and-Found-Primitive-Colonies-Orthodox-As-Hell-Defy-The-Evil-Forces-But-Let's-Not-Forget-Those-Yummy-Metropolitan-Prizes" Knaths. Anyway, I had stationery printed & for days now Ann and I have been knocking out letters to the heads of Romance Language & English depts. in all the noteworthy seats of learning, calculated to impress them with the dictum, what is your library without this peachy publication? Each letter is being individually typed (by us) & each is about 250 words in length; they have to be signed, folded, stuffed with a printed brochure, sealed, stamped, envelopes addressed, mailed, etc. On a good day we get out 50 letters or so. Now nearing the end. It's like typing two novels, only you type the same page—the least interesting one—over & over

again. —Then our furniture came, intact, scarcely anything broken,
and that meant a couple of days off for arranging, cleaning, wood-
creaming, sandpapering. In the meantime I've been trying to do a
piece of sculpture for Lou's next show. Two & a half days a week on
the movie; Ann has been doing some parttime secretarial work, too.
She's carried the biggest load on the letters. [. . .]

Kees's public high spirits did not at first seem seriously affected by his
continuing difficulty with publishing his book of poems, though he
complained about the crassness of publishers. On March 4 he wrote
to Jerry MacAgy: "Jim Broughton showed me several of the [short
movies] he's just finished, and one of them in particular is a dandy:
gets back to a sort of Buster Keaton flavor—a welcome direction. It is
the least arty experimental film I've ever seen, and damned amusing."
Broughton, after trying his hand at writing, had turned to cin-
ematography and now asked Kees to provide the score for *Adventures
of Jimmy,* his latest film. Kees wrote to Lou Pollack in New York, and
Pollack replied on May 18: "Couldn't help smiling to myself when
reading of your new activity on the coast. Arranging and composing—
that is. You've just about covered all the arts now except one. When
are you going to do a bit of architecture? I wouldn't be surprised one
of these days to read of a new building being built by Kees."

Tony Myrer sent the galley proofs of his novel to the Keeses, and
Weldon and Ann went through them with scrupulous care, giving the
text the kind of attention that Norris Getty had habitually given the
Kees poems. After returning the galleys, Weldon wrote to his friends
enclosing a limerick. For years he had amused himself and his correspondents with these limericks, most of them of very negligible
quality:

5 May 1951

Dear Tony & Judith, & *still* they come! Still *more* scintillating, gay,
yak-filled, earthy, riotous "limericks" from the busy pen of Point Richmond's beloved "Limerick King." Ever faithful to the hallowed traditions of Tennyson, Kipling, and Nick Kenney, he has "done it again"
with his *new,* NEW *seven-line* example of the poet's art! And now,
thanks to your foresight in becoming charter members of the Limer-

ick-of-the-Month Club (you *lucky* people!) at our low, low Bargain Rate, the Club brings you this month's BONUS limerick! Here 'tis:

There was a young lady named Mitzi
Who was diagnosed as a schitzy.
With loud cries of glee,
She would publicly pee
In such clubs in New York
As Larue and the Stork
And hotels like the Waldorf and Ritzi.

* * * *

I sent the galleys early in the week, insured. Hope you have them by now in order to continue your sordid dealings with Albert [Erskine] on house policy on the position of the dash, etc. This must be something that doesn't stretch back too far in history; certainly Random wd. have been hard put to lay down the law in the case of *Ulysses*. I looked through it for examples of the workings of their present cerebrum-activating policy and cd. not find any. [. . .]

I like yr. recommendations, Tony, about how to deal with the publishers when they keep mss. for over 60 days, and have sent them on to the Authors' Guild. However, I see the possibility of difficulties. That business of sticking bamboo shoots under their toenails has been tried; most of 'em don't feel a thing. And as for shutting their balls in a closet door, well, in most instances this has been found to be fairly ineffectual, since the above named parts of most publishers are reportedly manufactured by the Mssrs. Spaulding out of their sturdiest wear-resistant horsehide; even by subjecting them to your specified treatment in the doors of "21" or even the gates of the Tower of London has not brought forth the deeply desired result. Let us think about this problem more searchingly—do you know that rousing Dixieland tune, "Do What Caligula Say?"—and see if we can't come up with a more fool-proof schema.

Volkening is now handling the book for me—I don't think I am in any kind of mood for direct dealings with *any* publisher at the moment—and has it with Knopf. I have been going through this kind of stuff now for well over fifteen years and had it not been for a strain of Marcus Aurelius & Li Po in me, I could well have gone under with rage & despair. It is better to reserve this for one's work, where it properly belongs but needs just as careful control—in a rather different sense. But if the situation of poets continues to worsen at the same galloping rate it has been in recent years—it has *always* been lousy, from one standpoint or another: Shakespeare's ass-kissing lines to the Right Hon. Henry Wriothesley, Earl of Southampton and Baron of Titchfield, Baudelaire & the censors, Pound and the patriots, etc., etc., etc., etc., etc., etc.—not to mention the congenital Abe Northism of most poets—let's go down into the abyss. It won't be a really *awful* abyss: there'll be a lot of charming & good things in it: just no poets, that's all. Maybe we need a Byron to get the public interested in poetry again, though Byron's public wasn't any more interested in poetry than people today are: they were interested in Byron. I don't know *what* people are interested in today: but I can guess, and it ain't very pretty.

Maybe you know this: Abe North [in *Tender Is The Night*] was based on Ring Lardner. I was pleased that you think *Tender Is the Night* stands up. I have about worn it out, having read it at least seven times, a task I have found possible with only a very few novels, among them *Gatsby, Sentimental Education, A Handful of Dust, Madame Bovary,* and one or two others, some of James's shorter works. You are right about *Tender* and *The Sun also Rises* (and also right about the "fairly shallow reservoir of culture and experience") it comes out of. Which shld. maybe cause certain parties to revise their notions about "wide reservoirs of culture and experience" as it relates to fiction. I mean Fitzgerald's more thickheaded detractors. I have always been enormously moved by the last pages of *Tender* in their compression and as a triumph of dealing with years that are too sad to insist upon. The boys who see this book as a "parable of the artist being destroyed" by the haute bourgeoisie leave me limp. It is queer how people without the remotest understanding of the tragic sense of life react to a book that is soaked in it. [. . .]

Later in the month, on May 22, Kees began another letter, this time to Conrad Aiken, with "a limerick from my busy pen":

There was a French writer named Sartre
Who got off to a pretty good startre.
But as year followed year
It got painfully clear
He was longer on wind than on artre.

The grim facts must be faced: we like it out here enormously and our all too infrequent throbbings of nostalgia, so far as the East is concerned, relate to folks such as you & Mary & not to the locus or its geist. Never once have I caught myself humming "Give My Regards to Broadway," and it is an unconfined joy not to walk ankle-deep in NY's minglement of snow, slush, banana skins, burned newspapers and carbon bi-products of the Mssrs. Edison, not to experience that city's capacity for the type of Angst that has served Delmore Schwartz, et al., so faithfully through the years, not to have to do art pieces for Miss [Freda] Kirchwey's organ (*The Nation,* I mean), not to breathe that substance, half muck and half that delightful vapor that steams forth from carmel candy emporia, that passes for air, not to mention not to mention not to mention . . .

CHANGE NEEDLES AND SWITCH TO LP

I must confess that this time of year will always fill me with a yen for the Cape, which is a different matter; but I give Provincetown three summers more, by which happy time the queers & their followers will have taken over (a few particularly vigorously bull lesbians perhaps tolerated & allowed to remain) and the last of the artistes looking with interest at Red Hook or the East Side of Brooklyn as new and promising sites for colonies. * * *

The summer of 1951 was a bad one for Weldon and Ann. Both were sick again, as they had not been since the winter in New York. Nevertheless, by August 18 Weldon found the energy to write a long letter, full of gossip, to the Myrers:

Dear Tony & Judith, Yr. last letter came at a time when I cd. really use it: I had taken to the Beautyrest the night before with a very choice head cold that came on with awful suddenness; and when it arrived I was in the midst of a full day of using a Kleenex every minute on the minute. This shld. teach me not to forego my Enterol, which has staved off colds of Titanic dimensions for a couple of years. *This* one has been a thorough dandy; it has now settled happily enough in my long-suffering sinuses and in my chest; and this is the first day in six days that I've been able to breathe with anything like normality. —This has been (I hope) the coda to a series of unappealing melodies from these quarters. Ann went through a very excruciating time, both pre-operative and post-operative, the whole unfortunate business making doubly clear the expression, "pain in the ass"; but is now completely recovered; and we now await, one or the other, fresh developments on the ill-health front. * * *

Totally unconfirmed reports from NY:
Sam Kootz has closed his gallery & reopened in the same spot as a fish store, specializing in boned snapper.
Jackson Pollock is playing mellophone with a bop trio in a roadside gambling joint not far from Red Bank, N.J.
Archibald MacLeish has become a Unitarian minister.

IT IS WELL TO REMEMBER THAT THE CULTURE

Songs about painters:

"I Wonder Where My Easy Ryder's Gone?"
"I'll Be Glad When You're Dead, You Rothko, You"
"The Old Gromaire, He Aint What He Used to Be"

SOME AUTHORS, INCLUDING FUST

A few nights before my recent indisposition, we went over to la Jug Club with the [Douglas] MacAgys and heard [Paul] Lingle outdo himself. He stayed at the Wurlitzer for a good hr. and 15 minutes, doing unbelievable things. All of which is conclusive proof, for my money, that Western civilization is in firmer shape that anyone had supposed.

SOME OF THE CONTINENTAL WRITERS HAVE BEEN IMPRESSED

Bateson and I are about through with the picture [a study of nonverbal communications in families] we've been working on; held up by continual script revisions. Our collaborator, an old Bostonian gal, child psychologist named Wilma Lloyd, and a very sharp cookie, has been with us on many a session, grappling with the statements, and everyone finally feels it is the best we can do. Now, as soon as we get approval of funds for technical work, we will go ahead with final editing, titling, sound recording, etc. The picture has turned out to be a feature-length job, running at present about an hour and 15 minutes. Meanwhile, that loveable exponent of Viennese charm and a phallic symbol in every home, Jurgen W. McRuesch, is cooking up an unsavory broth we are busily stirring away at. This involves shooting (with a camera, I shd. add) the schizophrenic kids on the ward at Langley Porter. I have been around some adult maniacs of various kinds in my life, including some perfectly peachy paranoids, schizoids, and assorted manic-depressives; but young kids who are off their rockers are heartbreaking; and after a few hrs. with them I am reduced to a pulp. Gregory & I have also been doing some shooting of a very bright three-yr.-old boy in El Cerrito who doesn't talk, and is in other ways rather strange. After seeing the father, an Irishman who talks constantly, I don't wonder. The funds for all this movie-making have begun to run out, and rationing is in effect; so my take-home pay has lessened, and I shall no doubt soon be casting about for other methods of securing some dough. [. . .]

THROUGHOUT OUR ENTIRE DISCUSSION WE WOULD
DO WELL TO RECALL SHERBUSH'S OBSERVATION

The Flaubert came today, and a million thanks. Looks like one of the few vols. being published today fit to buy. *And* a very pretty jacket. It's very fine to have. —Incidently, for Christ's sake, speak up anytime you want to borrow any books I have, and keep them as long as you like. I think you know about what I have. Without any grandiose recommendations, I'm sending you E. Wilson's *I Thought of Daisy*, since I think you may find things in it to interest you. I guess it doesn't quite come off as a novel; but if you regard it as a memoir of considerable charm, slightly, oh so slightly, influenced by Proust, it has its points. It was an important book to me emotionally because, more than any other novel I know, it gets at the attractive (?) romantic side of intellectual New York life when that life still had something to be said for it, before it all went to pieces. And the period of *Daisy* was not the last gasp. That came a lot later. I think I saw it. —One's enjoyment of *Daisy* is deepened if one knows that Bamman is more or less Dos

Passos and Rita is Edna Millay; Grosbeake is Christian Gauss. I'm sending you this because I gather you're writing a New York book; and *Daisy* gets a side of New York better than any other familiar to me, and may be, shall we say, suggestive.

MANY OBSERVERS HAVE FOLLOWED GRÜNTHAL

Re the tune you suggested, "Louisiana." We were sitting around the Motorola one evening, listening to Jack Webb's new show, *Pete Kelly's Blues*, which features Ben Pollock's band, less Pollock, and they played a couple of choruses of it. With my amazing skill at picking up such things, I quickly learned it for the pianoforte. A splendid composition. And now I see that one of the bootleg labels has reissued Whiteman's recording of it.

CREAK NOTES A SIMILAR RESEMBLANCE

You ast me once who McKisco, in *Tender*, is. I think, more or less, Louis Bromfield. It is hard to remember that Bromfield was taken seriously in the 20's, but indeed he was. Anyway, this (p. 268, *Tender*, Scribner edition) seems to fit that worthy rather well: "His novels were pastiches of the work of the best people of his time, a feat not to be disparaged, and in addition he possessed a gift for softening and debasing what he borrowed, so that many readers were charmed by the ease with which they could follow him." [. . .]

OCCASIONALLY ONE IS STRUCK BY A POSITIVE WASSERMAN REACTION

I agree with you 100% on Bostonians. Schulberg's novel is a very good second-grade type book. Hank Rink is mistaken, I think, in contending Schulberg was definitely writing to hit the best seller list. The notable thing about that particular school that came out of that generation (mine, unfortunately)—[Budd] Schulberg, Daniel Fuchs (the best of the lot), Edward Newhouse, Jerome Weidman, Irwin Shaw, etc.—was their initial dedication to a very schizy set of allegiances: fellow-traveling, *The New Yorker*, sensibilities chiefly formed by Hemingway, and enormous ambitions for success. Sch. (now that Fuchs has lo these many years not written anything) had the most heart and also the most willingness to see contradictions & complexities along the way. Now nobody but a blooming idiot despises a best seller just because it's a best seller; over the years some of the best things are the best sellers; and once in a blue moon a very good book sells well over a short period of time. The two-bit editions show that first-rate books (that may have sold next-to-no copies in their original editions) can go into enormous editions, and hold their own along with Jack Woodford, Erle Stanley Gardner, and Thos. B. Costain. But what makes a best seller at a particular time is so whimsical a thing that a relatively "serious" character like Schulberg, I'm sure, doesn't sit down and formulate schema for turning one out. Also, he is at the mercy of his talent, which is precisely the same talent in *The Disenchanted* as it was in *What Makes Sammy Run?* and the prizefight book. I thought that stretch after stretch in *The Disenchanted* awfully engaging and almost very good, but the flaws are all over the place and the last couple of chapters are fearfully bad.

SUKHAREVA HAS APPLIED THESE CONCEPTS

Evil under the Sun is announced in the Summer announcements issue of Publisher's Weekly. When I was at the Richmond library the other day I inquired for the Fall number, which shd carry an ad & a news story on Random's fall list. It isn't out yet. Did you ask Albert if Random's policy is to supply clippings of reviews to its authors? Probably not, though some publishers do. If not, suggest you send $5 to Miss Dorothy M. Brandt, Literary Clipping Service, Walton, New York. For this you will get 50 clippings, which is very cheap service. You will probably have many more than that, though, and will have to shell out additional money. It is going to be damned interesting to see how the boys react.

EVER SINCE KRAEPELIN

I think it's possible to relax yr. method in the new book, which I gather is similar in method to *Evil,* to do anything you want with it. It is a mistake to go along as though there is one method (external, author-interpolation) and its opposite (organic revelation, interior monolog, immediacy, etc.) Based on actual results, proof positive, it wd. seem the best method is another one altogether, as based on the two most satisfactory works of this century (to me): *Remembrance of Things Past* and *Gatsby.* Both are told in the first person, roughly called autobiography: the only characters Fitzgerald & Proust get

19. Norris Getty, about 1952. Photograph courtesy of the Heritage Room, Bennett Martin Public Library

20. One-Man Show by Weldon Kees, October 1951, California Palace of the Legion of Honor, San Francisco. Photograph courtesy of the Heritage Room, Bennett Martin Public Library

21. Snapshot by Weldon Kees, in the Kees apartment, 1953. Left to right: Bob Helm, Ann Kees, Janet Richards, Charles Richards. Photograph courtesy of Janet Richards

22. Janet Richards and Ann Kees, about 1954. Photograph courtesy of Janet Richards

23. Charles Richards and Weldon Kees, Berkeley, 1953. Photograph courtesy of the Heritage Room, Bennett Martin Public Library

24. Robert Hagen, music critic on
the *San Francisco Chronicle;*
Weldon Kees; and Michael Grieg at
KPFA radio studio, 1954. Photograph courtesy of Michael Grieg

25. Weldon, Ann, and John Kees, Santa Barbara, California, about 1954. Photograph courtesy of Michael Grieg

26. Ann, Sarah, and Weldon Kees, Santa Barbara, California, about 1954. Photograph courtesy of Michael Grieg

27. Weldon and Ann Kees, Berke-
ley, about 1954. The painting is by
Weldon. Photograph courtesy of
Fritz Bultman

"inside of" are themselves.* But these books are in every way—both from the standpoint of structure and characterization—immense. And what cd. be more *succinct* than *Gatsby?* Ideally, the best method for a novelist (we are both talking all the time away from the *specific,* which is a way I don't much like to talk: I mean I can do better confronted by an actual, down-to-earth, livin-&-breathin paragraph by Anton O. Myrer than like this) is one that permits the greatest degree of modulation *if that is required.* Freedom to move in and out of characters at will, to use flashbacks, "objective" description, withhold vital information for later psychological effect, satire (which is *always* from the *outside*), freedom to view from any and all angles. This is more or less the method of Forster in *A Passage To India,* which is peppered with author-interpolation, and thank God, too [. . .]

—And then there are effects that the method you are advocating just can't get. Take the last two pages of *Tender Is the Night.* This is external (although it fools you a little by its pretense of all coming from Nicole's knowledge) and matter-of-fact as a police report. But what Fitzgerald wants here is remoteness, mystery, *lack* of news of Dick's life in America; and fifteen times as effective, *in this instance,* as fifty pages "told from Dick's point-of-view." —Another matter yr. method can't very well handle is what I wd. call objective irony. For instance, in *Evil,* there is a highly ironic point to be made from the fact that Kittering & Manny *can* get together *because* they have both fought in a war. But this is an irony that the reader gets or doesn't, and some sort of author-interpolation, however subtle (and the subtler the better) would give an added dimension. There are other instances—the one-eyed man business at the end. Actually I feel silly criticizing yr. method when it is capable of producing a book as good as *Evil.* And actually you adhere to your method less than you think: when you do feel the necessity for all-out satire, you switch (in the Walpurgis section) to the external (Aristophanic, Swiftian, Wyndham Lewis). I do not feel this is a violation.

IT IS HELPFUL TO RECALL

I suppose the most devoted practitioner of "absolutely-no-author-interpolation" is Jim Farrell. The case of Jas. is a warning. *Why* do we

---

* Really untrue. Proust "uses" everything. [W. K.].

have to be told every time Danny O'Neill lights a Camel, farts, or eats a meal at a greasy spoon? Do we have to go to *all* of the gangshags in which Studs Lonigan partook? At the other extreme is, say, somebody like Walter Pater. I think fiction that avoids the extremities of either Jim or Walt is what we need. Back to centrality!

ONE MAY TENTATIVELY CONCLUDE THAT NO SPECIFIC PATTERN

I suspect I'll be of more help when I see a draft of the new book. When do you think that'll be?

• • •

Norris Getty had received an appointment as a classics master at Groton School, the New England prep school modeled on Eton. On September 3, 1951, Kees wrote to him there:

I don't know what happened to my muse, but along the poetic front, things are quiet, very very quiet. Just not much of an impulse. Usual reaction to those I have is: "I've been over this ground before." Sometimes I incline toward the Scott Fitzgerald theory of emotional exhaustion, the idea that one has only so large an account to draw on, and once you've drawn on it, that's all there is. But I have endured longer periods of silence than this & discovered to my amazement that there was still something there. At least the condition does not stimulate a state of anguish as it sometimes used to, though I must say that these days I am frequently assailed with feelings that even efforts to produce art are both heartbreaking and absurd. But what else is there?

In these months and perhaps years, Weldon seemed increasingly preoccupied by thoughts of Fitzgerald, especially of *Tender Is the Night*. Some of his friends suggested that he identified himself with Dick Diver–Scott Fitzgerald, who was driven by circumstance and married to a troubled, dependent wife.

When *Evil under the Sun* was published, Kees wrote the Myrers:

Ruesch's Rustic Retreat
18 October 1951

Dear Tony & Judith, Joyous publication day! Don't know if you have as yet had a chance at an exhilarating glance onto the enclosed review, from this A.M.'s *Chronicle,* by Joseph Henry Jackass [Jackson]. Anyway, extra copies are always good to have around the house. Actually this seems one of his usual pieces, full of a sort of dim and woozy good will and with funny tinkly noises in the treble, a bit like Lee Sims on the old Brunswick label, playing *Paddling Madeline Home.* Funnier exhibits, I imagine, are yet to come.

Busy, rather, here. Finally in the last lap of the Bateson-Kees flicker (*A Meatball Named Expire*) after more snitches, shifts, ums, ahs, deliberations, recantations, policy & reversals, acts of God, etc., than I care to count. And in rather a bad state over a series of accusatory and strange letters from my folks, who, at the age of seventy, seem to be going through their second childhoods and being difficult as hell—not that my mother has ever been in the avant-garde of the stable as to understanding. [. . .]

Kees did not save the "accusatory and strange letters," but he did save a draft of his reply. Apparently he had asked Sarah and John for financial assistance to pay for the mounting of his San Francisco show; and they, or at least his mother, had replied sharply that he was now old enough to be paying his own expenses. In a letter to her, written probably in October 1951, Weldon said he had supposed

that both you and John took pride in my accomplishments—and that what I have been able to do in both writing and painting was a source of satisfaction and pride to you. Up until now, I have never had any indication that you thought otherwise. I gather from your letter you feel I have been wasting my time. I certainly do not feel defensive about my life or my way of life; although I have made many mistakes, I have always tried to the best of my ability to work hard and creatively and as well as I was able. I don't speak out of any conceit, but with a certain amount of pride in the fact that I have to my credit a body of work as creditable and sizeable as anyone my age. And if you know of anyone else, of any age, who has made something of a reputation for himself in both literature and art, I would like to know who it is. I remember how pleased both John and you were when I got in *Who's Who.* How do you think I got there? You know as well as I the praise my work has had. For instance, I have written 150 poems— all of which have been published and alone would be considered a

> lifetime's work for most individuals. My new book of poems will
> eventually find a publisher.

He comments on his emotional state:

> If you think it has been easy or without a struggle, or if you think it
> has all not been accompanied by the blackest kind of doubts and
> despair—or that many times I have wanted (but never for long) to
> chuck it all, you simply do not know. And believe me, I would never
> have taken a cent from you if I hadn't believed it was given freely and
> with faith in my abilities and beliefs. There is no question of my
> gratitude.

This letter is unusually disjointed, and though a copy was later found
among Kees's papers, perhaps it was never posted. The rough draft
lacks the finish that his work usually possesses. Kees's California
friends observed that Sarah Kees seemed to respect only popular success—stories in *Good Housekeeping*, verses in the *Ladies Home Journal*—and financial reward as evidence of it. This sort of thing Weldon
did not aspire to, and his mother did not understand.

• • •

In October, as planned, Jerry MacAgy mounted the Weldon Kees
exhibition at the California Palace of the Legion of Honor. "This show
is the best I've had," he wrote to Norris Getty when he sent him a flier
(undated) announcing its opening. He wrote to Lou Pollack on December 2, after the show had closed, that it "was stunningly installed
and otherwise not very noteworthy—sales, reviews, etc. There are
only two papers that carry reviews: Frankenstein in the *Chronicle*,
who gave it a good review (the collages puzzled him) and some cookie
on the Hearst paper who seems in league with the Sanity in Art
forces." On December 29, Weldon followed up with another letter:

> Somebody wrote me that Clem. G. is telling his little coterie at the
> Tibor-Nagy that "all-over" painting is washed up and that the Com-
> ing Painting will be "focal," i.e., painting that aims at a spot. All of
> which prompted me to compose the following 9-line limerick:
>
> An erstwhile "whole-surface" man, Clem
> Plucked himself off at the stem,

And sent out the word
To the avant-garde herd:
   "All-over" is over;
   It's finished; moreover,
   DeKooning does not,
   In a word, "hit the spot."
And that's the new gospel, pro tem.

All good wishes, Lou, for the New Year.

Send us some gossip & news.

• • •

Although Weldon Kees continued to be vitally concerned with what was new in New York, he wanted to know what was new in Los Angeles as well. He hoped that by staying for a few days in January 1952 as guests at the Huntington Hartford Foundation in Pacific Palisades, he and Ann might get in touch with whatever was happening in Southern California. This trip from San Francisco to Los Angeles turned out to be a greater adventure than they had planned for, in part because of storms. Even when they returned to Northern California, the weather so disturbed their plans that they could not make it into the Big Sur to see the Myrers. Weldon referred to the Big Sur as Henry Miller country since Miller held forth there in all his most recent fame. On February 3, 1952, he wrote to Norris Getty:

> We went down to Los Angeles for a week & managed to time our visit poorly enough: hit the rainy season with a vengeance. We were there during the worst of it; I suppose you saw stories on Venice-like L.A. We are only now beginning to dry out. I had to go down on some business in connection with the movie [*Communication and Interaction in Three Families*] that Bateson & I have finally completed,—tracked, scored & titled—(and premiered [for psychiatric and hospital personnel] here, in SF, last week, and handsomely received past all expectations). We had an invitation to stay at the Huntington Hartford Foundation, which kept our expenses down. What, you don't know about the Huntington Hartford Foundation? Well, it's in Pacific Palisades, about twenty minutes as the crow flies from Hollywood, out in the Thomas Mann–Aldous Huxley country,

and is the creation of one Huntington Hartford, 39-yr.-old heir to the A. & P. Tea Co. moola. He was formerly married to some society babe, but they are now divorced, and HH has a new wife, young & pretty, who (a) wants to be a movie star, (b) wants to be a Great stage actress, (c) wants to "do" "something" about "struggling artists." H. apparently gives every appearance of wanting to gratify all of these wishes; so has (a) put up the money for a movie in which she is now working, (b) is having her take lessons in diction & how-to-read-Shakespeare from Constance Collier, (c) recenty (2 yrs. ago) created the HH Foundation. Some of the ideas for this somewhat ill-starred venture seem to have come from the MacDowell Colony; he met Mrs. McD. at about the time his mind was churning with thoughts about what to do for struggling artists. Anyway, it is now the Jumbo West Coast Yaddo—some hundred acres of swank estate tucked away at the bottom of a canyon that may well feature cougars and timber wolves, with a huge iron gate at the entrance right out of a Norma Shearer movie of the 20's (it opens automatically by radar, or something, on the exit approach, and has to be opened with a key when you come in; they give you a key). The approach to the spot involves going over a road that in width cd. scarcely be called roomy, with a nice deep canyon on one side & what looks like none too secure shale on the other. The road has, by actual and intent count, 58 hairpin curves. This is fun to drive at night. The layout comprises a main building, Christ knows how many stables, and about fifteen studios, some of which were built by one of Frank Lloyd Wright's sons. These are very snazzy affairs, with wall-to-wall carpeting, jumbo fireplaces, terraces, kitchenettes, etc., any one of which wd. probably rent for $500 a mo. in NY if placed on top of a building in the East 60's. There is the inevitable kidney-shaped swimming pool. [. . .]

We came in at a nervous moment in the Foundation's life. It seems Mr. Hartford has been getting alarmed about the kind of painters who have thus far been admitted. Too many abstractionists. Before he started the Foundation, he hadn't realized what a lot of this kind of thing is around these days. I don't recall if you ever met or remember Hyde Solomon in Provincetown; he was there in the summer of 1950, the last year we were there. He's a nice fellow, and his work, though abstract, is quite tame and not very assertive. Anyway, Hyde had been approved by the Foundation's board—on the whole a very academic & safe group of men: Alfred Frankenstein, art critic of the *SF Chronicle,* Donald Bear, director of the Santa Barbara Museum, Millard Sheets, Lloyd Goodrich, and such. Mr. Hartford felt things had gone too far—all these daubs and smears, etc. So he overruled the board; Hyde, already informed that he had been accepted for a six month's period, was reinformed otherwise. I gather Hartford expected the board to just take this. Surprisingly enough, every last one of them resigned; and his literary board, which includes Isherwood (who has lived at the place a lot, but is now abroad), R. P. Warren, etc., are also apparently resigning. I don't know what gives among the men on the board in charge of composers. The resignation of the art boys was not, apparently, on the grounds of the treatment of Hyde (although this was no doubt the payoff), but on the grounds of Hartford's, shall we say, aesthetic ideas. These, I might add, he had now put in more permanent form by writing a pamphlet called "Has God Been Insulted Here?", sort of an up-to-date version of Max Nordau [19th century philosopher of artistic decadence]—an attack on modern painting, modern literature, modern music, and all done with the assurance of a man fearfully in need of just a rudimentary knowledge of all three fields. You don't know what he wants—well, maybe you do: Old Master techniques, forward-looking liberalism in the written word, etc.—but you sure aren't left in the dark as to what he's against.

"What has happened to the painter of the modern world? Where is the Raphael of the sixteenth century or the Rubens of the seventeenth . . . ?" etc. H. is now circularizing this pamphlet to every newspaper of over 500 circ. in the U.S. They'll love it. —Meanwhile, there are other indications that the Foundation is very possibly, among other things, an income-tax dodge. And Mr. H. is ready to lead us back to the good old days before Cezanne, Joyce, and Schoenberg. [. . .]

Kees's show at the Peridot in March was successful in that it got some attention, but none of the collages were sold. Stuart Preston in the *New York Times* on March 30, 1952, used it for a brief disquisition on collage as an art form: "Much taste and ingenuity have gone into Weldon Kees' collages at the Peridot Gallery. In many ways collage is the nihilist art form of this century. What would an old master have made of pictures composed like these? . . . The collage was the art of purest defiance to the kind of painting that was all finish and no heart. Now that academic art has trimmed its sails, due, as much to anything else as to the lamentable decline in technical standards of painting since 1914, this protest has lost its original point and become just another genre."

By March 1952, Weldon Kees had turned his mind quite seriously to filmmaking. Thanks to his job with Bateson (and Jurgen Ruesch), he had become relatively adept at managing a handheld movie camera, and thanks to his association with James Broughton's *Adventures of Jimmy,* he was learning how to integrate music and picture. Through his experience with collage, he had become professionally aware of the textures of papers, the relationships of materials, the effects produced by juxtaposing found objects. His film, finally called *Hotel Apex,* is like an animated collage, the camera ceaselessly moving over walls, up and down stairs, through doorways and over piles of refuse in a decaying building, an old hotel that had more recently become a whorehouse. All is stationary except the camera that searches surfaces. The music is atonal and discordant. On April 21, he wrote to the Myrers:

> Have been working hard on my little movie, on the destruction of the Point Richmond fleabag, and by tinkering around with the montage (excuse the expression), it has quite a nice lyricism. Thought first of using a Geo. Lewis blues, but the picture will run about 10 minutes, which lets out the Lewis, or for that matter, because of the length of time, most jazz on records. Then repeated viewings convinced me it needed something rather astringent, nostalgic, woebegone and marked by many changes of rhythm & beat; I thought of Hindemith & Bartok & some others. Today I showed it to a friend of ours up the road who knows a good deal about music & she suggested something of Alban Berg's—*Concerto for Violin, Piano, and 13 Wind Instruments.* We played it against the picture & it was damned spooky: almost scene for scene it was right; one might have thought the picture had been cut to fit the music. Now to shoot the titles and make some final adjustments.

> Letter from Willy Poster details the latest casualty of the Eastern
> Seaboard chute-the-chute: Bob Lowry. His wife had been away &
> came back to find him acting strangely; then big phases of depression
> and exaltation; then much worse. Now in a sanatarium. Diagnosis:
> paranoia. [. . .]

In the summer of 1952 Kees published three poems written during the
previous winter. Two of them are among his most significant pieces. In
"Guide to the Symphony," orchestral sounds reflect contemporary
culture:

> An agitated, almost angry theme ensues, in F.
> (Trombones.) A struggle (Flutes.) And then the
>   scherzo movement.
> Lachrymose, so often thought to deal
>
> With Western Man's religious hopes gone dim.
> Drums; and the famous "Wailing of the Damned" motif.
>   (Bassoons.)
> A horn sounds yearningly. A short ejaculation from
>   the fifes.

The second poem, of some seventy-five lines—a long poem for Kees—
dramatizes the ruminations of a mad murderer, confined in his prison
hospital. When Getty edited it, he reported later that he was disturbed
by the evident distress of its author; and when he returned the draft
with suggestions, he wrote of the "developing macabre streak" that he
had found in the Kees poems of late. Kees himself apparently had not
been aware of it. "The Testimony of James Apthorp" begins:

> A wall. A chair. A bed. A chiffonier.
> Ice fills the vacant places of the street.
> Not yet with silica or cinnabar
> Will I be healed.

The man whom Apthorp had clubbed was a druggist, an apothecary.
The meditation continues, a few lines later:

>   Now I hear the ice
> Filling the vacant places, frozen. Blackened seeds
> Drop from the peony; and once again

> The hinges of the heart creak open on
> A season echoed with iniquity,
> Predictable, and almost welcome now . . .

The mad murderer speaks of his dreams, of pygmies climbing or trying to climb, in sand.

> One of them floated downstream all night in the cold,
> After the long jump from the bridge . . .

The poem ends, the speaker still in his nightmare:

> Screaming and walking, upside down,
> While ice fills up the world.

In the third poem, "A Distance from the Sea," the speaker, who is one of Jesus's disciples, recalls how a raft was rigged to support what appeared to be walking on water. He speaks of "all the pain and worry every miracle involves," for "Life offers up no miracles, unfortunately, and needs assistance." The poems ends:

> It's dark here on the peak, and keeps on getting darker.
> It seems I am experiencing a kind of ecstasy.
> Was it sunlight on the waves that day? The night comes down.
> And now the water seems remote, unreal, and perhaps it is.

All three of these poems touch on religious matters, which is notable, for religion is not a frequent subject for Kees in letters, conversation, or published work. Two of them use ice and water imagery, both common in the Kees poems from earliest years. In a letter to the Myrers on August 7, he wrote:

> About "A Distance from the Sea" which has now appeared, along with "Apthorp" and "Guide to the Symphony" in the current *Furioso*. I agree with you Apthorp has more to offer, at least I like it better, in spite of the chorus of no's from Greg Bateson, Norris and Willy Poster. But I don't agree with you about the lack of ambivalence; if anything, there's too much. The poem is "about" the nature of art. That is, to be as down-to-earth as possible, even though art comes about through such mundane methods as building rafts under water, it is art in the end and we do experience the ecstasy. On another level I

intended it as a satire on the 19th Century German religious historians who attempted to reconstruct the historical Jesus in terms of
literal realism. But I have had other interpretations besides these, here
& there, and if people want to have 'em that way, it's quite okay with
me.

He continues discussing religion, but in a different context and with
an intensity unusual for him in letters or conversation; generally, he
prefers an ironic, satiric tone:

I must say that I guess I don't quite get you on Rahv's review of the
Whittaker Chambers, which I thought was an able piece & the best I
have seen on that book [*Witness*]. I really don't think he (Rahv) was
trying to make out a case for Dostoievsky "as a God-hater," as you
say—which would be pretty hard to do, although the references to the
Grand Inquisitor passage are a bit skimpy. But there is something,
surely, in the point Rahv is making here, for as I remember it, by
allowing the condemnation to come through the mouth of one of the
principal agents of the Roman Catholic Church (even though refracted
through Ivan), it gave Dostoievsky the opportunity of expressing his
hatred of Catholicism, which we know from other sources he detested
and which he often compares, in earlier works and in his letters, with
Socialism. The point Rahv makes is actually there, isn't it, quite aside
from considerations of Ivan or the later development of his character?
After all, there is a defense of free will here—a big item in the Dostoievsky creed; Dostoievsky demonstrably believed that both Catholicism & Socialism were to be condemned because both took away
men's personal responsibility. There was only one thing for Dostoievsky: Christ ("The whole planet, with everything on it, is mere
madness without that man," etc.) as opposed to secularized Christianity. This is not "making out a case for D. as a God-hater," as you
say, but pointing out that there is a distinct difference between D.'s
views of Christ (pure) and his views of organized Christianity (cor-
ruptible). Or do I misunderstand yr. point?—Anyway, I have been,
am, and am becoming more & more out of sympathy with the doctrines of Mssrs. Dostoievsky & Chambers, with their absolutisms &
assurance & intolerance; I think they insult human variability & that
they insult every human being who has tried to struggle for goodness
& decency without benefit of the particular dogmas of Dostoievsky &

Chambers. They insult every member of every other religious faith, whose views I would not for a moment admit are inferior to those of Dostoievsky & Chambers. They insult the dignity of every great moralist and philosopher and artist who has searched his own vision. They insult the good and decent and kind men I have known who did not believe, with Dostoievsky, that all nobility, all culture, receives its strength from the idea of God. Dostoievsky says that "if we do not acknowledge Christ we shall err in everything." But I think that men may acknowledge Christ until they are blue in the face & still do evil: for I have watched Whittaker Chambers, for instance, in operation, and it is not a pretty sight; and I believe deeply and with all my heart that moral and ethical values exist aside from religious belief. But I think that belief was more important to Dostoievsky, bursting into storms of jealous rage at his wife at the flimsiest pretexts & hitting the roulette tables while she pawned her wedding ring, than goodness, and dogma more important than anything else. In one of his letters he wrote: ". . . if anyone proved to me that Christ was not in the truth, and it really was a fact that the truth was not in Christ, I would rather be with Christ than with the truth." To such stuff as this, I say, resoundingly, loudly, and with spirit, No.

End of sermon on Dostoievsky.

Don't think I wrote you that I was ill a while back & in the hospital for a brief stretch, but quite okay now. Woke up one morning & had to go to the john badly, did so & proceeded to urinate blood. It got worse while I was at work & I got to a urologist fast, who slapped me into St. Luke's (who must also be the patron saint of the inflationists: $15 a day in a none-too-appealing ward). The ailment began to clear up before medication began, but the whole painful business (apparently prostatic) moved me to write a ballad entitled, "When You Piss Blood, It Scares the Shit Out of You, Baby, Blues." Since then I have done others, among them, "Make It Your Motto to Play it Legato, Mr. Raggedy Ragtime Man" and the appealing "I'd Rather Be Schizophrenic with You Than Well Adjusted with Somebody Else." But I have done none to match one of Turk Murphy's: "If I had It to Do All Over Again, I'd Do It All Over You" [. . .]

Ole Jurgen took off for the tall timber on his vacation, and I am getting some time off, with pay, too, and I must say that I can do without his smiling face for a bit. He has had Greg & me on a daffy project of photographing people's houses from top to bottom—this suggested itself to him by way of the movie on Michelangelo,—which has begun to bore us both a good bit. The Langley Porter Clinic was stirred up slightly when the head of its outpatient division attempted suicide by swallowing poison in the closet of the associate director. He lay there for four days before they found him, and what with anoxis & one thing and another, has been turned into more of a vegetable than a human being.

My little film got finished, premiered in Berkeley. [. . .] Maybe if & when we come down, I can snag a projector & the print. And you never did see *Adventures of Jimmy,* did you?

In 1952 Kees was sufficiently well known in the Bay Region to earn an invitation to contribute to a volume of essays on art and culture planned by the San Francisco Art Association. The little book, called *Painting and Sculpture,* was published by the University of California Press in 1952. He was paid $150 for his essay, "A Note on Climate and Culture." It contains a reply to those who thought that in devoting himself to painting, collage, music, cinema, and photography as well as poetry he was spreading himself too thin. He asks, "Should not the artist employ every means in his power, including his own uniqueness, to be entertainer, magician, prophet and conscience of society?" In the essay he observes the possibility of artistic flowering in the San Francisco area, just before the appearance of the Beat Generation and the City Lights group. As always, Weldon Kees was detecting the winds of change before the winds really rose. A formalist before the New Critics in the late thirties and early forties, an Abstract Expressionist in the postwar world, an enthusiast for New Orleans jazz and ragtime years ahead of the crowd, in the decade of the grey flannel suit, he plumped for versatility and pluralism.

In October 1952, Ann and Weldon Kees moved from Point Richmond to Berkeley, trading space for convenience. Weldon wrote on October 6 to Tony and Judith:

After protracted & various confrontations with crooked real estate operators (probably tautological, but let it pass), paranoid landladies, house numbers that don't exist, phony leads, wallpaper out of the later novels of Frank Norris, enough light green walls to divide the Stevens Hotel, neighborhoods of a Gogol-like cast, dead ends, dead-locks and dead centers, peeling bathrooms with colored pictures of chickens and rosy children by way of decalcomania—after all this, we found a place, dinky but delightful, and very near the UC campus, close to Ann's job, at 2713 Dana Street, Berkeley. We plan to move Monday. Hence this letter.

Their new place at 2713 Dana Street in Berkeley was so small that Weldon no longer had a studio in which to work, but the basement was available to him. He had not been highly productive for some time, nor was he here. Lou Pollack in New York and Kenneth Nack, director of the new Area Arts Gallery in San Francisco and an artist himself, both pressed Kees for pictures. He made some collages and wrote and published a few notable poems, but the late fall and winter of 1952–53 were marked by paralyzing depression.

In the spring of 1953, he and Jurgen Ruesch complete the book they had been working on for two years. Called *Message through Object*, it was eventually retitled *Nonverbal Communication: Notes on the Visual Perception of Human Relations*. For it Kees had supplied a thousand photographs, and he had worked over every sentence of the text, thinking that Ruesch's prose was excessively Germanic. Though the book was a joint product, its ideas were essentially Ruesch's. It has become a classic of its kind.

In spite of his low spirits, Kees turned his attention to writing lyrics, and sometimes music, in the popular idiom. Working with musicians associated with the San Francisco jazz revival, he found one of them, Bob Helm, especially compatible. On June 14, 1953, he wrote to Norris Getty:

> Dear Norris, The amount of effort that has gone into just getting the paper rolled into the typewriter I won't attempt to describe; maybe you can imagine it. Since you established a precedent for sloth in answering letters, I feel only mildly ravaged by my own. Anyway we were both pleased to have the silence shattered by yrs. of February 26th. The lacerating effects of middle age are dreadful, God knows, but seem to me to differ only in kind from those attending birth,

puberty, adolescence, etc. What the routes to wisdom along this particular terrain are I wish I knew. The trick of repeating, "It can't get any worse," is certainly no good, when all the evidence points to quite the opposite. And yet there are these periods of resilience, the reappearance of which I manage to count on most of the time. This last week I have been in such a state of torpor as to surpass Oblomov,* however.

Maybe it's just the weather. Everyone I know (when questioned in my most intent D.A. manner) says they just want to get as much sleep as possible & prefer not to move a muscle.

For the last four months have been devoting most of my spare time to writing songs, mostly for fun but with the not too dim hope of coming up with something marketable. It's been a prolific time. The all-out effort in this field was sparked by a request of Bob Helm, Turk Murphy's clarinetist, that I try my hand at doing some lyrics on "My Honey's Lovin' Arms," which the band plays, though Bob felt the original lyrics were too fearful for a grown man to sing. I knocked out some new ones, changing the possessor of the lovin' arms to a B-girl: ". . . She may request you buy/ Joe's best imported rye, / And when you do her smile is so sunny . . ." Helm thereupon suggested that we embark on some collaborating. He writes wonderful tunes; our watchword is "Back to the Twenties!"; and in a surprisingly short time we have come up with about fourteen tunes. During this time I've also done four or five of my own (both words & music), and have written lyrics for a new number of Turk Murphy's, "Five Aces." We are now about to try marketing these. The tunes are of all varieties, mostly pop rhythm numbers, a couple of ballads in the "April in Paris" tradition, some jazz tunes, even a western & a couple of novelty numbers. People seem to like them. —Helm has been a great pleasure to work with, a highly sensitive & aware sort of person, and unlike any jazz musician I've known before. His ability to write pop tunes at times gets him into a terrible state of anxiety: his devotion and commitment to hot jazz is so complete that he occasionally reviles himself as a traitor to the cause & has to be soothed & pacified. I don't know

---

* *Oblomov* (1859) by Ivan A. Goncharov is a Russian novel whose protagonist is characterized by lassitude and extreme ineffectualness.

if you know his work on records; I was never greatly impressed by his playing until I heard him in the flesh and am now convinced he is a great operator; he also plays jug & washboard about as well as those difficult instruments can be worked on. The Murphy band has recently been signed by Columbia & will record at least 16 sides a year for it; these records have used new recording techniques that present both Helm & the band itself in a far more favorable light than heretofore. Before long the band will also record under Helm's name for Grauer's new Riverside label, and he plans to use some of our rowdier tunes for this date. Turk will record "Five Aces," as well. And I hope to get down to L.A. soon to try to sell some of our pop numbers, a trip I rather dread.

Kees loved working with Bob Helm, a splendid musician, who was also, along with his beautiful wife, Kay, good company. Bob remembers their association as "one of the highlights of our life. We met once a week or so and tossed ideas around," he has said. "Pretty soon we'd have a tune going. It was great fun and excitement for all of us."[4] They set out to write tunes in the manner of the twenties and thirties, at least one in each of the prevailing styles: some serious, some tongue-in-cheek. He always thought that with effort Weldon could have made it as a professional pianist and singer, but Kees was not up to that standard when they worked together.

In the next two years, Kees copyrighted nearly a dozen songs, but he got none of them published, and his friends were not sanguine about his chances of breaking into a highly competitive, enormously professional business. The musicians liked Ann and Weldon very much, but "they did not like his being an intellectual, a poet, barging in on the music scene," Janet Richards said. "His dress put them off too. Never a bohemian, he dressed from Saville Row. He wore a mustache nicely trimmed when nobody else wore one. No, he was never a bohemian.[5]" Nesuhi Ertegun recently said, "The music was definitely in the Dixieland idiom, as Helm couldn't compose in any other terms (at least at that time). But the words were strange and very different from the popular music of the day. Again, I am sure Weldon tried to write what he felt would be commercial, but in fact, it really wasn't."[6]

On October 16, 1953, Kees wrote of the music business to Getty, who had introduced jazz to the Groton boys, with considerable success:

"—We went down [to Los Angeles] to see Nesuhi Ertegun, now working as a general trouble-shooter and recording director for Good Time Jazz, and found him up to his neck in woes of a deeply serious kind, but still able to operate out of a residue of élan rather amazing under the circumstances. He has been trying to help Helm and me peddle some of our tunes; but the recordings we made, it seems, were of too poor a quality for the publishers and recording executives to listen to. We made them on Bob's tape recorder and they seemed all right to me, but these days it appears that high fidelity is required. Managed, however, to find out quite a good bit about how the creepy semi-underworld of song-marketing operates, which is even more depressing than I had anticipated, and God knows my impressions had been sufficiently grim. —I had brought down the ms. copies of quite a few tunes, but these got me nowhere as it is no longer in the order of things to present material this way (most of the publishing and recording boys can't read music or don't want to be bothered), nor do publishing offices have pianos in them any more so that one can present a tune through on-the-spot performance (another vanishing piece of Americana). Nesuhi is currently running around with a very nice gal who used to be Mitch Miller's secretary and is now Rosemary Clooney's secretary; and the two of them racked their brains to think of one publisher who would even see me, or at least not give me the bum's rush in a couple of seconds. They finally agreed that there was one such person, apparently an unusually decent figure in a group they agreed outdid any other in the subhuman department. Finally got to see the guy and he was very decent and even flew in the face of protocol and looked over some of the tunes. He was frank enough to admit that he had long since abandoned any subjective principle when considering songs and thinks now solely in terms of what the recording execs of the big record companies "want." There are two kinds of songs: "lightweight" and "big"; what qualities distinguish these categories I am not at all sure. Seemed, however, from this by no means unauthoritative source that most of our numbers fall into the lightweight classification, though he pounced upon one with a gleam in his eye that I found welcome and announced that this one "might be *it*," i.e., BIG. Apparently what has been going on for some time now is that the ideas of a few record execs control all operations. No one is interested in anything that doesn't look like a great hit. And you can check your current hit parade, if your eardrums will bear it, to find out what these are. Maybe I'm all wrong, but they all seem to have melodies without originality or taste and with a determined repetitive cretinism in the lyrics. I gather that any wit or sophistication are actively feared. Such, indeed, is the state of things that a writer like Vernon Duke, with a fat assured income and an "A" Ascap rating from tunes like "April in Paris" and "I Can't Get Started," even though he continues to work prolifically and is writing good tunes, they are considered "lightweight" and he has been utterly unable to get a single number of his recorded in years. Well, that's it . . . Maybe with luck, pluck, grit, sand, and a ton of merde, Helm and I will try try again. Actually I suppose it's not much different than the situation that obtains in literary publishing these days, though it's probably slightly more honest, on the hard-boiled side.

The Keeses and the Helms continued to see one another through the fall and winter of 1953. In the fall, a local FM station, KPFA/FM, asked Kees to join its staff. According to Lawrence Ferlinghetti and Nancy Peters, historians of literary San Francisco, "In the early 1950s when television had yet to take over the mass consciousness of America, this small listener-sponsored radio station, located on the fringes of the University of California, became an intellectual center perhaps of more temporary influence than the university itself."[7] Kees refused what at another time might have seemed a professional opportunity, thinking the financial arrangements of the station altogether too shaky; but shortly he put together a radio "talk show." He and Michael Grieg, an engaging journalist later very well known in the Bay Area, were joined weekly by prominent, and not so prominent, writers, artists and people-about-town to discuss cultural topics. Pauline Kael appeared often, for she brought wit and openness to a program that tended to be ingrown. In 1953 she was not well known and seemed hardly more prepared than Kees for a remarkable career as movie critic. They became close friends, and remained so. The program was continued into 1954.

In the Bay Area, Kees was a man on the horizon, if not a commanding figure; but he was not forgotten on the East Coast either. In April 1954, the Poetry Society of America asked him to serve with Harry Levin of Harvard and Melville Cane of New York City on a panel

responsible for awarding the Shelley Memorial Award for poetry. In a
few weeks they settled on Leonie Adams. In 1955 he served a second
time, and at his suggestion this year the award went to Robert
Fitzgerald, the translator-poet. At age forty Weldon Kees was becoming a member of the literary establishment. Ann was "bitterly sorry
they had left the East and perhaps understood better than Weldon
did"[8] how much he needed that urban world of writers and painters,
Judith Rothschild has said; but Kees was not lost in California
obscurity.

By spring 1954 his book with Ruesch had found a publisher after
some trouble with the University of California Press, and he and
Ruesch worked at editorial revisions against a deadline. Still he found
time for a letter to the Myrers:

> 11 April 1954
>
> Dear Tony & Judith, I don't think I'm up to one of those extensive
> eighteenth century-type letters for which I've become justly notorious,
> but will do what I can. Hope that things are going better than passa-
> bly for you in this attractive world of ours, and in particular that those
> dexedrine tablets I gave you made for a pleasanter, saner and more
> euphoric Thursday, after you left us here a long time back. —I am
> now on a five-day week (and sometimes six-day), since Ruesch is
> anxious to finish up this damned book before he takes off for Europe
> on July 1st, & I still don't know whether we're going to make it or
> not, though the extra money is not exactly unwelcome. I did manage
> to get a pretty good subchapter written, ostensibly concerned with the
> codification systems of the insane, "schizophrenic art," and so on,
> which I think contains a fairly thoroughgoing wipeup job on the
> Freudians. I had occasion to re-read Old Sig's piece on the Moses of
> Michelangelo and it provided precisely the sort of data I needed for
> getting at the coarseness, irrelevance, and charlatanism that is per-
> vasive throughout the psychoanalytic approach to art. What is most
> striking, though, throughout the entire literature of this sort, whether
> it is Ernest Jones on *Hamlet* or the boys who attempt to prove that
> Cezanne was what he was because he liked to smear his excrement
> around, is a total lack of demonstration. They're utterly unable to
> *demonstrate* anything. And here and there in the book are other

passages that have been rather pleasant to do, though a good deal of
the time I think we are worrying our subject matter to death, and then
giving it a kick for good measure. From my own point of view it is
ironic that three publishers are after the book, and rather impassioned
about it, too. Meanwhile it has been six months since I sent my
poetry ms. off to Mr. Swallow's contest. I hear nothing. [. . .]

Kees had returned to writing poetry, after a brief note from Norris
Getty had said that he would be glad to see the latest work. All five
pieces that Kees sent were singularly autobiographical. "Waiting for
Pilgrims" grew out of his experience with his car the previous Thanksgiving when he and Ann had gone to Santa Barbara to be with
Weldon's parents. In "Travels in North America," the longest poem of
the group—about 125 lines—Kees considers his own state of being,
using geographical spots from his own experience as points of reference. The poem ends:

> . . . by a grapefruit crate,
> A ragged map, imperfectly enclosed by seaworn oilskin.
> Two tiny scarlet crabs run out as I unfold it on the beach.
> Here, sodden, fading, green ink blending into blue,
> Is Brooklyn Heights, and I am walking toward the subway
> In a January snow again, at night, ten years ago. Here is Milpitas,
> California, filling stations and a Ford
> Assembly plant. Here are the washboard roads
> Of Wellfleet, on the Cape, and summer light and dust.
> And here, now textured like a blotter, like the going years
> And difficult to see, is where you are, and where I am,
> And where the oceans cover us.

[*Poems 1947–1954*, 1954]

On June 7, 1954, Weldon wrote to Tony Myrer:

For the last ten days or so I've been waking up with maddening
regularity at the crack of dawn, wide awake & alert as Broyard at a
showing of pornographic movies. My mind is batting on all eight &
there's nothing to do but get up & work. I suppose it's because I'm so
damned snowed under with things I feel ought to be done; but by
midafternoon I am slavering for a Spansule. Jurgen & I are racing

against the Waltham to finish the book, and I only hope there is enough time for me to give the whole ms. a careful last revision. I was appalled to discover, while making some necessary calculations, that the text runs to almost 70,000 words *already*—and it is primarily a picture book. —Meanwhile there is markedly accelerated tempo (that repeats & repeats in my ear) on the Bateson project; and I have undertaken to become chairman of a jumbo jazz concert for the benefit of KPFA (which is in bad financial shape) which we hope to stage in September, with everybody & his brother in the area taking part, and think we can raise them $1500 or so. I have some good men working with me; so I don't forsee it turning into another Forum '49.

In between convulsions, I'm working away at poems.

In June, Howard Moss of *The New Yorker* returned proof of a Kees poem, "Colloquy," and asked to see others. Philip Rahv asked for an essay-review for *Partisan Review* dealing with a book that interested Kees. The University of California Press asked him for a chapter on "the intent of the artist" to be included in a forthcoming book; he suggested an essay on Jelly Roll Morton that would "show how his aims and stated ideas add up to a real esthetic, just as the ideas of a great painter or writer do." In June, Kees wrote to Emory Cook, publisher of Lizzie Miles, praising her as "the last of the great New Orleans blues singers who still operates in the tradition." He praised Bob Helm to Cook also, and wrote, "I wonder if you would be interested in creating a job for me as your part-time West Coast representative." In addition to his musical activity, in June he reopened negotiations with Henry Volkening, acknowledging that he might be willing now to undertake a novel. Volkening replied cordially. But in the midst of all this, a private storm was breaking.

None of Weldon Kees's letters in the winter and spring of 1954 suggest extraordinary psychic or marital difficulties. The references to Ann are of the usual kind: Ann sends her regards; Ann is well; we are planning a summer trip to the Northwest. He wrote that during May and June he was very busy completely rewriting the book Jurgen Ruesch and he had been collaborating on for several years; it ran to about 75,000 words and contained some three hundred photographs, most of which Kees had taken. When Ruesch went to Europe to lecture at Zurich, Kees put the manuscript into final shape and delivered it to the publisher. Kees was working under considerable pressure.

The Helms continued to see Ann and Weldon regularly, and Kay Helm remembers vividly the last time they visited the Keeses in the early summer of 1954. Asked over for dinner by Weldon, they found him cooking, but then he often cooked in these months. Ann was stitching in the living room and scarcely looked up. Kay and Bob, recognizing that something was wrong, suggested that they ought not to stay. Weldon did not protest overmuch. The Helms had arrived as the Keeses approached a breaking point; and over the weekend of the Fourth of July, the rising storm whirled to its climax. Ironically, one of the most successful of Kees's short stories was "The Evening of the Fourth of July," an apocalyptic vision in a Kafka world. Several months later, on September 22, he wrote an account of the weekend to Conrad Aiken:

I have been through a lot of rather grave personal difficulties, about which I'll be writing you very shortly. Just now I am terribly snowed under and must get ready to fly to Los Angeles. Briefly, Ann has been on a job in Berkeley [at the University's psychiatric clinic] for the last couple of years so strenuous and so wacky that things got pretty rough. I tried to get her to quit the job, but something or other—I'm not at all sure even now what or who it was—held her to it with a sort of fascination, I guess you would call it bordering on the pathological. About eight or nine months ago she got to drinking more than you, me, Malcolm Lowry and Tallulah Bankhead put together. I have never known what to do about any of the alcoholics I've known but to let them drink. I occasionally tried to talk to her about it; she was very touchy on the subject, on a couple of occasions said that she would try to cut down on the sauce, but every night it was the same thing. Then I began to see a lot of paranoid symptoms developing: the phone where she worked was tapped, our telephone at the apartment was tapped, all that sort of thing. It was very difficult for her to drag herself out of the house to see people and raised objections when I wanted to have people over for dinner or the evening. Over the 4th of July weekend she went completely paranoid; she drank continuously, and I was unable to get any psychiatric help, since all the boys and girls were off at the seashore and the mountains for that lovely weekend. Two nights a nice MD next door shot her full of sodium amytal, and occasionally she would have a lucid moment. Most of the time she was not sure who she was, who I was (sometimes I seemed to be one of her brothers), and there was a very deep certainty on her part that FBI men were outside the house. Well, Conrad, this ain't the half of it; finally, on Tuesday morning I got hold of one of the few psychiatrists around here of any real help on such cases and she finally agreed to sign herself in at Langley Porter Clinic. She improved greatly there, but left against advice after three weeks. We are now separated and she has agreed to a divorce, and I hope she will be all right. We were married for sixteen years and a lot of it was not so good. It's too bad that her life could not have been one long summer on the cape, because she was at her best then.

[. . .] The welcome mat is out. My job with US Public Health [and Ruesch and Bateson] went out with a whimper: Eisenhower is pulling out the rug from under all psychiatric and communications research that might indicate that there is more than one way to drive a person crazy. I am freelancing on writing and movie making, and, at the moment, am bushed but in good spirits.

Kees had tried without success to telephone Tony and Judith Myrer during that weekend of the Fourth of July. The Myrers did not have a private telephone. In desperation he got in touch with his parents, now living in Santa Barbara. His father replied immediately, alarmed, offering practical suggestions. "As things are, there are some business matters which we should talk about with you as soon as it can be done conveniently—for you. * * * The attic is safe and dry, so books & paintings will be safe there," John Kees wrote on July 18. In her uncomprehending way, Weldon's mother reached out to him. "You know you have a place [here] for as long as you want it," she wrote four days later. "I think egg nogs at least three times a day would give you strength. A few graham crackers with them." She ended, "If you need us, we will come at once. Would have come, but thought you'd rather we wouldn't." Tony Myrer responded to a letter, also on July 22:

> Weld, for pete's sake, let us know right off the bat and w/o any preliminaries if we can help out in any way. I mean *anything* at all. My God, you're our dearest friends and if there's anything we can do, sing out. What the hell are friends for. We gather this is a really bad siege from yr letter. Please don't hesitate at all. SF is only a few hours away, either way.

On the last day of July, Weldon replied:

> I apologize for not having dropped you a line before this. Thank you for the telephone call & yr. thoughtfulness.—These have been times to try men's souls—as Rilke once remarked to James B. Conant; and I don't mean just mine, either. Maybe someday they will find a name for this period, and it won't be the Age of Anxiety, either. The Age of Flying Apart, perhaps, or the Age of the Asps. Meanwhile quite a lot of pretty fair people get badly bunged up. —You know all this without me telling you, though.
>
> I think I am on the mend, and it looks as though Ann will be in much

> better shape soon. I have to give a lecture here the night of the *2nd* of August at SF State College; on the *3rd* (Tuesday) I plan to drive down to Monterey to see you.

He went briefly to Monterey and saw his parents, who came up from Santa Barbara, and then he rushed back to San Francisco. Kees wrote to Norris Getty on August 8 about "getting out of this country into another cultural climate for a change;" he repeatedly reminded his friends during the next year that Ambrose Bierce, also of San Francisco, had disappeared into Mexico, "tired of existence," in 1913. He told Getty, "Ann's plans seem rather uncertain. When I talked to her yesterday (she is staying on at the Berkeley apartment) she said she thought she would go back to her old job. Earlier, she had talked about looking for a job in San Francisco that wasn't so wearing, and finding a place to live here. Again, I don't know." In a brief postscript, he wrote, "The situation, I should add, had aspects not unlike the Nicole one in *Tender Is the Night*."

In the Fitzgerald novel, Dick Diver cared for his psychotic wife, Nicole, for years, protecting her both from herself and from the world, until at last he could sustain the support no longer. Subsequently Dick, though gifted with charm and high intelligence, drifted, ultimately to disappear. *Tender Is the Night* was a favorite novel of Weldon's; he particularly admired its understated conclusion. Anton Myrer wrote later: "You simply cannot minimize FSF's influence on Weldon; it ran *very* deep—right down to a predilection for witty racontage, expertise about jazz and jazz musicians, holding one's liquor ably, even sex. For instance, a lot of women were drawn to Weldon's dark, lean, good looks, his style and wit, and not a few of them made a play for him—I saw them; but he never to my knowledge played around; not till his marriage had gone to pieces."[1]

After returning from Monterey Kees stayed for two restless weeks with the Richardses, and then he went to Jerry MacAgy's apartment on Green Street. Though she was seriously diabetic, her manner of life was more undisciplined, more freely bohemian, than what Weldon Kees had ever experienced, and in September he moved to 1980 Filbert in the Marina. Janet Richards reports that Jerry MacAgy "having most useful connections, had found a wonderful little house for

Weldon, tiny and private. Within a day it was distinctly his, barely furnished though it was."[2] It became a party pad. Kay Helm remembers that once when she and Bob visited there, they found "some girl living with him. They had matching terrycloth robes, like towels, and were so absorbed in each other that we did not hang around long and were even a bit embarrassed by what we had come on."[3] Pauline Kael remembers it as a kind of stage set, complete with black towels and pseudo-romantic trappings. Kees now associated with people who had not known him or Ann before the breakdown of their marriage.

In these weeks and then months Kees was abnormally excited, filled with half-formed schemes for his future. His one firm commitment was to Adrian Wilson, an excellent printer. For some time Wilson had considered publishing occasional books in fine, limited editions. Kees, encouraging him, advised him on titles, distribution, and sales; and after much hesitation, Wilson undertook to print Kees's poems for a first venture. The proposed collection contained forty-two poems, twenty-six of which had appeared in magazines before 1950; three poems had appeared in 1951, three in 1952, and only one had been published in 1953. The volume, called *Poems 1947–1954,* surveyed Kees's entire career. Its publication was supported by an advance of $500 from John and Sarah Kees, and Weldon himself spent an additional $150 on promotion and advertising. In one of his evenings of long conversation with Pauline Kael, he complained bitterly that here he was, forty years old, still having to take money from his parents— and his mother, at least, expected "success" from him.[4] On August 24, 1954, he had written to Norris Getty about his plans for the book:

> I think I am going to publish my poems of the last six years out here. Have a good printer who wants to do it—Adrian Wilson—as good as the Grabhorns or Cummington, etc. on typography and format—and a nice person in addition. The last publisher to have the ms. kept it for a year, thought he was going to do it, then no word for months; I finally called him long distance after he didn't answer my letters. He said he was terribly sorry. This had happened, more or less, with publisher after publisher.

Through Jerry MacAgy, he had become involved with a theatrical and

184

museum set, and he now spent days with actors and journalists. He and Michael Grieg had struck up a particular friendship and at one point even considered sharing a house. A number of Kees's old friends had reservations about Grieg, feeling that he "attached himself" to Weldon, but Grieg's affection was deep and tenacious. The separation of Ann and Weldon Kees, which seemed natural enough to these new people, struck old friends as unbelievable. Nesuhi Ertegun said many years later:

> A word about Ann Kees. She looked much older than Weldon, and I often wondered whether there was a sort of mother-son relationship between them. She must have been extremely attractive when she was younger and was attractive still when I knew her. She never used make-up or perfume and didn't seem to care how she was dressed. Even though she never said very much—in fact she was one of the quietest people I have ever seen—she always looked wise and intelligent and distinguished and detached in an almost aristocratic manner. Weldon seemed deeply attached to her, but I was never able to figure out which needed the other more.[5]

• • •

All during the fall of 1954 Weldon kept feverishly busy. He wrote to his New York friends, offering to review books and write articles; he planned the promotion of his volume of verse; he undertook free-lance film projects; he got in touch with recording companies on behalf of neglected jazz artists; he plotted to get himself sent to Hawaii on a writing assignment; he promoted Conrad Aiken's play, *Mr. Arcularis;* he told Edmund Wilson and others that Adrian Wilson was planning to establish a "little press" for neglected works of art (Edmund Wilson nominated Nabokov's novel *Lolita*); he wrote sketches and music for a local revue temporarily named *The Seven Deadly Arts;* he worked on several essays, including a long piece dealing with Louise and Walter Arensberg as patrons of contemporary art and another on Jelly Roll Morton; he sent for those collages that were still in New York so he could have an exhibition in San Francisco; he corresponded with Bob and Kay Helm, on tour in the East, about recording their songs; he continued his weekly radio program for KPFA with Michael Grieg, "Behind the Movie Camera."

Weldon now led a very active sexual life. One of his new friends remembers that he "railed against the homosexual conspiracy against him and his heterosexual kind"[6] but that he seemed to have a fundamental quarrel with women. In company he was always in good temper, cheerfully sardonic; but several of his new friends understood that he was in deep psychic trouble. Pauline Kael thought him an exceedingly sensitive, fragile man who was close to desperation. Watching the schizophrenic children whom he filmed for Jurgen Ruesch, he became terribly distressed, she recalls, fearing that, far from improving under treatment, the children were sinking. Michael Grieg remembers that his desperation was always understated, but "I felt it was on the tip of his tongue: 'If I did not feel it was in bad taste, I would unburden myself. I am in despair. Let's go off where I can tell you about it.' But he never did."[7] Several people recall that in addition to Ambrose Bierce, he talked of the poet Hart Crane. Crane's life ended with his disappearance into the sea, he reminded his friends. In a short film dealing with the Golden Gate Bridge that he was making at this time with William Heick, he used Crane's famous poem, "The Bridge." Some people remember that his two poles of reference seemed to be the Bridge and James Agee, his movie critic friend who like himself was a man of great versatility.

Kees and Adrian Wilson proceeded with their plans for the publication of the book of poems, sharply aware of distribution problems. Kees wrote to Bob and Kay Helm on October 22: "It must be the busy season. I have been scraping by on five or six hours sleep, a regular stint by now, and my metabolism seems to be holding up. So damned many irons in the fire it looks like branding time at the old Bar Z. Adrian & I have shipped out over 1500 brochures on my book (did you get yours? It was sent to that distinguished hostelry, the President) and orders have begun to trickle in. It isn't great, exactly, but not too discouraging."

He kept up his connections with established literary figures, whatever his state of mind. When Wallace Stevens subscribed to his patron list and ordered one of his special volumes, he wrote to thank him. He did not hesitate to ask Malcolm Cowley, Conrad Aiken, Allen Tate, and Stevens for endorsements of his poems, hoping that with their stated approval his book might reach a larger audience. Though Aiken was in Massachusetts, Stevens in Connecticut, and Tate in Minnesota, Kees seemed to feel himself in a community of writers. Myrer later wrote, "He knew that West Coast writers and artists were largely ignored by the East, that the Manhattan intelligentsia certified the reputations; he had a very shrewd (and hard-earned) sense of how recognition—and its consort, power—was bestowed; and why. . . ." Malcolm Cowley in New York offered help when he was asked, with his usual, disarming generosity. In November 1954, he sent a testimonial for the cover of Weldon's book:

> These are poems about Robinson, the average popular, despondent man, shipwrecked by middle life and cast away on a waterless island. They are felt poems about unfeeling, and liquid poems about the dry heart of an era. In his own voice, recognizable in every line, the poet speaks for us all.
>
> MALCOLM COWLEY

Cowley sent along a personal note:

> Dear Weldon:
>
> Try this on your harmonica. Then take another look at K. Burke's "Book of Moments"—it's unprofessional and as witty in places as any collection of poems I have read. Nothing sells these days, but I hope it gets attention.
>
> As ever,
> Malcolm

To which Weldon replied:

> 30 Nov. 1954
>
> Dear Malcolm, I tried it on my harmonica—the E♭ one that has a chromatic scale—and it sounded fine to me. Particularly that long cadenza at the end. Thanks a great deal. I'll send you a copy of the book when it's ready. A little binding trouble, but it looks as though it will be out in a couple of days.
>
> Best, as ever,
> Weldon

Poems 1947–1954 appeared in December. Very elegant, the volume
deserved its praise as a handsome piece of bookmaking: Adrian
Wilson had produced prize-winning limited editions for a number of
clubs and presses, and he had designed books for both the University
of California and the Stanford University presses. After so many rejec-
tions and so many disappointments, *Poems 1947–1954* was important to Kees, more significant perhaps than his friends may have
understood. On its title page, he quoted a fragment from Chapter
XXIX of *The Marble Faun* by Nathaniel Hawthorne. In Hawthorne's
"romance," in the passage immediately preceding Kees's quoted lines,
two young men stand on the battlements of an Italian castle. The
sculptor says to his Italian friend:

> "I am one of those persons who have a natural tendency to climb
> heights, and to stand on the verge of them, measuring the depth
> below. If I were to do just as I like, at this moment, I should fling
> myself down . . . a man would leave his life in the air, and never feel
> the hard shock at the bottom."

The friend replies:

> "He does not leave his life in the air! No; but it keeps in him till he
> thumps against the stones, a horribly long while; then, he lies there
> frightfully quiet, a dead heap of bruised flesh and broken bones! . . .
> Yes, yes; I would fain fling myself down, for the very dread of it, that I
> might endure it once for all, and dream of it no more!"

The sculptor knew, Hawthorne says, that the friend's "condition must
have resulted from the weight and gloom of life, now first, through the
agency of a secret trouble, making themselves felt. . . ." Then the
sentence follows from which Kees quoted for his epigraph:

> It was perceptible that he had already had glimpses of strange and
> subtle matters in those dark caverns, into which all men must de-
> scend, if they would know anything beneath the surface and illusive
> pleasures of existence.[8]

It was these words about "those dark caverns" that Kees caused to be
printed on the title page of his collection of poems.

The publication of Kees's volume was celebrated by a party in the loft where Wilson had his press. Everybody came and signed a copy of the new book. Knowing the ways of editors and reviewers, Weldon Kees thereafter made every effort to get his book reviewed in the national journals. He had some success. An anonymous critic in the (London) *Times Literary Supplement* perceptively linked Kees with Hart Crane, whose poem, *The Bridge*, was much in Kees's conversation in these months. In the review on August 17, 1955, the *TLS* writer said that in the poetry of both men "is the nostalgia of the uprooted metropolitan, whose steel and concrete environment constantly changes, caught in the buffeting slipstream of the urban rush to nowhere." He concluded: "It is the authority of the individual voice that counts; and by this test, no one is likely to dispute the authenticity of Mr Kees's gifts."

Kees's activity did not lessen after the book was published. Theatrical ventures took time, and he worked hard on his revue, now called *Pick Up the Pieces*. All his artistic and literary life, Kees had sought to reconcile the high achievements of Joyce, Proust, and Eliot with the popular arts of film and jazz. His critical friends thought him a romantic because he believed it possible that Hollywood could produce art—he cited *Citizen Kane* and *Sunset Boulevard* as evidence—and he thought popular music could be reclaimed from the philistines. He was concerned with quality, not with kind; to him no "kind" was of itself inferior. Kees was the enemy of the superficial, the ready-made, the clichéd, which he found in some of the most celebrated artists of his generation as well as in some of the most successful of the entertainers. His latest venture into the performing arts was a last effort to bring the popular arts and the elitist arts into equilibrium. If it did not finally work out, it at least defined what many thoughtful critics of American culture saw as its principal problem: how to keep democratic ideals of equality from destroying excellence.

In midwinter the revue was temporarily laid aside when Kees and Michael Grieg produced a pick-up, nearly spontaneous entertainment called *The Poets' Follies of 1955*. The *Follies* may have had more dash than precision, but it attracted unusual national notice; and this success, or at least notoriety, gave Kees big ideas. He dreamed of television and the New York stage, and in his euphoria even wrote (on April 2, 1955) to T. S. Eliot asking permission to adapt his poem, "Sweeney Agonistes," to television. Kees schemed endlessly. He tried

189

to get his own songs recorded, and he acted as agent for his musician friends and a young singer, Ketty Frierson, whom he had discovered in "The Purple Onion," a San Francisco cabaret of local fame. With five friends he founded San Francisco Films, but the plans were more elaborate than substantive, and of course Kees had no money. That spring Kees wrote a one-act play for his theatrical friends, his first play since undergraduate days. "The Waiting Room" was like what was appearing on the world's stages, notably like Samuel Beckett's *Waiting for Godot.** In it three women who are vaguely symbolic or representational or typical talk and talk, but not with each other. Each seems to be listening for something to happen, suspended in time and in life. Each reaches out but establishes no contact with anyone.

Two reviews written in the spring of 1955 reveal Kees's state of mind. Considering a book that he had solicited for review, *Love and Hate in Human Nature,* he wrote for the *San Francisco Examiner* of April 3, 1955:

> In our present atmosphere of distrust, violence, and irrationality, with so many human beings murdering others and themselves—either literally or symbolically—Dr. [Arnold A.] Hutschnecker's book has appeared, offering itself as a work that will "help you to find a happier life by recognizing and resolving . . . your basic loves and hates. * * *
>
> Doctor Hutschnecker offers self knowledge as a set of rules, a gimmick, essentially, and concludes with a list of numbered "basic beliefs" to get us through these times of strain. "Respect for Life," "Reason for Life," "Responsibility," "Tolerance," "Adjustment" are some of them—and there are probably not many who will deny that these are all qualities worth attaining.
>
> Presented as they are here, however, "self-knowledge" is turned into a mere by-product of "modern psychology," with the doctor's assumption that "we are now able to penetrate the mystery of the unconscious self."
>
> Have we? Has Doctor Hutschnecker? Socrates, Proust and Coleridge, for instance, had more "self-knowledge" and knew more at first hand

---

* "The Waiting Room" was published for the first time in the *Prairie Schooner* 60 (Spring 1986): 5–18.

of love and hate than the doctor will ever know; they also wrote very well indeed unlike the Doctor; and never believed for a moment that "self-knowledge" could save them—or us.

With all his wisdom, Socrates had one of the most horrendous domestic lives on record and was sentenced to death for his ideas; Proust's masterpiece came out of an existence of incredible emotional suffering; Coleridge found release in opium.

The liberal assumption that self-knowledge will lead to "adjustment" and "happiness" is a curious one [. . .]

Kees's review for the June 20, 1955, issue of *The New Republic* might have alerted his friends to his desperate state of mind, if any of them had read it. He wrote:

I suppose that everyone thinks that his life is interesting to some extent or the suicide rate would be even higher than it is; consider the number of persons who keep journals, diaries, write their autobiographies or talk about the most humdrum aspects of their days to each other or even pay for the privilege of doing so in the company of such professional listeners as psychiatrists. I am willing to be persuaded that every life *is* interesting [. . .].

• • •

July 1955 was exactly one year after Kees's separation from Ann—.

Weldon Kees had been fascinated by suicide from his earliest years, and his friends recalled that he talked about it a good deal. Recurring themes in his poems were death, darkness, and covering water. A person sensitive to others' psychic states might perhaps have seen that Weldon's busyness during that last year covered a mortal anguish, but one doubts if anybody short of a psychiatrist equipped with a full pharmacopoeia could have prevented a tragic denouement. Janet Richards, a very sensitive woman indeed, had had some premonition: "I knew it could come only to a crashing end. I made feeble efforts to coax him back from what very clearly seemed to me his last-ditch stand." Yet when his efforts were at last exhausted and he called her, she was unable to breach the chasm. She has written an account of Monday, July 18:

One afternoon about four Charles and I, dressed in our reluctant best, were trying to endure our anxieties on the way out of the door to go to the airport to meet Millie's plane. She [Charles's mother] was arriving for her semi-yearly visit of three weeks. The phone rang. It was Weldon, speaking from some distant depth into which his plunge back from carnivals had plummeted him. I knew it was a cry for help and stood transfixed, the sweat dripping down my palms and up my wrists. "I'd like to see you," he said.

Never before had I faced so fearsome a decision. In those days Charles and I were still the captives of Millie's iron will. [. . .]

"My God, Weldon, we're on our way out the door this minute to meet Millie's plane."

In a second he saw that we were no good either. I felt like a murderer. I wonder if we were the last resort?

He knew, having a Millie of his own, that we would never get away from her during a visit that was like the gift of a pair of handcuffs.

"Things are pretty bad," he said, as soldiers, the three left out of their company, may say to one another as they wait in their mudhole for their bomb.

"I'm sorry, sorry," I said, staring at Charles, standing in the open doorway.

"Nobody seems to be doing anything," he said.

"Let's get together, Weldon. I'll call you as soon as we get away from Millie tonight."

A silence. "I may go to Mexico. To stay," he said.

"Right away?" I cried, aghast.

"I don't know."

"Weldon, for God's sake don't go without seeing us."

"I won't." And those were the last words he spoke to me.[9]

During the afternoon of July 18, Weldon called Pauline Kael. The last thing he said on the telephone was, "What keeps *you* going?" and the

28. Adrian Wilson and Weldon Kees, fall 1954. Photograph courtesy of the Heritage Room, Bennett Martin Public Library

29. Flier for *The Poets' Follies of 1955*, San Francisco. Courtesy of the Heritage Room, Bennett Martin Public Library

30. The Barbary Coast Five, playing for *The Poets' Follies*, San Francisco, 1955. Left to right: Horace Schwartz, percussion; Carol Leigh, washboard; William Ackridge, jug; Weldon Kees, piano; Adrian Wilson, clarinet. Photograph courtesy of the Heritage Room, Bennett Martin Public Library

31. Weldon Kees, spring 1955. Photograph by Bill Heick. Courtesy of the Heritage Room, Bennett Martin Public Library

32. Ann Kees, 1954. Photograph courtesy of Michael Grieg

remark combined with his tone of voice made her so uneasy that she kept calling him all evening without answer. She "somehow knew" that his life was coming to a turning point, and she could do nothing about it. When finally Michael Grieg reported that his car had been found abandoned on the north approach of the Golden Gate Bridge, she was not surprised, just profoundly disheartened. Kay Helm remembers that the fog was so dense that Monday one could not see more than a foot ahead and the bridges were lost in a gray oblivion.[10] Greig had spent part of the previous weekend with Weldon. He later published an account of it:

> We were both going through some sad times. He asked if I'd go to Mexico with him but my problems weren't that desperate and I didn't have enough money to make the trip seem appealing. He talked of selling his books, the whole lot of them. That seems strange now that it's known he had some $800 in the bank, still untouched. We discussed Dostoievksy's *The Devils,* the last book he had been reading, and how the novel came close to how he was feeling. (I recall now that *The Devils* ends with a similar disappearance/suicide.) He also quoted something from Rilke, that every so often we have to change our lives completely.
>
> I had gone to his little apartment in the Marina to drink to his decision to go to Mexico. That seemed a lot more sensible than suicide which he sheepishly admitted trying the week before. "I just couldn't get my foot over the rail," he had said. Months before we had been planning a book on suicide, a How-Not-To-and-Why-Not-To-Do-It with studies of such suicides as [James] Forrestal, Lupe Velez, Alexander Berkman and Hart Crane. He had accumulated some of the material with his friend, the late Jim Agee. I joked about his attempt. "It's a hell of a useless way to get research," I remember telling him. He joked also. We discussed how suicide was a statistical whim. It happened most often in the summer months. It could be triggered by a poor diet (and Weldon hadn't been eating well since his separation from his wife the year before [. . .]
>
> I called him the next morning to tell him about an overseas job I had heard of. He seemed interested. We talked of seeing one another that week. It was Monday, July 18, 1955.

He wasn't home when I called that evening. I called during the following day. No one home. I went down to his place that evening. Dark and quiet, not even a sign of Lonesome his cat. Then I got a call from the highway patrol at Golden Gate Bridge. His car had been found parked at the north end with the keys in it. With Adrian Wilson, Weldon's local publisher, we went back to his place. We got in. It was almost as I had left it the Sunday before.

Most of the Jack Daniel was left. On his piano were some sheet music blues. There was the copy of *The Devils* and Unamuno's *Tragic Sense of Life* near his bed. A note was on the telephone table, the details of the job I had told Weldon about. There were a pair of red socks soaking in the bathroom sink. Near the bookcase in the kitchen was a plate with congealed milk.

His suitcase was in the basement. The only clothes missing were those he was wearing.[11]

Janet Richards describes Weldon's parents at that time:

Michael notified Weldon's parents in [Santa Barbara] that he might be missing. When they registered in the morning at the St. Francis they called us, and that night we went to see them.

We had heard about Weldon's parents for years. [. . .] Sarah Kees, a smallish, plain, expensively, tastefully dressed woman with blue-gray hair, who kissed us and pathetically burst into tears, held my hand throughout our visit simply because Weldon had spoken well of us, and brought tears of sympathy to my own eyes. She was voluble. What was the trouble? Could we please tell her what had been going on? Was it Ann, had she been making unhappiness? Did we think Weldon had just gone off on a trip and forgotten to tell anybody, and would be back tomorrow?

"And would he leave Lonesome [his cat] alone in his apartment for days?" put in John Kees, and I seemed to hear Weldon himself in the dry, sardonic little question, which the mother ignored.

John Kees said very little that night. He was a small man, quietly the American middle-western gentleman, who read history and biographies when he came home from his business, who was twenty years younger than he looked, and who knew Weldon was dead.

We were as reassuring as we could be. John had offered us a drink, and had a bottle of Scotch sent up. He did not drink. [. . .]12

The circles that Weldon Kees had frequented were filled with speculation. Luther Nichols, book columnist for the *San Francisco Examiner,* reported on July 24, 1955, that "when he vanished into the fog of the Golden Gate Bridge, he had a new book in progress. The subject: Famous Suicides." Such a manuscript was not among his papers, though a list of famous suicides, historical and fictional, was there. In the wider, national circles there was considerable interest in his disappearance. Kenneth Rexroth wrote an account to Malcolm Cowley, and Cowley quoted it in a letter to Conrad Aiken: "I should say Weldon killed himself out of intolerable madness—a manic-depressive psychosis which, because it took socially approved forms, was not recognized as delusional: 'Looky Papa I'm a *Time* cover man.' I was very fond of Weldon—knew him all his life as a writer. New Directions first published him." John Kees found some explanation for Weldon's disappearance in Cowley's book, *The Literary Situation* (1954). Speaking of the profession of writing, one of Cowley's characters says:

> It's a good life, and I'd choose it again, but it has some bad years in it, especially around the age of forty. That's the time when writers have to face up to what they've been doing, like everybody else. They are halfway through their active careers, and perhaps they've made a little success, but not the sort they were hoping for, and now the future begins to look like the past and not so interesting. They begin to wish desperately that everything could be changed, starting tomorrow— wives, jobs, friends, places, everything, before the walls close in. It's the forty-year-old crisis [. . .].13

Two years later Ann Kees wrote of the summer of 1955 to Conrad and Mary Aiken. She had long been out of touch with the friends she and Weldon had had in the Bay Area: she did not respond to their overtures of friendship.

2530 College Avenue
Berkeley 4, California
May 25, 1957

Dear Conrad and Mary—

After a rackety Berkeley day, one of buying a piece of luggage that I couldn't afford, two pairs of Woolworth earrings that I could, a broiling chicken and a bottle of gin, it seems an appropriate time to tap out an answer to your good letter. I was so pleased to receive it and I love you both.

It would be impossible to tell you the whole story in a letter, or even in a series of letters, so I shan't try. Our breakup and my breakdown were simultaneous. I spent an edifying month at Langley Porter Clinic while Weldon was in the process of moving to San Francisco from Berkeley. I didn't see much of him after that—a brief, unpleasant meeting in January and an accidental meeting at a restaurant that Spring. He was wound up and manicky, something like the Forum 49 phase, but much more so. On a day in the middle of July two years ago his car was found abandoned at a parking lot on the Marin side of the Golden Gate Bridge. This was a Wednesday and no one had seen him since Monday. Several of his friends called me that evening, thinking I might have heard from him, but I hadn't. This was the first I'd heard of his genuine disturbance and it was a shock. He talked to one of his friends of suicide and had even set the date on his calendar for the previous Sunday. I don't know what the accumulated bad news was in the letters he wrote you. At a distance, I had thought things were going very well. There were frequent mentions of him in the *Chronicle*—favorable reviews of his book of poems, reviews by him, stories of the Poets Follies that he organized, etc. etc. He was obviously driving himself and there obviously had to be a letdown, and it must have been during this most trying period of all that he disappeared. He had called Jurgen Ruesch, with whom he wrote *Nonverbal Communication,* and told him that he was going to Mexico. He also called his mother and asked her if she minded if he went to Mexico. His bank balance was down to eight dollars and he had been trying to sell his library, something I find almost impossible to believe. I think his friends and his family hoped against hope that he would reappear—from the hills of Mexico or the wilds of Schweitzer's Africa, or wherever. I accepted his disappearance as a suicide from the beginning because it was something he had talked about ever since I've known him—and that goes a long way back. There was no suicide note and there were certain papers missing that a suicide does not take with him. This led the San Francisco police to advise his parents that his disappearance was just that. And that's about all I'm going to write about that, for now anyway. It's the first time I've written anyone a letter about it and no doubt explains why it took me until May to answer yours. But I know you were genuinely fond of him and deserve something more than the notice in *Poetry.* I didn't see it, myself.

It was rough. But I think I *am* beginning to flourish a little, as you said you hoped. I've got a perfectly maddening job that interests me and pays starvation wages. I'm a secretary at the psychiatric clinic for students of the university. It's run by a man with turquoise eyes who looks most like a tall Ghandi (sp?). He's a Freudian analyst who spends most of his time dissenting, and subtle as all getout. The rest of the staff are a fascinating bunch of ex-rebels who manage never to agree about anything. My job is part nursemaid, part policeman and part (no doubt) mother figure. The students who come there are a healthy bunch of neurotics and psychotics and mostly extremely intelligent. Five days there and I need two days to rest up.

I think I am trying to say that it took more than the court's sayso to divorce me from Weldon, but that has finally come about. [. . .]

Ann Kees stayed on at the campus clinic for many years. She died alone in her Berkeley apartment in August 1975. Even her family in Douglas, Wyoming, had lost track of her. Like Weldon, she had withdrawn into the fogs of San Francisco.

• • •

For twenty years, Weldon Kees was at the cutting edge of his time. Alert to shifts in sensibility, aware of changes, he moved with his generation. Indeed he moved in advance of it. He stood a bit apart, and the parade came along later, often down his street. Kees had more than one string to his fiddle, and this was both his strength and his limitation. Not content with writing poetry that earned him a place among the prominent poets of his generation, he tried his hand at painting and collage. As he had published his poems in the most prestigious journals, he exhibited his pictures with the most distinguished painters. And more: before it was fashionable, he was investigating what we now call "pop culture." He was devoted to New Orleans jazz and especially Jelly Roll Morton and Fats Waller when only a handful celebrated their achievements. He was eager to search out the possibilities of art in standard Hollywood features, this in a generation which scorned the films that later generations would make objects of cult adulation. Interested in the cinema as an art, he tried his hand at both still and moving photography. He got to the new enthusiasms before others and understood more than the crowd.

From abstract expressionism on canvas he moved to abstract expressionism in the cinema, and he wrote experimental background music for films. Then he went to what we now call "multimedia." He tried to combine music, anecdote, poetry, even criticism in one "entertainment," one "happening"—this a decade before the sixties. In his last, posthumous book, he investigated nonverbal communication. Later that subject was topic for cocktail chatter, but when he worked with it, the subject was fresh. Weldon Kees did not so much move with his time—rather he anticipated new times.

And through it all we can detect one constant theme. From his first letters and stories, he investigated "those dark caverns into which all men must descend, if they would know anything beneath the surface and illusive pleasures of existence."[14] In the stories of his apprenticeship, Kees skirted the surreal, the symbolic, that took him into subterranean regions where no daylight comes. In the poems, he alludes to a half identified world of isolation and shadow. The paintings gave form to terrors that he recognized but could not tame. He shaped his apprehensions into color and pattern; and in collage he sought order among miscellaneous experiences. His music and lyrics expressed an ironic detachment from life, anticipating the witty, expressive lyrics of a new generation. Weldon Kees documented one voyage through dark caverns from which, alas, he did not emerge.

Chapter 1

1. Rudolph Umland, "Looking Back at the Wimberly Years," 39 pp; "More Beerdrinking with Wimberly," 40 pp, [1978?], MSS, Heritage Room, Bennett Martin Public Library, Lincoln, Nebraska.

2. Norris Getty, "Weldon Kees," *Sequoia: Stanford Literary Magazine* 23, no. 2 (Spring 1979): 21–22.

Chapter 2

1. *Prairie Schooner* 12, no. 2 (Spring 1938): 68–69.

2. Robert D. Harper, "Weldon Kees' Denver Years," 12 pp, 1980, MS, Heritage Room, Bennett Martin Public Library, Lincoln, Nebraska.

Chapter 3

1. William Barrett, *The Truants: Adventures among the Intellectuals*
(New York: Anchor/Doubleday, 1982), pp. 64, 67.

2. Umland, "More Beerdrinking with Wimberly."

3. Norman Podhoretz, *Making It* (New York: Random House, 1967), p. 238.

4. Janet Richards, *Common Soldiers: A Self-Portrait and Other Portraits* (San Francisco: The Archer Press, 1979, 1984), p. 149.

5. Janet Richards, *Common Soldiers,* p. 145.

6. Janet Richards, *Common Soldiers,* p. 148.

7. John Kees published the letter in both of the Beatrice, Nebraska, papers (the *Beatrice Times* and the *Beatrice Sun*), on August 13, 1946.

Chapter 4

1. "Catalogue Notes for a Show of Paintings by Byron Browne" Kootz Gallery, 15 East 57 Street, New York, November 1–10, 1946.

2. Russell W. Davenport, with the collaboration of Winthrop Sargeant, "A *Life* Round Table on Modern Art," *Life*, 25, no. 15 (October 11, 1948): 56–79.

3. Dorothy Gees Seckler, "History of the Provincetown Art Colony," in *Provincetown Painters 1890's–1970's,* edited and with a foreword by Ronald A. Kuchta (Syracuse, New York, Everson Museum of Arts, 1977), p. 65.

4. Anton Myrer to Robert E. Knoll, July 13, 1981.

5. Judith Rothschild to Robert E. Knoll, January 2, 1983.

6. Anton Myrer to Robert E. Knoll, July 13, 1981.

7. Fritz Bultman, "Enemy of Obfuscation," 9 pages, November 1979, MS at Sheldon Memorial Art Gallery, University of Nebraska-Lincoln.

Chapter 5

1. Janet Richard to Robert E. Knoll, July 13, 1981.

2. Janet Richards, *Common Soldiers,* p. 288.

3. Thomas Albright, *Art in the San Francisco Bay Area 1945–1980* (Berkeley: University of California Press, 1985). See also Mary Fuller McChesney, *A Period of Exploration: San Francisco 1945–1950* (Oakland: Oakland Museum Art Department, 1973).

4. Bob Helm in conversation with Robert E. Knoll, San Francisco, June 16, 1982.

5. Janet Richards in conversation with Robert E. Knoll, San Francisco, June 18, 1982.

6. Letter to Robert E. Knoll, September 23, 1981.

7. Lawrence Ferlinghetti and Nancy J. Peters, *Literary San Francisco: A Pictorial History from Its Beginnings to the Present Day* (San Francisco: City Lights Books and Harper and Row, 1980), p. 159.

8. Judith Rothschild to Robert E. Knoll, January 2, 1983.

Chapter 6

1. Anton Myrer to Robert E. Knoll, January 2, 1983.

2. Janet Richards, *Common Soldiers,* p. 295.

3. Kay Helm in conversation, San Francisco, June 17, 1982.

4. Pauline Kael in telephone conversation, August 31, 1982.

5. Nesuhi Ertegun to Robert E. Knoll, September 23, 1981.

6. Byron Bryant in telephone conversation, San Francisco, June 18, 1982.

7. Michael Grieg in conversation, San Francisco, June 17, 1982.

8. In the Centenary Edition of the Works of Nathaniel Hawthorne (Columbus: Ohio State University Press, 1968), vol. 4, Matthew J. Bruccoli, gen. ed. Chapter XXIX begins on p. 260 and Kees's epigraph is quoted from a sentence on p. 262.

9. Janet Richards, *Common Soldiers,* pp. 299–300.

10. Pauline Kael in telephone conversation, August 31, 1981.

11. Michael Grieg, *Intro Bulletin: A Literary Newspaper of All the Arts* [New York], 1, no. 8 (May 1956), p. 4.

12. Janet Richards, *Common Soldiers,* pp. 301–2.

13. Malcolm Cowley, *The Literary Situation* (New York: Viking Press, 1954), pp. 214–15.

14. Epigraph on title page of *Poems, 1947–1954,* quoted from Nathaniel Hawthorne, *The Marble Faun,* Chapter XXIX; in the Centenary Edition of the *Works of Nathaniel Hawthorne,* vol. 4, Matthew J. Bruccoli, gen. ed. (Columbus: Ohio State University Press, 1968), p. 262.

This list contains names of persons mentioned in the Kees letters with vital statistics as they are available. Kees's references, which often provide additional information, may be found by consulting the index.

LIONEL ABEL (b. 1910), one of the *Partisan Review* Intellectuals, published essays, poems and translations in the forties and prizewinning plays later. His autobiography, *The Intellectual Follies: Memoirs and Reflections over Five Decades*, appeared in 1984.

JAMES AGEE (1909–55) was the kind of man about whom legends grew. His novel, *A Death in the Family* (1955), was partly autobiographical; and his letters to his old teacher, Father Flye, were published posthumously in 1962.

CONRAD AIKEN (1889–1973) wrote poetry, criticism, novels, and dramas. After he graduated from

Harvard University in 1912, he "devoted all his time to literature," he said. His autobiography, *Ushant,* was published in 1952.

ELIZABETH AMES organized Yaddo, the artists colony, and was its executive director from 1924 until 1970, whereupon she became its director emeritus. In 1959 she received the Distinguished Service Award from the National Institute of Arts and Letters.

HAROLD ARLEN (Hyman Arluck) (b. 1905) was a prominent composer of popular music from 1929 through the 1950s. A pianist in the Buffalo area by age fifteen, he had a dozen Broadway hits. Among his perennial favorites are "Stormy Weather," "I've Got the World on a String," and "That Old Black Magic." He wrote the score for the movie, *The Wizard of Oz* (1939).

JEAN ARP (1887–1966) was born in Strassburg when it was still under German rule. He exhibited his paintings with Kandinsky, Klee, and others of the *Blaue Reiter* group (1911) and was later associated with the Dadaists (1916–19). His writings on art were widely published.

NEWTON ARVIN (1900–1963) was a professor at Smith College and part of the *Partisan Review* circle. His study of Herman Melville won a National Book Award (1951); and in 1952 he was elected to the National Institute of Arts and Letters. He was a director of Yaddo from 1939 to 1954.

NATHAN ASCH (1902–64) was the son of Sholem Asch. Born in Poland but brought to America by age 13, he was in Paris with the Lost Generation. He later wrote for *The New Yorker* and other leading periodicals.

W. H. AUDEN (1907–73), the poet, emigrated to the United States in 1939. His "baroque eclogue," *The Age of Anxiety* (1947), was said to define his generation.

BURT BALES recorded "Down among the Sheltering Palms" with Joe Darensbourg, the New Orleans jazz clarinetist, and "Jazz from the San Francisco Waterfront" with Marty Marsala in the early 1950s.

GEORGE BARKER (b. 1913) wrote his first novel at eighteen and W. B.

Yeats included his verse in the *Oxford Book of Modern Verse* in 1936. From 1940 to 1943 he was in the United States.

DJUNA BARNES (1892–1982) was born in New York City but lived for many years in Europe. Her novel of five psychotic people, *Nightwood* (1936), was admired by T. S. Eliot. A biography, *Djuna: The Life and Times of Djuna Barnes* (1983), is by Andrew Field.

MARY BARRETT was a prominent member of the Washington D.C. staff of the Federal Writers' Project. She was "a pink-faced former schoolteacher from Michigan, with silver-gray hair tightly clinging to her scalp," according to Jere Mangione in *The Dream and the Deal: The Federal Writers' Project, 1935–1943* (1972).

WILLIAM BARRETT, a native New Yorker (b. 1913), was an editor of *Partisan Review* from 1945 to 1953 and a professor of philosophy at New York University from 1950. His autobiographical essay is called *The Truants: Adventures among the Intellectuals* (1982).

IRIS BARRY (1895–1969), a pioneer in film criticism, was the director of the film library of the Museum of Modern Art. Though born in England, she did most of her work in the United States.

GREGORY BATESON (1904–80) graduated from Cambridge University in 1925 and thought of himself as an anthropologist. After field study in the South Pacific with Margaret Mead, he studied psychotherapy. His daughter, Mary Catherine Bateson, has written of him in *With a Daughter's Eye: A Memoir of Margaret Mead and Gregory Bateson* (1984), and David Lipset has written a biography, *Gregory Bateson: The Legacy of a Scientist* (1980).

WILLIAM BAZIOTES (1912–63) studied with Leon Kroll at the National Academy of Design and taught in the Federal Arts Project from 1936 to 1938. He was cofounder of the school, Subjects of the Artists, in 1948 with Robert Motherwell, Barnett Newman, and Mark Rothko in New York City.

CECIL BEATON (1904–80), photographer, stage and film designer, and artist, was born in London and educated at Harrow and Cambridge. Author of many books and collections of pictures, he had great panache.

SAUL BELLOW was born in Canada in 1915 but moved to Chicago in 1924, where he has chiefly lived and worked. His novels have won all the prizes, including the Nobel Prize in 1977.

HERB BERNSTEIN was named Herbert Spencer Bernstein by his rich, eccentric father. He was Willy Poster's brother.

JOHN BERRYMAN (1914–72), born in Oklahoma, was educated at Columbia and Cambridge and taught at Harvard, Princeton, and the University of Minnesota. From their first appearance in the thirties, his poems got critical attention; and his biography of Stephen Crane (1950) was admired. Eileen Simpson has written of him in *Poets in Their Youth: A Memoir* (1982).

FRANCIS BIDDLE (1886–1968) was educated at Groton and Harvard and became private secretary to Justice Holmes (1911–12). In 1940 he was U.S. Solicitor General, and from 1941 to 1945 he was U.S. Attorney General. His autobiographical volumes are *In Casual Past* (1961) and *In Brief Authority* (1962).

KATHERINE GARRISON BIDDLE (1890–1977) was privately educated. In 1918 she was married to Francis Biddle. Author of some ten volumes of poetry, she was honorary consultant in American Letters, Library of Congress, 1944–54.

ELIZABETH BISHOP (1911–79) was born in Massachusetts and educated at Vassar (1934). She devoted herself wholly to poetry, for which she won a Pulitzer Prize in 1956. For many years she lived in Brazil.

BERYL BLACK managed the book shop at Ben Simon's, a department store in Lincoln, Nebraska, from 1935 to 1938.

MARC BLITZSTEIN (1905–64) studied at the Curtis Institute of Music and in Paris with Nadia Boulanger and Arnold Schoenberg. His one-act opera of social significance, *The Cradle Will Rock,* opened on Broadway in 1937. Later he collaborated with Kurt Weill, translating *The Three Penny Opera* (1954). He died of brain injuries sustained from an altercation in a bar following a political argument.

BRUCE BLIVEN (1889–1977) was on *The New Republic* after 1923 and its editorial director after 1946. His autobiography is *Five Million Words Later* (1970).

PETER BLUM was born in Russia in 1906 but came to the United States in 1911. He began exhibiting his paintings in New York in 1926 and they have been shown in the Museum of Modern Art and abroad since that time.

MAXWELL BODENHEIM (1893–1954) was a resident of Greenwich Village in its most bohemian days. In his last years he was reduced to begging in the streets and peddling his poems in bars.

LOUISE BOGAN (1897–1970) was poetry critic on *The New Yorker* from 1931 to 1969. In 1945–46 she had the Chair in Poetry at the Library of Congress, and in 1955 she received the Bollingen Prize for poetry. Ruth Limmer edited her selected letters (1920–70) in 1973.

TOM BOGGS (1905–52) edited an anthology, *American Decade: 68 Poems for the First Time in an Anthology,* in 1943 for the Cummington Press, one of the small presses that specialized in producing beautiful books.

HENRY BOTKIN was born in Boston in 1896 but after 1950 he worked in Provincetown. His paintings were nonrepresentational, sometimes combined with collage.

C. M. BOWRA (Sir Cecil Maurice) (1898–1971) was a distinguished English classicist. His *Memories: 1898–1939* was published in the United States by the Harvard University Press.

ERNEST BRACE published *Commencement* (1924) with Harper's, and *Buried Stream* with Harcourt, Brace (1946). In the midthirties several of his stories were anthologized as the "best of the year."

HARVEY BREIT (1913–68), a New Yorker, was assistant editor and columnist on the *New York Times Book Review* from 1948 to 1957. At one time he was on the advisory board of *Partisan Review.*

ANDRÉ BRETON (1896–1966) was a leader in the surrealist movement. In 1938 he went to Mexico, and from there he went to New York City. He organized an important surrealist exposition in 1945, and in 1946 he returned to France.

LOUIS BROMFIELD (1896–1956) grew up on an Ohio farm, and after attending Cornell University became an ambulance driver in World War I. His early work, *The Green Bay Tree* (1924) and *Early Autumn* (1926), was highly praised, the latter getting a Pulitzer Prize. He published two volumes of autobiography in 1945 and 1948.

CLEANTH BROOKS (b. 1906), critic, was a member of the Fugitives at Vanderbilt University (1922–25) and a leader in the New Criticism of the forties and fifties. A founder and editor of the *Southern Review* (1935–42), he has been a professor at Yale since 1947.

JAMES BROUGHTON (b. 1913) made his first experimental film, *The Potted Palm,* in 1946 and his second, *Mother's Day,* a black comedy, in 1948. They are said to be classics of their kind.

HARRY BROWN (b. 1917) was in the Harvard class of 1940 but left before taking a degree. His poetry was first published in *Poetry* in 1934, and his novel, *A Walk in the Sun,* appeared in 1944. After 1946 he wrote scenarios for many films in Hollywood and got an Oscar for *A Place in the Sun* (1952).

BYRON BROWNE (1907–61) was a charter member of American Abstract Artists. His first one man show was at the New School for Social Research in 1936. From 1952 to 1961 he worked at Provincetown on the Cape.

ANATOLE BROYARD was born in New Orleans in 1920 but was educated and lived in New York City. He became a prominent reviewer and feature writer on the *New York Times.* It was said of him that "whatever arouses his passions he can communicate fully; hence his reactions are infectious." *Aroused by Books,* a selection from his reviews, was published in 1974.

BYRON R. BRYANT was part of the San Francisco artistic-theater group of the early fifties, just before the appearance of the Beat Generation. In the summer of 1955 he joined the staff of St. Mary's College of California, Oakland, as a professor of English.

FRITZ BULTMAN (1919–85) was born in New Orleans and studied at the New Bauhaus in Chicago (1937–38) and with Hans Hofmann (1938–41). From 1938 on he worked in

Provincetown and was one of the founders of *Forum 49*.

MARGUERITE CHAPIN CAETANI, Duchess of Sermoneta, (1890–1963) was the American wife of the seventeenth Duke of Sermoneta, Prince of Bassiano, whom she married in 1911. After publishing *Commerce,* a French review, with Paul Valéry and others, she founded *Botteghe Oscure* in 1948. In its twelve years of existence this review published 650 writers of thirty nationalities.

MARIA CALAS (1923–77) was the most influential opera singer of her time.

ERSKINE CALDWELL (b. 1903) won fame with *Tobacco Road* (1932). Much of his work dealt with social problems in the South. A popular writer, since 1940 he has received little critical attention.

MELVILLE CANE (1897–1980) was a poet and essayist, but he was also a lawyer. He served as legal counsel to such persons as Sinclair Lewis, Thomas Wolfe, Upton Sinclair, William Saroyan, and others of similar fame and literary accomplishment.

ROBERT CANTWELL was born in the state of Washington in 1908, but lived in New York City after 1929. In the thirties he wrote two "proletarian" novels, *Laugh and Lie Down* (1933) and *Land of Plenty*

(1934). After serving on the staff of *Time,* he became literary editor of *Newsweek* in 1945.

TRUMAN CAPOTE (1924–84) was born and raised in the South. His novel *Other Voices, Other Rooms* (1948), created some stir. At first something of an *enfant terrible,* in time he became a "personality."

WHITTAKER CHAMBERS (1901–61) translated Felix Salten's classic for children, *Bambi,* in 1929, but he is better known for his charges (1948) that Alger Hiss had been a spy for the Russians. His account of American Communism and the Communist plot is told in *Witness* (1952).

JOHN CHEEVER (1912–82) is regarded as one of the best writers of short stories in his generation. He published often in *The New Yorker.* For some years he lived at Yaddo as a "general factotum." His daughter Susan has written her memories of him in *Home before Dark* (1984).

SERGE CHERMAYEFF (b. 1900) was educated at Harrow and Cambridge in England, though born in Russia. Primarily an architect, he taught at Yale University after 1940.

ELEANOR CLARK (b. 1913), novelist and essayist, was educated in the United States and Europe and graduated from Vassar. Her first novel, *The Bitter Box* (1946), earned considerable critical acclaim, and her long essay, *Rome and a Villa* (1952), an "intricate re-creation of the spirit and charm of the Eternal City," has become a classic. She has been married to Robert Penn Warren since 1952.

ROBERT M. COATES (1897–1973) wrote "the first Dada novel in English," *The Eater of Darkness,* published by McAlmon in Paris in 1926. After 1928 he was on the staff of *The New Yorker.*

CYRIL CONNOLLY (1903–74), a founder of the English journal *Horizon* in 1930, was its editor from 1939 to 1950.

VINCENT CONNOLLY was a well-known radio announcer in the days before television. Kees met him when they both worked for Paramount News in the forties.

EDWARD CORBETT (1919–71) studied at the California School of Fine Arts and taught at the San Francisco State College and other institutions after 1947. His first one-man show was held in 1956, and he had a retrospective exhibition at MIT in 1959.

THOMAS B. COSTAIN (1885–1965) was a popular novelist. Between 1942 and 1952 he published seven full-length novels, each a selection of a major book club; two volumes of history; and a biography. He specialized in historical romance.

MALCOLM COWLEY (b. 1898) is a poet, essayist, and critic. His *Exile's Return* (1934, revised 1951) deals with the Lost Generation, and his studies of poets and novelists have helped establish many reputations. After 1948, he was literary adviser to Viking Press.

KYLE CRICHTON (1896–1960) was a successful journalist. Born in Pennsylvania, he contributed to *The Daily Worker, The New Masses* and *Collier's Weekly* simultaneously. He also wrote novels and, in 1950, a biography of the Marx Brothers.

PETE DAILY had his own jazz combo on the West Coast after 1946, where he was a leader in the Dixieland revival. Born in 1911 in Indiana, he spent the Depression years playing the cornet in Chicago.

JOE DARENSBOURG played the clarinet in the traditional New Orleans style. Born in Baton Rouge in 1906, he played on riverboats to St. Louis, toured with the Al G. Barnes circus, entertained on West Coast liners, and in the forties played with Kid Ory.

D. A. DAVIDSON saw his novels distributed by the Book-of-the-Month Club, Fiction Book Club, Bantam, and other popular publishers. Born in

New York City in 1908, he wrote for radio, the newspapers, and television.

MORRIS DAVIDSON (1898–1979) was a painter and teacher of painting. In New York he directed the Morris Davidson School of Art, and he had his own art school in Provincetown, Massachusetts, as well.

MARION DAVIES (1897–1961) began her career as a screen actress in 1917. She appeared in films opposite some of the most prominent leading men of her time, but she was perhaps better known for her enduring friendship with William Randolph Hearst.

GEORGE DAVIS (b. 1914) was born in Indiana and educated at the University of Southern California. He was art director of more than two hundred feature films, including *All About Eve* and *The Diary of Anne Frank*, and more than two thousand television segments.

STUART DAVIS (1894–1964), American painter, developed a style characterized by bold abstraction of color and shape based on synthetic cubism; but he drew inspiration and subject matter from the American scene.

WILLEM DE KOONING was born in Rotterdam (1904) and came to America in 1926. Supporting himself first as a house painter, he was a commercial artist until 1935. His first influential one-man show was in 1948.

REUEL DENNEY graduated from Dartmouth at nineteen in 1932. After working for *Time* and *Fortune* (1942–48), he began teaching at the University of Chicago, where he won prizes as teacher and writer.

NIGEL DENNIS was born in England in 1912 and lived both in Africa and Germany as he was growing up. He came to New York City in 1934 for what he thought a "short visit" and remained for fifteen years as a journalist, first as book review editor of *The New Republic* and later as a staff reviewer for *Time* (1940–49).

GENE DERWOOD (1909–1954) a poet and painter, was married to Oscar Williams, the anthologist. Her only volume, *Poems,* was published in 1955.

BABETTE DEUTSCH (1895–1982) published poetry from early years. She graduated from Barnard (B.A. 1917) and got an honorary doctorate from Columbia University in 1946. Her volume of criticism, *Poetry in Our Time* (1952), was much praised.

DENIS DEVLIN (1908–59), Irish poet and translator, left the seminary to take a degree in languages. His poems are often marked by a religious fervor, and his translations of St.-John Perse have been much admired. Between 1940 and 1947 he was in the United States as a member of the Irish foreign service.

HOWARD DEVREE (1890–1966) was born in Michigan and educated at the University of Michigan (B.A., 1913). After serving on the *Kansas City Star* and the *New York Globe,* he joined the *New York Times* in 1926 as an art critic, where he remained until his retirement.

PETER DE VRIES (b. 1910) has been a successful free-lance writer since 1931, when he graduated from Calvin College, Grand Rapids, Michigan. An editor of *Poetry* from 1938 to 1944, he has been on the staff of *The New Yorker* since. He is best known for his stories and novels of suburban life.

JOHN DEWEY (1859–1952) continues to have wide influence. In his later years he taught at Columbia University, where he tried to wed philosophy to the practical affairs of the time.

DAVID DIAMOND, composer, was born in 1915 in Rochester, New York, and educated at the Eastman School. He studied with Roger Sessions and Nadia Boulanger and won many prizes. In addition to symphonies, he composed music for films.

JOHN DOS PASSOS (1896–1970) went to Harvard and from there to World War I as an ambulance driver. His novel *Three Soldiers* (1921) attracted attention; and his trilogy, *USA* (1937), was much talked about. His later work shows a steady drift from the political left to the right.

PAUL DRAPER (b. 1909), a tap dancer, toured the country with Larry Adler, an artist on the harmonica. A writer and teacher as well as a dancer, he was known for his leftist sympathies.

KATHERINE DUNHAM was born in Chicago in 1910, where she established her first school of dance in 1931. It was said that she added to the vocabulary of modern dance form with innovations from her studies of ethnological dance. Her autobiography is called *A Touch of Innocence* (1959).

ALAN DUNN (b. 1900) joined *The New Yorker* in 1926 as writer and cartoonist. His paintings and cartoons have been in many international exhibitions and collections, and he has published such books as *Who's Paying for This Cab?* (1946) and *East of Fifth* (1948).

RICHARD EBERHART (b. 1904) was graduated from Dartmouth in 1926 and had taught there since 1956. Author of many volumes of poetry and winner of many prizes (Pulitzer in 1966), he is said to have "an even temper, a healthy optimism, a muscular good-will."

LEONARD EHRLICH was born in New York City in 1905 and graduated from City College in 1928. His novel about John Brown, *God's Angry Man* (1932), was much praised and he got a Guggenheim Fellowship in 1933.

LOREN EISELEY (1907–77) published his first verse in the *Prairie Schooner* in 1927. He took his Ph.D. in anthropology at the University of Pennsylvania in 1937, where he became provost and professor. His autobiography is *All the Strange Hours: The Excavation of a Life* (1975). Leslie Gerber and Margaret McFadden have written his biography (1983).

DONALD ELDER was an editor for Doubleday in the thirties. In 1956 he wrote a biography of Ring Lardner, and in 1960 he compiled an anthology, *The Good Housekeeping Treasury.*

ALBERT ERSKINE was on the editorial staff of Random House for a number of years and edited successful anthologies with Robert Penn Warren in 1954 and 1955. In 1949 he wrote, "I seriously doubt that the present (whether this year, this decade, or this century) is any harder for [serious] writers than almost any other past period was for their counterparts."

NESUHI ERTEGUN was an early student of jazz. In the forties he recorded some of the best jazz musicians from New Orleans. A "profile" of his

brother, Ahmet Ertegun, by George W. S. Trow, Jr., in *The New Yorker* for May 30 and June 5, 1978, contains information about both men.

STOMP EVANS (1900–1930), jazz saxophonist, played with the King Oliver band.

WALKER EVANS (1903–75) was born in St. Louis and studied at the Sorbonne. He supplied the pictures in *Let Us Now Praise Famous Men* (1941), for which James Agee wrote the text. His photographs have been collected in *American Photographs* (1938), *Many Are Called* (1966) and elsewhere.

CLIFTON FADIMAN (b. 1904) was book editor of *The New Yorker* from 1933 until 1943 and has been on the selection committee of the Book-of-the-Month Club since 1944.

LESLIE FARBER (b. 1912) took his M.D. at Stanford University in 1938. He practiced as a psychiatrist in and around San Francisco from 1946 to 1953 and at the National Institute of Mental Health in Bethesda, Maryland, from 1954 to 1968. He is the author of a number of essays and books, including *The Ways of the Will* (1966).

MANNY FARBER first published movie criticism in *The New Republic* in 1941. Born in Arizona and educated in California, he is prominent in

Common Soldiers (1979, 1984), Janet Richards's memoir. *Negative Space: Manny Farber on the Movies* was published in 1971.

JAMES T. FARRELL (1904–79) was a literary naturalist and much talked of when his novels, chiefly those about Studs Lonigan (1932–35) were published. Born in Chicago, he had radical views but was violently opposed to orthodox Communism.

WILLIAM FAULKNER (1897–1962) published his first novel in 1926 but got little popular attention for twenty years. He received the Nobel Prize for literature in 1950.

KENNETH FEARING (1902–61) went to New York after graduating from the University of Wisconsin. He wrote poetry and novels "in the Whitman tradition." His novel, *The Big Clock* (1946), a "psycho-thriller," was made into a successful movie. *New and Selected Poems* was published in 1956.

LAWRENCE FERLINGHETTI (b. 1920) has been long associated with San Francisco, but he was educated at the University of North Carolina, Columbia University, and took the Doctorat de l'Universite at the Sorbonne in 1951. Though his father had shortened the family name to Ferling, in 1954 Lawrence restored the final syllables.

LESLIE FIEDLER was born in New York in 1917 and associated with the *Partisan Review* group, but he wrote his controversial books on literature and American culture from Missoula, Montana, where he taught at the state university for many years. He has been at Buffalo since 1964.

ALFRED YOUNG FISHER (1902–70) taught at Smith College from 1937 to 1967. He specialized in Shakespeare and Renaissance literature.

ROBERT FITZGERALD (1910–85) is perhaps best known as a translator of Greek and Roman classics, especially Homer. He wrote book reviews for *Time* off and on from 1937 to 1949.

HILDEGARDE FLANNER (b. 1899) published her first volume of poetry in 1920 and has written a number of volumes of verse and some plays since then. She is the sister of Janet Flanner.

JANET FLANNER (1892–1978) was born in Indianapolis. She was the Paris correspondent of *The New Yorker* from its inception in 1925. Her *Paris Journal 1944–1965,* edited by William Shawn, appeared in 1965.

FORD MADOX FORD (1873–1939) was a distinguished editor of *The English Review* (1909) and *transatlantic review* (1924) and a prolific novelist. His series of novels published under the general title *Parade's End* (1924–28) attracted some attention when they appeared, and his reputation revived after 1950 when they were republished.

MICHAEL FRAENKEL (1896–1957) was the model for Boris in Henry Miller's book, *Tropic of Cancer* (1939). His theme in writing and talk was death, a preoccupation that he said was "his way to achieve meaning and vitality in life."

WALDO FRANK (1889–1967), novelist and essayist, was educated at Yale (BA 1911) and lived in Europe and South America for long periods. His work reflects his continuing involvements with Latin America. Admired by other writers, he never achieved popular success.

LLOYD FRANKENBERG (1907–75) edited *Pleasure Dome,* a collection of contemporary English poetry and then prepared an "audible anthology" for Columbia Records in 1947. Married to Loren MacIver, the painter, he was in Provincetown during the summer of 1949.

DANIEL FUCHS (b. 1909) has written novels, short stories, and plays. He was a scriptwriter in Hollywood after 1937, working on such movies as *Panic in the Streets* (1950) and *Love Me or Leave Me* (1955).

J. HARRIS GABLE was the state director of the Federal Writers' Project in Lincoln, Nebraska, after 1937. He was responsible for *Nebraska: A Guide to the Cornhusker State* (1939, 1979) and twenty-two Nebraska Folklore Pamphlets.

ERLE STANLEY GARDNER (1889–1970) wrote mystery stories that sold many millions of copies and influenced all detective fiction. His approach to his work was commercial, not literary, but he has always had critical admirers.

CHRISTIAN GAUSS (1878–1951) was one of the influential teachers of his generation. First a professor of modern languages at Princeton, he was dean of the college from 1925 to 1945.

NORRIS GETTY was the youngest child in a large farming family. He entered the University of Nebraska in 1932, but his undergraduate career was irregular and he took his B.A. only in 1947, majoring in Greek, after serving in the army, first with black troops at Fort Huachuca, Arizona, and then in the South Pacific. Following study at Harvard he taught the classics at Groton School from 1951 until he retired in 1978. He died in Nebraska in 1983.

ROBERT GOLDWATER (1907–73) was an American art critic, scholar, and teacher. At one time he edited the *Magazine of Art.*

IVAN GOLL (1891–1950) published poems in French in *The American Scholar* in 1942. In 1953 a society called American Friends of Yvan Goll was founded at Berkeley by "admirers of the late French poet." Its first publication was an exhaustive bibliography of his work in French and German from 1912 to 1953.

PAUL GOODMAN (1911–72) was a writer of extreme virtuosity whose most famous book was *Growing Up Absurd* (1960). Educated at City College (BA 1931) and the University of Chicago (Ph.D. 1940), he became a psychotherapist who wrote essays, stories, plays, and letters to editors and public figures on city planning and American culture. A man of "startling individuality," he was witty, talkative, lively, and fascinating.

ADOLPH GOTTLIEB (1903–74) studied at the Art Students League with John Sloan and Robert Henri after 1919. In 1923 he was a founding member with Mark Rothko of The Ten, an organization dedicated to abstract painting. His first one-man show was in 1930.

JANE GRABHORN was a member of a distinguished West Coast publishing family. The Grabhorn Press won prizes annually after 1923. The Huntington Library has a considerable collection of material related to it. Jane Grabhorn was associated with

William Roth on the Colt Press in the forties.

JULIAN GREEN, the bilingual novelist, was born in Paris in 1900 of American parents. His autobiography in English, *Memories of Happy Days,* appeared in 1942. He came to the United States after the fall of France to Hitler but returned to Paris after World War II. His *Diary 1929–1957* was published in 1964.

CLEMENT GREENBERG was educated at Syracuse University (B.A. 1933) and came to art criticism after working for the Civil Service. *Partisan Review* published his work in 1938 and he became an editor in 1940. From 1941 to 1949 as art critic on *The Nation,* he championed the New York school of Abstract Expressionism. His essays have been collected in a number of volumes, including *Art and Culture, Critical Essays* (1961).

GRAHAM GREENE (b. 1904) is one of the leading British novelists of his generation. *This Gun for Hire* (1936) and *Brighton Rock* (1938) established his reputation in the United States as a popular novelist; and his later work, *The Power and the Glory* (1940) and *The Heart of the Matter* (1948), got him critical attention.

HORACE GREGORY (1898–1982), poet, critic, translator, was educated at the University of Wisconsin, but he has been associated with New York from the beginning of his career. He won the Bollingen Prize for poetry in 1964, and his translations from Catullus, Ovid, and other classic poets are standard. With his wife, the poet Marya Zaturenska (Pulitzer Prize, 1938), he wrote *A History of American Poetry, 1900–1940,* published in 1946.

MICHAEL GRIEG (b. 1922) was educated at City College, New York, but his career as journalist has been on the West Coast. On the *San Francisco Examiner,* he was successively book critic, writer, and Sunday editor (1959–63). Since 1963 he has been a special contributor to the *San Francisco Chronicle.*

GEORG W. GRODDECK (1866–1934), psychoanalyst, wrote in a letter to Freud, "The distinction between body and mind is only verbal and not essential." His book, *The Unknown Self: A New Psychological Approach to the Problems of Life,* went through four editions in English between 1929 and 1951.

BERNARD HAGGIN (b. 1900) was music critic for *The Nation* from 1936 to 1957. Developing a polemical manner of personal journalism, he published a number of volumes of musical essays.

ALBERT HALPER was born in Chicago in 1904 and, though he went to New York City in 1928, his literary

roots remained in Chicago. He was sometimes identified as a "proletarian writer." His novel, *The Golden Watch* (1953), is semiautobiographical.

ELIZABETH HARDWICK was born in Kentucky in 1916 and educated at the state university (B.A., 1938; M.A., 1939). She has written novels and criticism, publishing in leading journals. A founder of the *New York Review of Books,* she is now one of its editors.

ROBERT D. HARPER grew up in Denver and took his Ph.D. at the University of Chicago. After serving as professor of English and dean of the College of Arts & Sciences at the Municipal University of Omaha, he returned to Colorado, where he now lives.

HUNTINGTON HARTFORD (b. 1911) is a patron of the Lincoln Center for Performing Arts and the New York Cultural Center. He founded the Huntington Hartford Foundation in 1949 and the Huntington Hartford Theater in Hollywood in 1954.

H. R. HAYS (Hoffman Reyhold Hays) was born "of New York stock" in 1904 and educated at Cornell (B.A. 1925) and Columbia. He has translated Spanish-American poetry and the poetry of Bertolt Brecht in addition to writing television dramas and plays.

BEN HECHT (1894–1964) was a literary bohemian in Chicago after World War I but he became a commercial playwright with such successes as *The Front Stage* (1928) and *Twentieth Century* (1932). His autobiography is *A Child of the Century* (1954).

WILLIAM HEICK is a West Coast photographer. In 1955 he collaborated with Weldon Kees on films dealing with the Golden Gate Bridge and California romantic architecture.

ROBERT AND KAY HELM have lived their lives on the West Coast with only occasional tours to the East. A distinguished jazz clarinetist, Bob has also written music, most of it in the New Orleans idiom. In 1984 Santa Rosa, California, held a festival entitled "Bob Helm Day."

CECIL HEMLEY was a founder of Forum 49 with Fritz Bultman and Weldon Kees. In the fall of 1949 he went to the University of Chicago, and in later years he became an editor with Farrar, Straus, & Giroux.

JAMES HENLE was president of Vanguard, the publishing house, from 1926 to 1952. He died in January 1973.

JOSEPHINE HERBST (1897–1969) born in Iowa, was in New York City by 1920; but later she lived in France, Mexico, the Soviet Union, Hitler's Germany, Cuba, Spain and South America. Elinor Langer's biography, *Josephine Herbst: The Story She Could Never Tell* (1984), gives an account of "the turbulent literary life of the 1920s and 30s as it moved from bohemianism to radicalism."

JOHN HERRMANN (1900–1959) was one of the group of writers surrounding Eugene Jolas and *transition,* the international magazine for experimental writers published in Paris, 1927–38. He married Josephine Herbst in 1925.

GRANVILLE HICKS (1901–82) was a leading Communist critic in the thirties and wrote a Marxist interpretation of American literature, *The Great Tradition* (1933). His autobiography, *I Like America* (1938), is a kind of apologia for the Communist critic. He became disillusioned with Communism, and *Part of the Truth* (1965) is a later autobiography.

HILAIRE HILER (1898–1966) was an artist and a writer on art. He published *Why Abstract?* in 1948.

WILDER HOBSON (b. 1906), worked on *Time, Life,* and *Fortune* in the forties, and for a number of years wrote a column on music, primarily jazz, for the *Saturday Review of Literature.*

HANS HOFMANN (1880–1966) studied and taught in Europe before coming to the United States, where he became a citizen in 1941. He was the dean of the Abstract Expressionists and an influential teacher; he gave up teaching in 1958 at age 78. A semiportrait of him appears in Anton Myrer's novel, *Evil under the Sun* (1951). He and his wife, Miz, were regarded with particular affection by both painters and writers.

SIDNEY HOOK was born in New York City in 1902 and has taught at New York University after 1929. Long a student of Marx, he was a leading Anti-Stalinist for many years.

LINDLEY WILLIAMS HUBBELL was born in Connecticut in 1901 and educated by tutors. Long a resident of Kyoto, where since 1953 he has been professor of English literature at Doshisha University, he became a Japanese citizen in 1960, taking the name Hayashi Shuseki. His volumes of poetry have been published by Yale, Knopf, Alan Swallow, and others.

ROBERT HUTCHISON was one of the "advanced writers" of the thirties who were on various art, writer, and theater projects supported by the WPA in both Denver and elsewhere. In 1937 Kees reported that he "had just finished his own adaptation of the *Antigone*," and that he "lived on $5 a week which is doled out to him by a grasping and wealthy uncle."

ALDOUS HUXLEY (1894–1963), British novelist, made his reputation with such books as *Crome Yellow* (1921), *Point Counter Point* (1928), and *Brave New World* (1932). In 1938 he settled in the United States.

CHRISTOPHER ISHERWOOD (1904–86), the novelist and essayist, collaborated with W. H. Auden on several works. He made his home in America for many years.

JOSEPH HENRY JACKSON (b. 1894), an unofficial historian of San Francisco, was literary editor of the *San Francisco Chronicle* and served on the juries for Pulitzer Prizes, Harper Prize novels, O. Henry Memorial Awards, and for other awards.

HENRY JAMES, JR. (1879–1947) was the son of William James, nephew of the novelist. His two-volume biography of Charles W. Eliot (1930) earned him a Pulitzer Prize. He was on the Harvard Board of Overseers, and he was a trustee of the New York Public Library. He also served on the boards of the Carnegie Corporation, the Rockefeller Institute of Medical Research, and other philanthropic organizations.

RANDALL JARRELL (1914–65), poet, critic and novelist, was born in Tennessee and taught at Kenyon College with John Crowe Ransom. In his volume of poems *Little Friend, Little Friend* (1945), he makes use of his wartime experience, and his literary essays, *Poetry and the Age* (1953), are highly regarded for their common sense. His satirical novel, *Pictures from an Institution* (1954), a *roman à clef*, concerns the faculty of a progressive women's college.

EUGENE JOFFE published two stories in *Contact,* the little magazine that William Carlos Williams edited in 1932.

RICHARD JOHNS founded and edited *Pagany: A Native Quarterly* in 1930 when he was 21, with the encouragement of William Carlos Williams. An account of the periodical can be found in *A Return to Pagany,* edited by Stephen Halpert with Richard Johns (1969).

MAURICE JOHNSON (1913–78) graduated from the University of Nebraska (B.A., 1935), where he was an associate editor of *Prairie Schooner.* He took his Ph.D. at Columbia University (1949). After teaching at the Carnegie Institute of Technology and at Syracuse, he went to the University of Pennsylvania in 1950, where he remained until his death. His first book was called *Sin of Wit: Jonathan Swift as a Poet* (1950), and his second was *Fielding's Art of Fiction* (1961).

EUGENE JOLAS (1894–1952) was a founder and editor (with Elliot Paul) of the international journal *transition,* published in Paris (1927–38). Portions of Joyce's *Finnegans Wake* first appeared in these pages.

PAULINE KAEL was born in California in 1919 and educated at Berkeley (1936–40). She managed a film theater in Berkeley in the forties and appeared as movie critic on the radio. After 1953 she became a free-lance writer with an encyclopedic knowledge of films and film history. Movie critic on *The New Yorker* since 1968, she has a formidable following.

ALFRED KANTOROWITZ published two pieces of fiction in John Lehman's British literary magazine, *New Writing,* in 1936 and 1937, and in this country he published expository prose in *Direction,* an "independent liberal monthly . . . seeking to present a true picture of the social scene."

ALFRED KAZIN, born in New York City in 1915, has written about his urban youth in *A Walker in the City* (1951), and his young manhood in *Starting Out in the Thirties* (1965). His study of American prose, *On Native Grounds* (1942), surveys the moral history of the United States since 1880.

HARRY KEMP (1883–?) wrote poems, plays, and several novels. In 1939 he brought out a collection of essays in collaboration with Laura Riding, Robert Graves, and Alan Hodges, entitled *The Left Heresy in*

Literature and Life. Some of his poems and songs were published by Provincetown Publishers in 1946 and 1952.

PAUL KLEE (1879–1940) was one of the most influential painters of his generation. Of Swiss birth, for ten years he was with the Bauhaus group (1921–31); but he invented his own pictorial methods of representing "the roots of things and their place in the cosmic scheme."

KARL KNATHS (1891–1971) was active in Provincetown from 1919 until his death. Associated with the Abstract Expressionists in the forties, he won many prizes and awards and in 1955 was elected to the National Institute of Arts and Letters.

SAMUEL M. KOOTZ set out to study law at the University of Virginia; but becoming interested in painting, especially the International School, he started writing about it in 1929. In 1945 he opened his first New York gallery. On his roster were young American painters: Robert Motherwell, William Baziotes, Byron Browne, and Carl Holz. Only two of his painters were not American.

LEON KROLL (b. 1884) studied at the Art Students League, the National Academy of Design, and in Paris. His paintings hang in all the major galleries of this country and in many galleries abroad. Winner of more than two

dozen prizes, he painted the murals for the Justice Building in Washington, D.C.

LOUIS KRONENBERGER (1904–80) was drama critic for *Time* (1938–62) and wrote books on manners and tastes. Anthologist and critic, he also wrote histories and fiction.

STANLEY KUNITZ (b. 1905) has won many prizes for poetry, including the Pulitzer in 1958. A graduate of Harvard (summa cum laude, 1926), he has been editor of reference books for many years, sometimes under his own name but sometimes under the pseudonym, Dilly Tante.

ERLING LARSEN, born in Iowa in 1909, was educated at St. Olaf College (B.A., 1930) and the University of Iowa (M.A., 1932). A poet, he was also a theater manager at Northfield, Minnesota, from 1932 to 1947 and a farmer. He taught literature at Carleton College from 1956 to 1974.

ROBERT LASCH graduated from the University of Nebraska (B.A., 1928) and studied at Oxford University as a Rhodes Scholar (1928–30). As an undergraduate he served as an associate editor on *Prairie Schooner*. In 1966 he won a Pulitzer Prize for "distinguished editorial writing" on the *St. Louis Post-Dispatch*.

M. J. LASKY was born in New York City in 1920. Before his military service, he was literary editor of *The*

New Leader (1942–43), but he has been a foreign correspondent and editor of European journals, including the London-based *Encounter* since the end of World War II.

JAMES LAUGHLIN IV (b. 1914) established New Directions in the Depression years to give advanced writers a place to be published. He has had an important and generous place in midcentury American writing.

D. H. LAWRENCE (1885–1930), novelist and poet, published *Sons and Lovers* in 1913, and many other novels subsequently. Both he and they were extremely controversial, and though he is generally regarded as a modern classic now, he remains a figure about whom discussion continues to rage.

FRIEDA LAWRENCE (1879–1956) eloped with D. H. Lawrence in 1912 and married him in 1914, when her divorce was final. They traveled widely and lived in many places, including New Mexico.

MAX LERNER was born in 1902. Columnist and commentator on national and world affairs, he is professor emeritus of world politics and American civilization at Brandeis University.

HARRY LEVIN (b. 1912) was on the faculty at Harvard after 1939. His first book on James Joyce was published in 1941, but he wrote books on many writers in many languages during his long career.

GEORGE LEWIS (1900–1968) was a jazz clarinetist in the New Orleans style. In his early years he played with Buddy Petit, Kid Ory, and other leading jazz musicians; and in the fifties he made a number of recordings.

PAUL LINGLE, jazz pianist, was born in Denver (1902), the son of a cornetist, and was on the Chautauqua Circuit as early as 1915. Much interested in Scott Joplin and other ragtime musicians, especially Jelly Roll Morton, he also played for Al Jolson in *Sonny Boy* and *Mammy,* and by the forties had become a legend. In 1952 he moved to Honolulu where he directed his own jazz band.

HARRY LINK, jazz composer, wrote tunes for lyrics by Billy Rose in 1929 and collaborated with Bert Lown, Chauncy Gray, and others in the thirties. In 1936 he composed the music for "These Foolish Things," which was an immediate and continuing success.

FREDERICK LONSDALE (1881–1954) was a dramatist who wrote "highly varnished comedy about upper class sin," according to Brooks Atkinson; according to Walter Kerr he wrote "polished flippantry," and was "witty about trifles and iconoclastic about everything else." His most famous plays were probably *The Last of Mrs. Cheyney* (1925) and *On Approval* (1927).

ROBERT LOWELL (1917–77) studied at St. Marks School and Harvard, but went then to Kenyon College to work with John Crowe Ransom. He won a Pulitzer Prize with his second volume of verse, *Lord Weary's Castle* (1946). *Life Studies* (1959) consists of semiautobiographical prose and poetry.

MALCOLM LOWRY (1909–57) is a cult figure. His novel, *Under the Volcano* (1947), has been called a "work of genius," ranking with the fiction of James Joyce. This symbolic and semi-hallucinatory work deals with an alcoholic British consul in Mexico where Lowry lived after 1939.

ROBERT LOWRY was born in Ohio in 1919. He taught himself printing in order to publish The Little Man books in Cincinnati: "nobody had seen the likes before." These occasional volumes introduced promising and unusual writers. After World War II, he became production manager for New Directions.

MABEL DODGE LUHAN (1879–1962) was a leader in liberal intellectual and aesthetic movements in Italy, New York, and after 1918 in Taos, New Mexico. Her autobiography, *Intimate Memories*, comprises four volumes (1933–37).

DOUGLAS MACAGY (b. 1913) was director of the California School of Fine Arts in San Francisco (1945–50) and brought Clyfford Still there. He joined the Museum of Modern Art in New York City in the early fifties and became director of the Hirshhorn Museum and Sculpture Garden, Washington, D.C., in 1972.

JERMAYNE MACAGY received a Ph.D. from Western Reserve University in art history and joined The California Palace of the Legion of Honor in 1941. She died of diabetes at age fifty-five. An account of her is contained in Janet Richards's memoirs, *Common Soldiers* (1979, 1984). She was married to Douglas MacAgy.

ROBERT McALMON (1895–1956) was an expatriate publisher in the twenties. He brought out Hemingway's first books (*Three Stories and Ten Poems*, 1923; and *in our time*, 1923) and works by James Joyce, Gertrude Stein and all "the crowd." His autobiography, *McAlmon and the Lost Generation*, is a self-portrait created from fragments by Robert E. Knoll (1962, 1976).

MARY McCARTHY was born in Seattle in 1912 and reared by relatives, about whom she wrote in *Memories of a Catholic Girlhood* (1957). She wrote about some of her Vassar classmates in her novel *The Company She Keeps* (1942) and, after acting as drama critic for *Partisan Review*, wrote a novel *The Oasis* (1949) in which various New York intellectuals can be identified.

ROBERT McCHESNEY, the painter, was born in Missouri in 1913 but has lived in California most of his productive life. He taught at California State University, Hayward, for many years, and the San Francisco Art Institute had a retrospective show of his work in 1974.

CARSON McCULLERS (1917–67) was born in Georgia. Her first novel, *The Heart Is a Lonely Hunter* (1940), created some stir; and her second, *Reflections in a Golden Eye* (1941), dealing with violence in a southern army camp, had a certain topical interest. *The Member of the Wedding* (1946) was dramatized with great success in 1950.

HUGH MacDIARMID (C. M. Grieve) (1892–1978) was an important literary figure in Scotland in the generation of Pound and Eliot. Inspiring a literary renaissance, he was said to be the most powerful intellectual and emotional fertilizing force Scotland has known since the death of Burns. Much of his poetry is in the Scottish idiom.

DWIGHT MacDONALD (1906–83) graduated from Yale University (B.A. 1928) and worked for *Fortune* from 1929 to 1936. An editor of *Partisan Review* from 1938 until 1943, he edited his own periodical, *Politics,* for five years thereafter. He joined the staff of *The New Yorker* in 1951. He called himself a "conservative anarchist" and at various times was a socialist, a Marxist, and a revolutionary. It has been said that he was "perhaps the wittiest and liveliest polemicist on the American scene." He published *Memoirs of a Revolutionist* in 1957.

VINCENT McHUGH (b. 1904) began his first novel at twenty; in the thirties he was on the Federal Writers' Project in New York City. He wrote book reviews for *The New Yorker* until 1943, when he went to the West Coast. His novel, *I Am Thinking of My Darling* (1943), was celebrated in its day.

MAVIS McINTOSH was Weldon Kees's literary agent from 1939 to 1942 and attempted without success to get his fiction published by New York houses.

LOREN McIVER, painter, was born in New York in 1909 and studied at the Art Students League. Her pictures hang in the Whitney Gallery, the Metropolitan Museum of Art, the Museum of Modern Art, the Corcoran

Gallery in Washington, D.C., and other leading galleries. She is a member of the National Institute of Arts and Letters.

WILLARD MAAS (1911–71) was an American poet and pioneer filmmaker. His papers are in the archives at the University of Texas.

NORMAN MAILER (b. 1923) first came to national attention with *The Naked and the Dead* (1948), a novel of the war in the South Pacific. Later novels are *Barbary Shore* (1951) and *The Deer Park* (1955), a satire of motion picture people.

JEAN MALAQUAIS was born in Warsaw in 1908. He first wrote in Polish, but his novels were in French, earning him distinguished French prizes. After being a prisoner of the Germans during the war, he went to Mexico and in 1952 became an American citizen.

KLAUS MANN (1906–49) wrote plays and novels in German in the thirties, but he left Germany in 1933 to become an American citizen in 1943. *The Turning Point* (1942) is autobiographical. After the war he founded and edited *Decision,* a journal of opinion and criticism. Thomas Mann was his father, and he wrote several books with his sister, Erika Mann.

WILLIAM MARCH, (William Edward March Campbell) (1893–1954)

served in the marines in World War I, after which he was one of the organizers of the Waterman Steamship Corporation, the largest steamship company in the world. He lived in New York City from 1937 to 1947. His novels and short stories deal with smalltown life in the South. *The Bad Seed* (1954), about an eight-year-old murderess, was dramatized by Maxwell Anderson.

BORIS MARGO, painter and printmaker, began experimenting with graphics in 1930, and was well known by 1947 for his nonrepresentational pictures, which often required as many as fifteen plates for completion. "Today the artist creates his own symbols, his own mythology," he said in 1947.

LEONORE G. MARSHALL (1897–1971) published volumes of verse, but she was active also in anti-war groups, including the Committee for Nuclear Responsibility (1971).

MARGARET MARSHALL (1900?–1974) was literary editor of *The Nation* in the forties. After twenty-four years on the liberal weekly, in 1951 she was released when, in the opinion of many, *The Nation* became an apologist for the Soviet Union.

MATTA (Roberto Sebastian Antonio Matta Echaurren) was born in Chile in 1911 of a Spanish family. After studying architecture in Paris in Le

Corbusier's office, he came to America in 1939. According to J. T. Soby in 1947, Matta was the "last important painter of the surrealist movement."

T. S. MATTHEWS was born in Cincinnati in 1901 and educated at Princeton (B.A., 1922) and Oxford. He worked for *The New Republic* from 1925 to 1929, when he joined *Time*. He was its managing editor from 1943 to 1950. His autobiography is *O My America!* (1962).

FRANCIS O. MATTHIESSEN (1902–50) was educated at Yale (B.A. 1923) and became a professor at Harvard. Particularly interested in the art and cultural history of America, his study, *American Renaissance* (1941), has become a classic.

ELSA MAXWELL (1883–1963) was a professional party-giver and a "personality" in café society.

EDNA ST. VINCENT MILLAY (1892–1950) was the most famous poet of her time. Living in Greenwich Village in its "Golden Age" of bohemianism, she was the creator of her own legend.

HENRY MILLER (1891–1980) decided to make writing his career in 1924, after what he described as a shiftless life of vagabondage. In 1930 he went to Paris, where he remained for nine years. His semiautobiographical novel, *Tropic of Cancer* (1931), became no-

torious for its sexual frankness and scatology. Returning to the United States in 1940, he reported what he found in *The Air Conditioned Nightmare* (1945). After 1944 he made his home in Big Sur, California.

ARTHUR MIZENER (b. 1907) was educated at the Hill School, Princeton and Harvard, and was a professor at Cornell University after 1951. His biography of F. Scott Fitzgerald, *The Far Side of Paradise* (1951), is standard.

MARIANNE MOORE (1887–1972) was educated at Bryn Mawr in 1909 and lived in New York most of her life. Her first volume of poetry appeared in 1921, a second in 1924. Her *Collected Poems* (1951) won the Pulitzer Prize. Her total oeuvre consisted of only 120 poems and her *Complete Poems* (1967) occupies only 242 pages.

MERRILL MOORE (1903–57) was one of the Fugitive group of poets at Vanderbilt (1922–25). Born in Tennessee, the son of the poet and novelist, J. T. Moore, Merrill produced a prodigious body of poetry, mostly sonnets. He was a practicing psychiatrist in Boston for many years.

JELLY ROLL MORTON (Ferdinand Joseph) (1885–1941), jazz pianist, combo leader, and composer, started his musical career playing in the sporting houses of New Orleans. He published his jazz composition, *Jelly Roll Blues* (1917), in Chicago and recorded for Victor (1926–30). Alan Lomax recorded Morton for the Archives of the Library of Congress (1939–40).

HOWARD MOSS has been poetry editor of *The New Yorker* since 1948. Born in 1922, he has written and edited some twenty volumes of verse, children's fiction, and satire.

ROBERT MOTHERWELL, born in Aberdeen, Washington, in 1915, was educated at Stanford, Harvard, and Columbia. An important Abstract Expressionist painter, he has had a lifelong interest in philosophy and psychoanalytic theory. He has written extensively on aesthetics and the history of art.

GORHAM MUNSON (1896–1969) edited *Secession* (1922–24), one of the little magazines, but after 1932 he became more concerned with economic than with literary journalism and wrote scores of articles on social credit. By 1947 he had become an editor with Prentice-Hall, and later he was vice president and editor of Hermitage House.

TURK MURPHY (Melvin Murphy) was born in California in 1915 and has lived most of his life there. With Lu Watters he helped revive an interest in traditional jazz. Trombonist, composer, and band leader, he has been an outspoken opponent of the conventional neo-Dixieland jazz of the Eddie Condon variety.

ANTON MYRER was born in Massachusetts in 1922 and educated at the Boston Latin School and Harvard. In the Pacific with the Marine Corps in World War II, his second book, *The Big War* (1956), gives a vivid account of that experience. His first novel, *Evil Under the Sun* (1951), is laid in a Cape Cod art colony like Provincetown.

GILBERT NEIMAN (b. 1912) was a practicing poet when Kees knew him in Denver. Upon Kees's suggestion, Jay Laughlin published his translation of Lorca's *Blood Wedding* in 1939. In 1959 he took his Ph.D. and has taught creative writing and romance languages at Clarion State College, Clarion, Pennsylvania, since 1963.

HOWARD NEMEROV was born in New York in 1920. Educated at Harvard (1941), he taught at Bennington College and then went to Washington University in St. Louis, where he has remained. He has won many prizes for poetry, but he has also written novels and critical essays.

EDWARD NEWHOUSE (b. 1911) is a writer of novels and short stories. He was on *The New Yorker* after 1936.

His books include *You Can't Sleep Here* (1934), *Anything Can Happen* (1941), and *The Iron Chain* (1946).

FRANKIE (WILLIAM FRANK) NEWTON (1906–54) had his own band at Cafe Society in 1939 and played in a variety of Harlem clubs. He was one of the foremost swing trumpet players of his generation.

LUTHER NICHOLS was a San Francisco journalist and a stringer for the *New York Times* in the fifties. With Michael Grieg, Adrian Wilson, and others, he was part of a literary-artistic group prominent in the Bay Area just before the Beat Generation.

RED NICHOLS, cornetist, was born in Utah in 1905, the son of a professor of music. As a bandleader, he introduced many gifted musicians to a wider public. They included Jimmy Dorsey, Joe Venuti, Benny Goodman, and Glenn Miller.

JOHN FREDERICK NIMS was born in Michigan in 1913. He published verse in *Poetry* before he was eighteen. Teaching first at Notre Dame and later at the University of Illinois, he has been on the staff of *Poetry* since 1945 and is now its editor.

EDWARD J. O'BRIEN (1890–1941) was born in Boston and educated at Boston College and Harvard. While a reporter on the *Boston Transcript* he devised a method of evaluating short stories and began publishing annual collections of *Best American Short Stories* in 1915. Not a writer himself, he seldom frequented literary or bohemian circles.

BARNEY OLDFIELD (b. 1909), called "King of PR" by Charles Kuralt recently, studied at the University of Nebraska and served as entertainment editor of the *Lincoln State Journal* while an undergraduate in 1936 and 1937.

KID (EDWARD) ORY, trombonist, leader and composer, was born in Louisiana in 1886. In 1911 he brought his own band to New Orleans. Mutt Carey, King Oliver, and Louis Armstrong held the trumpet chair successively in his band, in that order; but others, almost as famous, also played with him. In 1919 he went to California and in 1924 to Chicago. He toured Europe in 1956 and 1959.

LOUELLA O. PARSONS (1881?–1972), gossip columnist, was a power in the Hollywood of her day.

KENNETH PATCHEN (1911–72), born in Ohio, was said to be among the Leftist poets in the thirties. He published six volumes of verse in the forties, plus a surrealist allegory and three novels. Raymond Nelson has written *Kenneth Patchen and American Mysticism* (1984).

NORMAN HOLMES PEARSON
(1909–75) spent his academic career
at Yale University. He collected manuscripts and memorabilia of twentieth-
century writers and served as their literary adviser.

MAXWELL PERKINS (1884–1947),
the editor, was associated with Scrib-
ners, where he advised Hemingway,
Fitzgerald, Thomas Wolfe and a
number of other celebrated writers.
John Hall Wheelock published *Editor
to Author: The Letters of Maxwell
Perkins* in 1950, and Andrew S. Berg
has written a biography, *Max Perkins: Editor of Genius* (1978).

KAPPO PHELAN was the drama critic on *Commonweal* from 1946 to
1950.

WILLIAM PHILLIPS was one of the
founding editors of *Partisan Review*
with Philip Rahv (1934), and remained at the center of the New York
Intellectuals. William Barrett reported
that his apartment during the late
1940s was a center for whatever currents were alive at the time.

WILLIAM PLOMER (1903–73), English novelist, was born in Africa, educated at Rugby, and lived in Japan
and Greece for extended periods. His
reputation rests on his work of comparative youth. In 1943 he published
an autobiographical volume, *Double
Lives*.

NORMAN PODHORETZ (b. 1930)
turned *Commentary* into one of the
two or three most influential journals
of opinion then being published. A
younger member of the New York Intellectuals, he has moved steadily to
the political right. *Making It* (1967)
is his autobiographical account of the
New York literary scene.

LOU POLLACK (1921–70) had a
gallery, the Peridot, at 6 East 12th
Street in the late forties. In addition
to Weldon Kees, he showed Louise
Bourgeois, Willem de Kooning,
Seymour Franks, Hans Hofmann, Reginald Pollack, Melville Price, Bradley
Tomlin, Arthur Drexler, and other
"advanced" artists. The Peridot continued until 1970.

JACKSON POLLOCK (1912–56)
studied with Thomas Hart Benton at
the Art Students League (1930–32)
and was part of the WPA Federal Art
Project from 1935 to 1943. In 1947
he developed a technique of dripping
and splattering that was enormously
influential. He was a leader among
the Abstract Expressionist painters in
the New York school.

KATHERINE ANNE PORTER (1890–
1980) wrote short stories, novellas,
and one novel. Her volume, *Flower-
ing Judas* (1930), won her enormous
critical acclaim. Her only novel is
Ship of Fools (1962).

WILLY POSTER was a New York eccentric who periodically practiced journalism. Born William Shakespeare Bernstein, brother of Herbert Spencer Bernstein, he was the son of a self-made dealer in real estate and lived a mysterious nighttime life, appearing and disappearing from various social circles. An account of him is contained in Janet Richards, *Common Soldiers* (1979, 1984).

EZRA POUND (1885–1972) was incarcerated in St. Elizabeth's Hospital, Washington D.C., in 1945 as mentally unfit to stand trial for treason because he had broadcast for the Fascists during the war. He was released in 1958, whereupon he returned to Italy.

LOUISE POUND (1872–1958) was internationally famous among academicians for her work on the origins of the ballad and her study of American speech. She spent her entire career at the University of Nebraska. In 1955 she was elected the first woman president of the Modern Language Association. Roscoe Pound, the jurist, was her brother; she was not related to Ezra Pound.

DAWN POWELL (1897–1965) wrote novels and short stories and published in the leading periodicals of the forties and fifties. She lived in Greenwich Village, near Washington Square, and worked on television scripts and Broadway musicals and plays for many years.

DICK POWELL (1904–63), screen actor, began in such musicals as *Gold Diggers of 1933* but turned later to dramatic roles in movies like *The Bad and the Beautiful* (1952).

JOSEPHINE PRÉMICE was a Haitian singer and dancer. It was said that "The carnival and voodoo songs which form the basis of her performance combine the sophistication and naïveté which characterize Prémice herself."

FREDERICK PROKOSCH (b. 1908), poet, was the son of a distinguished professor of linguistics, and took his Ph.D. at the University of Pennsylvania in 1933. He spent years in Europe, first with the Office of War Information in Stockholm (1942–45) and later in Rome (1947–53). He is said to have thought that "politics had done American writing vast harm during the last decade" (1942).

WALTER QUIRT (1902–68) was born in Michigan and educated in Milwaukee. His painting was originally in a realistic style, but it became surrealistic and then increasingly abstract.

PHILIP RAHV (1908–78) was born Ivan Greenberg in Russia but changed his name to Rahv (Rabbi) when he became a Communist in the United

States. Cofounder (with William Phillips) of *Partisan Review* (1934) during what in retrospect was "a golden age of criticism," he was its editor until 1970. He returned to the Marxist-Leninism of his youth toward the end of his life. In 1978 Arabel J. Porter and Andrew J. Dvosin edited his *Essays on Literature and Politics 1932–1972.*

JOHN CROWE RANSOM (1898–1964) taught at Kenyon College after 1937. His book, *The New Criticism* (1941), gave a name to a school of critics.

MAN RAY (1890–1976) as a painter was associated with the Dadaists but is better known for his remarkable photographs. His book, *Self Portrait,* appeared in 1963.

KENNETH REXROTH, the poet, was born in Indiana in 1905 and supported himself from the age of thirteen. After hoboing around the country, he came to San Francisco in 1927, where he was active in the John Reed Club and other left-wing groups. Entirely self-educated, he claims to have been one of the first abstract painters in America. An account of his personality is contained in Janet Richards, *Common Soldiers* (1979, 1984).

PHILIP BLAIR RICE (1904–56) was a graduate of the University of Illinois (B.A., 1925) and a Rhodes Scholar at Oxford (1925–28). After 1937 he taught at Kenyon College in Ohio, and was an editor of the *Kenyon Review* from 1938 to 1950. A professional philosopher, he was a celebrated teacher.

CHARLES RICHARDS, a Texan, has lived in San Francisco for many years. A student and practitioner of jazz, he has been associated with all the literary and artistic movements in the Bay Area.

JANET RICHARDS (1915–85) grew up in San Francisco but lived in Manhattan in the forties as one of the New York Intellectuals. She was then married to Manny Farber. She and her second husband, Charles Richards, lived in San Francisco after 1950. She was a painter, novelist, and essayist, but her work has been almost totally neglected. Her memoirs, *Common Soldiers: A Self-Portrait and Other Portraits* (1979, 1984), gives a vivid picture of the writers' world on both coasts across the middle of this century.

LAURA RIDING (b. 1901) is primarily a poet, but she has written a number of volumes of criticism and fiction as well, sometimes collaborating with Robert Graves.

PAUL ROBESON (1898–1976), American singer and actor, played such roles as Emperor Jones in Eugene O'Neill's play and Othello in the

Shakespeare play. He became a controversial figure because of his leftist political affiliations.

BOARDMAN ROBINSON (1876–1952) was born in England, educated on the continent, and became the director of the Colorado Springs Fine Arts Center (1930–47). He was an instructor in the Art Students League from 1918 to 1929 and at various times was on the staff of *The New Masses, Harpers Weekly,* and *Outlook* (London).

EDOUARD RODITI (b. 1910) wrote poetry and history and translated writings of André Breton (1946), Albert Memmi (1956), and miscellaneous prose pieces by Pablo Picasso.

THEODORE ROETHKE (1908–63), poet, taught at the University of Washington after 1947. His career began with *Open House* (1941). His work brought him many prizes: the Pulitzer (1953), the Bollingen (1958), and others.

HAROLD ROSENBERG was born in Brooklyn in 1906 and educated at City College (1923–24) and St. Lawrence University (1927). He was the national art editor for the WPA American Guide Series (1938–42) and worked for the Office of War Information during World War II. Art critic on *The New Yorker* after 1967,

he has written numerous books on twentieth-century art.

ISAAC ROSENFELD (1918–56) was a member of the staff of *The New Republic* in the forties and wrote reviews for it and other leading periodicals. In 1962 Theodore Solotaroff edited *An Age of Enormity: Life and Writings in the Forties and Fifties,* with a foreword by Saul Bellow, a collection of his essays and reviews.

HARRY ROSKELENKO, poet, was on the Federal Writers' Project in New York City in the thirties, with Lionel Abel, Harold Rosenberg, and others of the *Partisan Review* circle. His autobiography is *When I Was Last on Cherry Street* (1965).

JAMES ROSS published short fiction in the *Partisan Review* in 1940 and in the *Sewanee Review* in 1945.

WILLIAM ROTH established the Colt Press in San Francisco in 1938 and published a distinguished list of limited editions. Among his writers were George R. Stewart, Edmund Wilson, Henry Miller, Janet Lewis, Paul Goodman, J. V. Cunningham, Philip Rahv, and Weldon Kees. Jane Grabhorn was associated with him on the Colt Press.

MARK ROTHKO (1903–70) was born in Russia and came to Portland, Oregon, in 1913. After study at Yale

University (1921–23) and at the Art Students League with Max Weber, he had a one-man show in 1933. His painting became increasingly abstract after 1940, and by 1950 he had developed a unique style of abstract expressionism.

JUDITH ROTHSCHILD, painter and collage artist, was born in New York and studied at Wellesley College, the Cranbrook Academy, the Art Students League, and with Hans Hofmann. In 1946 she became a member of American Abstract Artists. Since 1945 she has had more than thirty one-man shows, both here and abroad.

RICHARD ROVERE (1915–79) contributed a column of political news and comment to *The New Yorker* from 1944 to 1979. In 1976 he published *Arrivals and Departures: A Journalist's Memoirs.*

JURGEN RUESCH, M.D. (b. 1909) is a Swiss psychiatrist, active on the West Coast for the better part of his working life. In addition to the book that he wrote with Weldon Kees, *Nonverbal Communication: Notes on the Visual Perception of Human Relations* (1956), he has written several other books about psychiatric aspects of communications.

MURIEL RUKEYSER (b. 1913), poet, was educated at Vassar. She is widely known as a campaigner for civil liber-

ties. Her poetry has received a number of major prizes.

JOE RUSHTON played in Red Nichols's band in the early fifties. Weldon Kees wrote to Norris Getty on November 11, 1950, that Rushton was "probably as good a white hornblower [as is] extant . . . Rushton, by the way, is a Yale man, the black sheep of a 'good' family, who bears a spookily-close resemblance to Chester Morris; he's enormously witty."

MARI SANDOZ (1896–1966) first published *Old Jules,* a biography of her father, in 1935 and followed it with a number of volumes dealing with the high plains. Helen Winter Stauffer has written her biography: *Mari Sandoz: Story Catcher of the Plains* (1981).

WINTHROP SARGEANT (b. 1903) has been a contributing editor and music critic on *The New Yorker* since 1950. He wrote for *Time* and *Life* between 1937 and 1950, and before that played in a number of symphony orchestras, including the New York Philharmonic (1928–30).

WILLIAM SAROYAN (1908–81) wrote impressionistic, rhapsodic stories. In 1939 he rejected a Pulitzer Prize offered for his play, *The Time of Your Life.*

MEYER SCHAPIRO was born in Russia in 1904 but came to the United States at an early age. Educated entirely at Columbia University in New York, he has been a professor of art history and criticism there since 1928.

BUDD SCHULBERG (b. 1914) has written novels, short stories, and plays; and he was a screenwriter in Hollywood from 1936 to 1939. His books include *What Makes Sammy Run?* (1941), *The Harder They Fall* (1947) and *The Disenchanted* (1950).

DELMORE SCHWARTZ (1913–66), the poet, attracted considerable attention with his brilliant first fiction, *In Dreams Begin Responsibilities* (1938). He was an editor on *Partisan Review* from 1943 to 1955, and he taught at Harvard from 1940 to 1947. He is the subject of a novel by Saul Bellow, *Humboldt's Gift* (1975), and of a biography by James Atlas (1977).

WINFIELD TOWNLEY SCOTT (1910–68) was born in Massachusetts and stayed close to home all his life. After graduating from Brown University (1931), he began working on the Providence (R.I.) *Journal* as its literary editor, resigning in 1951. Rudolph Umland has said that his volume of verse, *Elegy for Robinson* (1936), suggested the name "Robinson" to Weldon Kees for his poems. Scott Donaldson has written a biography of him (1972).

MICHAEL SEIDE published some stories in literary quarterlies before

World War II. His collection, *The Common Thread: A Book of Stories* (1944) was reissued in 1975 and his novel, *The Common Wilderness,* appeared in 1982.

BEN SHAHN (1898–1969), American painter, developed a highly personal fusion of Expressionism and Cubism. His pictures were often concerned with social justice.

KARL SHAPIRO was born in Baltimore, Maryland (1913), and drafted into the army in 1941. While he was in Australia and New Guinea, *Person, Place and Thing* (1942) and *V-Letter and Other Poems* (1944) were published, and he won a Pulitzer Prize for the latter. In 1950 he became editor of *Poetry.*

IRWIN SHAW (b. 1913) wrote for the radio and became drama critic for *The New Republic* in 1934. *The Gentle People* (1939) was a successful play, and his novel *The Young Lions* (1948) was much talked about. His short stories were collected in several volumes.

LEE SIMS (1898–1966) was a piano stylist of the twenties and thirties. He published books of advanced piano arrangements and through them and his performances on radio had a wide influence on popular music.

AGNES SMEDLEY (1894–1950) was an American radical journalist. First a

Socialist, then a Communist, she participated in the Chinese revolution and learned to speak and write Chinese. After 1929 she attempted to "interpret Chinese communism to the world." She died in Oxford, England.

A. J. M. SMITH, born in 1902, is a leading Canadian poet, critic, and editor. Since 1929 he has taught in the United States, most recently at Michigan State University.

DALE AND MARGARET SMITH were part of the Wimberly group in Lincoln during the thirties. Dale was on the Federal Writers' Project, and Margaret was a librarian. In 1950 they moved to Oakland, California, where for a number of years they owned a bookstore.

HASSEL W. SMITH, JR., was born in Michigan in 1915. He studied at Northwestern University and the California School of Fine Arts. He was active on the West Coast with retrospective shows of his paintings in Pasadena in 1961, San Francisco in 1964, and in Santa Barbara in 1969, but he has lived in Britain since 1966, most recently in Bristol.

OLIVER SMITH (b. 1918) has been a prolific and imaginative scenic designer for the stage and screen. Among his stage shows were *Pal Joey,* and *West Side Story,* and among his movies was *Oklahoma! The New*

Yorker published a profile of him in its issue of September 10, 1955.

ROBERT PAUL SMITH (1915–77) wrote continuity for the radio, working for the Columbia Broadcasting System after 1936. Author of many novels, plays, and collections, he wrote *The Tender Trap* with Max Shulman in 1955.

JAMES THRALL SOBY (1906–79), art critic, grew up in Hartford, Connecticut, and was educated at Williams College and in the Paris of the twenties. Associated with the Museum of Modern Art after 1942 and the *Saturday Review of Literature* after 1946, he published books on twentieth-century painters and painting.

HYDE SOLOMON (b. 1911) studied at Columbia University with Meyer Schapiro and was exhibited at the Peridot Gallery in 1954, 1955, and 1956. In recent years he has lived in New Mexico.

HERBERT SOLOW (1903–64) was educated at Columbia University (B.A., 1924; B. Litt., 1925). After serving as assistant to the president of the New School for Social Research from 1940 to 1943, he became a contributing editor on *Time* and then editor of *Fortune* (1945).

STEPHEN SPENDER (b. 1909) was one of the Auden group in the thirties. He was an editor on *Horizon* until 1941 and after 1953 edited *Encounter*. An autobiographical volume, *World Within World*, appeared in 1951.

JEAN STAFFORD (1915–79) took years to finish her first novel, *Boston Adventure* (1944), which received great praise. Born in California, she took an M.A. at the University of Colorado (1936).

DONALD STAUFFER (1902–52) studied at Princeton University and became a Rhodes Scholar before returning as a professor to his alma mater. An inspired lecturer and author of books on a number of subjects, he liked to think of himself as a "Renaissance man."

ORIN STEPANEK was educated at the University of Nebraska, Lincoln, and at Harvard University. He returned to Nebraska, where he taught comparative literature at the University until his death in 1955. He was among the vivid personalities of his academic generation.

JAMES STERN an English novelist and translator (primarily from German), wrote for the *New York Times, The New Republic,* and *Partisan Review,* as well as for British periodicals.

WALLACE STEVENS (1879–1955) published the bulk of his poetry after he was fifty; he made a career in business as a vice-president of an insurance company. His letters were edited in 1966 by his daughter, Holly Stevens, who has written *Souvenirs and Prophecies: The Young Wallace Stevens* (1976).

CLYFFORD STILL, born in North Dakota in 1904, was educated in Washington and worked in the Bay Area. He is usually classified among the Abstract Expressionists though he was somewhat separated from the New York group.

FRANK SULLIVAN (1892–1976) wrote humorous pieces for *The New Yorker* and became known as the "national cliché expert" because of his amusing dialogues exploiting the trite language of sports, journalism, politics, and entertainment. In the thirties the *Saturday Review of Literature* called him "the best slapstick satirist now writing."

GERALD SYKES had a career as a free-lance writer. He wrote and edited more than half a dozen books, lectured at leading universities here and abroad, and contributed to leading American periodicals.

GORDON SYLANDER published poetry in the *Partisan Review*. Kees wrote to Norris Getty on December 4, 1941: "I was telling Harold [Rosenberg] that Clement Greenberg said what a mistake Gordon Sylander had made by not leaving Madison and coming to New York. 'It would have been the making of him,' said Clem. . . . Harold said, 'That's the trouble with Clem; *he* didn't come to New York soon enough. He stayed in Brooklyn too long.' "

ALLEN TATE (1899–1979), poet, was one of the Fugitives at Vanderbilt University (1922–25) and wrote biographies, a novel, poetry, and criticism. A successful editor for Holt, he later taught at the University of Minnesota until he retired.

ERSKINE TATE (b. 1895), violinist and band leader, played with Louis Armstrong and other jazz greats but became a teacher late in the thirties.

FRANK J. TAYLOR (1894–1972) was born in South Dakota and studied at Stanford University (1914–17). He was a free-lance magazine writer on the West Coast, long attached to the *Reader's Digest*.

DOROTHY THOMAS was born in Kansas in 1898, and her novels were humorous, sympathetic portrayals of farm people. H. L. Mencken's *American Mercury* said in the thirties that she was "one of the ablest of American short story writers." The University of Nebraska Press reprinted *The Home Place* (1936) in 1966 and *Ma Jeeter's Girls* (1933) in 1986.

DUNSTAN THOMPSON was born in Connecticut in 1918 and educated at Harvard. His first book of poems was published in 1944 while he was in service and widely acclaimed that year.

RUTHVEN TODD (b. 1914), British poet, editor, novelist and essayist, studied painting before turning to poetry. He came to the United States in 1947, becoming a permanent resident after 1948. Mark Schorer said that he was "a gifted exemplar of the long British tradition of amateur scholarship."

LIONEL TRILLING (1905–75) spent his entire life associated with Columbia University. His essays, *The Liberal Imagination* (1950), established him as a leading critic. His novel, *The Middle of the Journey* (1947), deals with the political and moral atmosphere of the thirties and forties, especially in New York.

PARKER TYLER (1907–74) became one of the leading critics of film in his time. Born in New Orleans he published volumes of poetry, a novel, studies in art, and a monumental biography of Pavel Tchelitchew, as well as several volumes of film criticism.

RUDOLPH UMLAND was associated with the *Prairie Schooner* from its founding in 1927. He joined the Federal Writers' Project in 1935 and became state editor, where he remained until the coming of the war. His lengthy manuscript memories of

L. C. Wimberly are deposited at the Heritage Room, Bennett Martin Public Library, Lincoln, Nebraska.

IRITA VAN DOREN (1891–1966) was the editor of the Sunday book section of the *New York Herald Tribune* when Kees lived in New York City.

JOSE GARCIA VILLA was born in Manila in 1914. He came to the United States in 1930 and took his B.A. at the University of New Mexico (1933). Edward J. O'Brien dedicated his 1932 volume of *Best Short Stories* to him. He was associate editor of New Directions from 1949 to 1951.

HENRY VOLKENING (1902–72) studied at Princeton (B.A., 1923), Harvard, and Fordham. He and Russell Diarmuid set up an office as literary agents in 1940. Among his clients were Saul Bellow, Wright Morris, Barbara Tuckman, Alan Watts, and Jessamyn West.

NANCY WALKER (b. 1922) first made her mark as an actress in the Broadway musical *Best Foot Forward* (1941–42). She starred in *On the Town* (1944–46) and *Pal Joey* (1952–53) as well.

TEDDY WEATHERFORD (1903–45) was one of the most admired jazz pianists of his generation. He moved from New Orleans to Chicago to California to the Far East.

JACK WEBB (1920–82) wrote mystery, crime, and suspense fiction under several names. He was active as a radio and television actor, but he was a producer and director as well. He was best known for the television series "Dragnet."

MAX WEBER (1881–1961) was an American artist associated with Alfred Stieglitz who fused elements of Expressionism and Cubism in paintings often religious in subject matter.

JEROME WEIDMAN (b. 1913) wrote novels and screenplays and edited *The Somerset Maugham Reader* (1943). His novel, *I Can Get it for You Wholesale* (1937), became a Broadway musical in 1962 and later a film.

GLENWAY WESCOTT (b. 1901), author of fiction and essays, was one of the Paris expatriates. His *Images of Truth* (1962) is a collection of remembrances and critical judgments.

RAY B. WEST, JR. (b. 1908) edited the *Rocky Mountain Review* at the University of Utah after 1938, before he moved it as the *Western Review* to the University of Kansas in 1946 and the University of Iowa in 1949. West published the work of Walter Van Tilburg Clark, Wallace Stegner, Kenneth Burke, and William Carlos Williams. Kees was a "contributing editor" while the magazine was still based in Utah.

REED WHITTEMORE (b. 1919) edited the literary quarterly, *Furioso,* from 1939 to 1953. On the faculty at Carleton College from 1947 to 1962, he was consultant in poetry at the Library of Congress in 1964–65.

THORNTON WILDER (1897–1975) got his first Pulitzer Prize for *The Bridge of San Luis Rey* (1927), his second for *Our Town* (1938), and his third for *The Skin of Our Teeth* (1943).

LEE WILEY (1915–75) was a jazz singer with the Paul Whiteman band and sang in the 52nd Street clubs in New York during the thirties. Lee Wiley is associated musically with Mildred Bailey, Sarah Vaughan, and Billie Holiday.

OSCAR WILLIAMS (1900–1964) published a volume of poetry in 1921 and, after a silence of sixteen years, returned to verse and brought out a second volume in 1940. According to Robert Lowell, he was "probably the best anthologist in America."

WILLIAM CARLOS WILLIAMS (1883–1963), the poet, was a practicing physician in Rutherford, New Jersey, for most of his working life; and much of his writing grew from his daily experiences. While studying at the University of Pennsylvania, he became a friend of Ezra Pound. His *Autobiography* appeared in 1951 and *Selected Letters* in 1957.

ADRIAN WILSON spent his entire career on the West Coast, where he became known as one of the finest printers of his time. Retrospective shows of his work have been held at the University of California, Berkeley, and elsewhere. His papers are at the Bancroft Library, Berkeley.

EDMUND WILSON (1895–1972) became America's most highly praised critic after the publication of *Axel's Castle* (1931). His novel, *I Thought of Daisy* (1929), dealt with bohemian life in Greenwich Village in the twenties. From 1944 to 1948 on *The New Yorker,* he practiced journalism "in the grand historical manner."

LOWRY C. WIMBERLY (1890–1959) founded the *Prairie Schooner* at the University of Nebraska in 1927 and edited it until 1956. In addition to *Folklore in English and Scottish Ballads* (1929, 1959), he published *Famous Cats of Fairyland* (1938).

WALKER WINSLOW was a novelist-poet whom the Keeses knew in Colorado. A very heavy drinker and irresponsible, he was a prototypical bohemian whose antics filled Ann Kees's letters to Getty.

JOHN WITTWER, jazz pianist from Seattle, Washington, recorded for the Exner Label there, and for Jazzman and Good Time Jazz in Hollywood in the forties. In more recent years he has played and taught in Seattle.

BERT WOLFE, painter, was one of the "Provincetown regulars" whom the Keeses saw occasionally in New York City. Ann Kees reported to Norris Getty on November 2, 1948: "The other night we were at Bert Wolfe's, and met Louis Fisher (Fischer?) who hates cats and gets asthma when they come near him. He threatened to leave if the Wolfe's didn't do something about their cat Dopey."

THOMAS WOLFE (1900–1938) of Asheville, North Carolina, wrote rhapsodic, autobiographical novels that were much talked about in the thirties and early forties. *Look Homeward Angel* (1929), *Of Time and the River* (1935), and *You Can't Go Home Again* (1940), continue to have their admirers.

VICTOR WOLFSON (b. 1910) wrote plays and novels. He published short stories in *The New Yorker, Harper's,* and other leading periodicals and adapted novels by Dostoevsky, Ignazio Silone, and others to the theater with uneven success.

JACK WOODFORD (Josiah Pitts Woolfolk) (1894–1971) wrote fiction and scenarios for the movies. An ex-convict, he drew on first-hand experience in his writing about prisons.

MONTY WOOLLEY (1888–1963) was popularly known for acting in *The Man Who Came to Dinner* (1939), but he was a director and teacher as well. Bearded and outspoken, he was a "personality."

MALCOLM GLENN WYER (1877–1965) librarian at the Denver Public Library from 1924 to 1951 and dean of the School of Librarianship, University of Denver, established the Bibliography Center for Research, Rocky Mountains Region, of which Weldon Kees was acting director. Wyer was president of the American Library Association in 1936–37.

MORTON D. ZABEL (1901–64) took his Ph.D. at the University of Chicago in 1933 and became a professor there in 1946. He was an editor on *Poetry* after 1926 and established himself as a leading critic of modern literature.

BOB ZURKE (1910–44), jazz pianist, was a leading boogie-woogie performer. He joined Bob Crosby's band late in 1936 and played at the Hangover Club in Los Angeles for the last three years of his life.

Note: References to persons and other subjects occurring in separate letters have been indexed separately, even when the pagination overlaps. Thus a sequence like 92–95, 95–97, 97 indicates that the referent appears in three different letters.

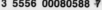